BOUNDARIES

readings in
DEVIANCE, CRIME AND CRIMINAL JUSTICE

A Customized Reader

General Editors

Bradley R.E. Wright
University of Connecticut

Ralph B. McNeal, Jr.
University of Connecticut

Compiled by

Dr. Divya Sharma
Thomas M. Ryan, M.B.A., B.S.
Criminology/SOC274
Utica College of Syracuse University
Criminal Justice

PEARSON

Custom
Publishing

Director of Database Publishing: Michael Payne
Senior Sponsoring Editor: Robin J. Lazrus
Development Editor: Catherine O'Keefe
Assistant Editor: Ana Díaz-Caneja
Marketing Manager: Kathleen Kourian
Operations Manager: Eric M. Kenney
Production Manager: Jennifer Berry
Rights Editor: Francesca Marcantonio
Cover Designer: Renée Sartell and Kristen Kiley

Cover Art: "Chain with Broken Link," courtesy of Emanuele Taroni/PhotoDisc; "Fence," courtesy of PhotoDisc; Ernesto Rios Lanz/Sexto Sol (photographers), "Shadow Hands image," courtesy of Ernesto Rios Lanz and Sexto Sol/Getty Images; JoSon (Photographer), "Shatter Glass image," courtesy of SuperStock, Inc.

Please visit our website at *www.pearsoncustom.com*
Attention bookstores: For permission to return any unsold stock, contact Pearson Custom Publishing at 1-800-777-6872.

ISBN-13: 978-0-536-93535-9   ISBN-10: 0-536-93535-1

PEARSON CUSTOM PUBLISHING
75 Arlington St., Suite 300
Boston, MA 02116

CUSTOMIZABLE SOCIOLOGY READERS
FROM PEARSON CUSTOM PUBLISHING

Create the reader that matches your syllabus!

Effective pedagogical apparatus — headnotes, end-of-selection questions, and optional introductions included with all selections!

Intersections: Readings in Sociology
www.intersectionsreader.com

- Suitable for all sociology survey courses, including Macrosociology, Conflict Approach and Marriage and Family.
- An archive of more than 380 selections of the best classic and contemporary writing for any introductory sociology course.
- Select only the content you wish to use in your course to reflect your teaching methods and course perspective.

Inequalities: Readings in Diversity and Social Life
www.inequalitiesreader.com

- Ideal for sociology studies in Racial and Ethnic Relations, Gender, Social Stratification, Religion and Disabilities.
- The most comprehensive collection of high-quality readings on multiple forms of inequality and how they intersect. More than 175 classic and contemporary articles reflect theoretical, conceptual, and global perspectives.

Crossroads: Readings in Social Problems
www.crossroadsreader.com

- Suitable for introductory level courses in social issues such as Alcohol and Drug Abuse, Marriage and the Family, Urban Sociology.
- An essential source of over 300 essays and readings that illuminate and help explain central ideas and issues in the study of social problems.

Boundaries: Readings in Deviance, Crime and Criminal Justice
www.boundariesreader.com

- More than 400 classic and contemporary readings that cover all the topics addressed in deviance, criminology, and criminal justice course.

Reading Women's Lives: The Customizable Reader for Women's Studies
www.readingwomenslives.com

- Nearly 500 selections are available including literature, pieces that reflect multicultural and cross-cultural diversity, readings drawn from the social sciences and third-wave feminism readings.

Learn more at
www.customsociology.com

ACKNOWLEDGEMENTS

The success of *Boundaries* could not have occurred without the attention of our reviewers. Those who have reviewed the content are experts in the field of sociology and criminal justice, and have influenced our decisions about the direction that a revision should take. With sincere thanks, we acknowledge:

Ann M. Borden, Peter M. Carlson, *Christopher Newport University*; *University of Central*; Mirelle Cohen, *University of Puget Sound*; Norman Conti, *Duquesne University*; Christopher T. Godialis, J.D., *Iona College* and *Sacred Heart University*; Andy Hochstetler, *Iowa State University*; Alan Horowitz, *University of Delaware*; Jo Ellyn Johnson, *Richard J. Daley College*; Joyce D. Meyer, *Parkland College*; P.J. McGann, *University of Michigan*; Marilyn D. McShane, *University of Houston-Downtown*; Stacey Nofziger, *University of Akron*; Timothy O'Boyle, *Kutztown University*; Peter Parilla, *University of St. Thomas*; Curt Sobolewski, *Indiana University South Bend*; Paul Stretesky, *Colorado State University*. Yvonne Villanueva-Russell, *Texas A&M University, Commerce*; Kimberly A. Vogt, *University of Wisconsin, La Crosse*; Patrick D. Walsh, *Loyola University New Orleans*

FOREWORD
By William J. Chambliss

One of the most effective classroom pedagogies available is to have students read original research in the form of published articles. This provides the students not only with the data and theories that drive the discipline but it also enables them to get a sense of the craft. In the past, books have traditionally served the purpose of bringing together the literature on a particular subject. Often these books fail to provide an instructor with the most important articles to the course and often contain many articles the instructor does not want to assign.

Now there is an alternative to the traditional "reader" that enables instructors to pick and choose precisely those articles that are most important to their method of teaching the course. *Boundaries: Readings in Deviance, Crime, and Criminal Justice* creatively edited by Bradley R. E. Wright and Ralph McNeal, both of the University of Connecticut, provides a collection of more than 400 of the most influential articles in the field of sociology and criminal justice. It is an unbiased, eclectic collection of academic journal articles and book chapters which survey the past 70 years in both fields. Classic and contemporary selections can be found within the collection, and they range from the harshest criticism to the most defensive posture in the literature. To add additional perspective, every article is introduced with an editor-written headnote, and concludes with several thought-provoking discussion questions. More importantly, the collection represents what the editors claim: there is a wide range of articles covering deviance, crime, and criminal justice.

Instructors will find this collection timely and unlimited in its flexibility. Each reader can be easily updated and modified at the beginning of each semester. The end result is an attractive paperback reader with the articles arranged in accordance with the professor's own choice. I have been using *Boundaries* for several years and am very happy with the results.

Contents

The Normal and the Pathological
Emile Durkheim.. 1

Social Structure and Anomie
Robert Merton.. 8

The Rich Get Richer and The Poor Get Prison
Jeffrey H. Reiman.. 23

Lower Class Culture as Generating Milieu of Gang Delinquency
Walters Miller.. 53

Social Support as an Organizing Concept for Criminology
Francis T. Cullen 72

Social Learning Theory
Ronald L. Akers... 112

V

Is White Collar Crime Crime?
Edwin Sutherland... 125

The Culture of the Corporation and Illegal Behavior
Marshall Clinard and Peter Yeager... 145

Fighting a War Against Terrorism, at Home and Abroad
Cole.. 166

The Fall and Rise of Restorative Justice
Braithwaite.. 189

The Normal and the Pathological

EMILE DURKHEIM

What is normal for a society? What is pathological? Though many people consider crime "non-normative" and therefore believe it should be eliminated from society, Emile Durkheim disagrees. In this classic essay, Durkheim addresses the conditions under which pathological behavior emerges. He then uses crime to illustrate the functional necessity of such behavior for society.

. . .

If there is a fact whose pathological nature appears indisputable, it is crime. All criminologists agree on this score. Although they explain this pathology differently, they none the less unanimously acknowledge it. However, the problem needs to be treated less summarily.

. . . Crime is not only observed in most societies of a particular species, but in all societies of all types. There is not one in which criminality does not exist, although it changes in form and the actions which are termed criminal are not everywhere the same. Yet everywhere and always there have been men who have conducted themselves in such a way as to bring down punishment upon their heads. If at least, as societies pass from lower to higher types, the crime rate (the relationship between the annual crime figures and population figures) tended to fall, we might believe that, although still remaining a normal phenomenon, crime tended to lose that character of normality. Yet there is no single ground for believing such a regression to be real. Many facts would rather seem to point to the existence of a movement in the opposite direction. From the beginning of the century statistics provide us with a means of following the progression of criminality. It has everywhere increased, and in France the increase is of the order of 300 per cent. Thus there is no phenomenon which represents more incon-

"The Normal and the Pathological," by Emile Durkheim, reprinted from *Rules of Sociological Method*, 1938, pp. 85–107. Copyright © 1938 by The Free Press.

trovertibly all the symptoms of normality, since it appears to be closely bound up with the conditions of all collective life. To make crime a social illness would be to concede that sickness is not something accidental, but on the contrary derives in certain cases from the fundamental constitution of the living creature. This would be to erase any distinction between the physiological and the pathological. It can certainly happen that crime itself has normal forms; this is what happens, for instance, when it reaches an excessively high level. There is no doubt that this excessiveness is pathological in nature. What is normal is simply that criminality exists, provided that for each social type it does not reach or go beyond a certain level which it is perhaps not impossible to fix in conformity with the previous rules.[1]

We are faced with conclusion which is apparently somewhat paradoxical. Let us make no mistake: to classify crime among the phenomena of normal sociology is not merely to declare that it is an inevitable though regrettable phenomenon arising from the incorrigible wickedness of men; it is to assert that it is a factor in public health, an integrative element in any healthy society. At first sight this result is so surprising that it disconcerted even ourselves for a long time. However, once that first impression of surprise has been overcome it is not difficult to discover reasons to explain this normality and at the same time to confirm it.

In the first place, crime is normal because it is completely impossible for any society entirely free of it to exist.

Crime, as we have shown elsewhere, consists of an action which offends certain collective feelings which are especially strong and clear-cut. In any society, for actions regarded as criminal to cease, the feelings that they offend would need to be found in each individual consciousness without exception and in the degree of strength requisite to counteract the opposing feelings. Even supposing that this condition could effectively be fulfilled, crime would not thereby disappear; it would merely change in form, for the very cause which made the well-springs of criminality to dry up would immediately open up new ones.

Indeed, for the collective feelings, which the penal law of a people at a particular moment in its history protects, to penetrate individual consciousnesses that had hitherto remained closed to them, or to assume greater authority—whereas previously they had not possessed enough—they would have to acquire an intensity greater than they had had up to then. The community as a whole must feel them more keenly, for they cannot draw from any other source the additional force which enables them to bear down upon individuals who formerly were the most refractory. For murderers to disappear, the horror of bloodshed must increase in those strata of society from which murderers are recruited; but for this to happen the abhorrence must increase throughout society. Moreover, the very absence of crime would contribute directly to bringing about that result, for a sentiment appears much more respectable when it is always and uniformly respected. But we overlook the fact that these strong states of the common consciousness cannot be reinforced in this way without the weaker states, the violation of which previously gave rise to mere breaches of convention, being reinforced at the same time, for the weaker states are no more than the extension and attenuated form of the stronger ones. Thus, for example, theft and mere misappropriation of property offend the same altruistic sentiment, the respect for other people's possessions. However, this sentiment is offended less strongly by the latter action than the former. Moreover, since the average consciousness does not have sufficient intensity of feeling to feel strongly about the lesser of these two offences, the latter is the object of greater tolerance. This is why the misappropriator is merely censured, while the thief is punished. But if this sentiment grows stronger, to such a degree that it extinguishes in the consciousness the tendency to theft that men possess, they will become more sensitive to these minor offences, which up to then had had only a marginal effect upon them. They will react with greater intensity against these lesser faults, which will become the object of severer condemnation, so that, from the mere moral errors that they were, some will pass into the category of crimes. For example, dishonest contracts or those fulfilled dishonestly, which only incur public censure or civil redress, will become crimes. Imagine a community of saints in an exemplary and perfect monastery. In it crime as such will be unknown, but faults that appear venial to the ordinary person will arouse the same scandal as does normal crime in ordinary consciences. If therefore that community has the power to judge and punish, it will term such acts criminal and deal with them as such. It is for the same reason that the completely honourable man judges his slightest moral failings with a severity that the mass of people reserves for acts that are truly criminal. In former times acts of violence against the person were more frequent than they are today because respect for individual dignity was weaker. As it has increased, such crimes have become less frequent, but many acts which offended against that sentiment have been incorporated into the penal code, which did not previously include them.[2]

In order to exhaust all the logically possible hypotheses, it will perhaps be asked why this unanimity should not cover all collective sentiments without exception, and why even the weakest sentiments should not evoke sufficient power to forestall any dissentient voice. The moral conscience of society would be found in its entirety in every individual, endowed with sufficient force to prevent the commission of any act offending against it, whether purely conventional failings or crimes. But such universal and absolute uniformity is utterly impossible, for the immediate physical environment in which each one of us is placed, our hereditary antecedents, the social influences upon which we depend, vary from one individual to another and consequently cause a diversity of consciences. It is impossible for everyone to be alike in this matter, by virtue of the fact that we each have our own organic constitution and occupy different areas in space. This is why, even among lower peoples where individual originality is very little developed, such originality does however exist. Thus, since there cannot be a society in which individuals do not diverge to some extent from the collective type, it is also inevitable that among these deviations some assume a criminal character. What confers upon them this character is not the intrinsic importance of the acts but the importance which the common consciousness ascribes to them. Thus if the latter is stronger and possesses sufficient authority to make these divergences very weak in absolute terms, it will also be more sensitive and exacting. By reacting against the slightest deviations with an energy which it elsewhere employs against those what are more weighty, it endues them with the same gravity and will brand them as criminal.

Thus crime is necessary. It is linked to the basic conditions of social life, but on this very account is useful, for the conditions to which it is bound are themselves indispensable to the normal evolution of morality and law.

Indeed today we can no longer dispute the fact that not only do law and morality vary from one social type to another, but they even change within the same type if the conditions of collective existence are modified. Yet for these transformations to be made possible, the collective sentiments at the basis of morality should not prove unyielding to change, and consequently should be only moderately intense. If they were too strong, they would no longer be malleable. Any arrangement is indeed an obstacle to a new arrangement; this is even more the case the more deep-seated the original arrangement. The more strongly a structure is articulated, the more it resists modification; this is as true for functional as for anatomical patterns. If there were no crimes, this condition would not be fulfilled, for such a hypothesis presumes that collective sentiments would have attained the degree of intensity unparalleled in history. Nothing is good indefinitely and without limits. The authority which the moral consciousness enjoys must not be excessive, for otherwise no one would dare to attack it and it would petrify too easily into an immutable form. For it to evolve, individual originality must be allowed to manifest itself. But so that the originality of the idealist who dreams of transcending his era may display itself, that of the criminal, which falls short of the age, must also be possible. One does not go without the other.

Nor is this all. Beyond this indirect utility, crime itself may play a useful part in this evolution. Not only does it imply that the way to necessary changes remains open, but in certain cases it also directly prepares for these changes. Where crime exists, collective sentiments are not only in the state of plasticity necessary to assume a new form, but sometimes it even contributes to determining beforehand the shape they will take on. Indeed, how often is it only an anticipation of the morality to come, a progression towards what will be! According to Athenian law, Socrates was a criminal and his condemnation was entirely just. However, his crime—his independence of thought—was useful not only for humanity but for his country. It served to prepare a way for a new morality and a new faith, which the Athenians then needed because the traditions by which they had hitherto lived no longer corresponded to the conditions of their existence. Socrates's case is not an isolated one, for it recurs periodically in history. The freedom of thought that we at present enjoy could never have been asserted if the rules that forbade it had not been violated before they were solemnly abrogated. However, at the time the violation was a crime, since it was an offence against sentiments still keenly felt in the average consciousness. Yet this crime was useful since it was the prelude to changes which were daily becoming more necessary. Liberal philosophy has had as its precursors heretics of all kinds whom the secular arm rightly punished through the Middle Ages and has continued to do so almost up to the present day.

From this viewpoint the fundamental facts of criminology appear to us in an entirely new light. Contrary to current ideas, the criminal no longer appears as an utterly unsociable creature, a sort of parasitic element, a foreign, unassimilable body introduced into the bosom of society.[3] He plays a normal role in social life. For its part, crime must no longer be conceived of as an evil which cannot be circumscribed closely enough. Far from there being cause for congratulation when it drops too noticeably below the normal level, this apparent progress assuredly coincides with and is linked to some social disturbance. Thus the number of crimes of assault never falls so low as it does in times of scarcity.[4] Consequently, at the same time, and as a reaction, the theory of punishment is revised, or rather should be revised. If in fact crime is a sickness, punishment is the cure for it and cannot be conceived of otherwise; thus all the discussion aroused revolves round knowing what punishment should be to fulfil its role as a remedy. But if crime is in no way pathological, the object of punishment cannot be to cure it and its true function must be sought elsewhere.

£ndnotes

[1]From the fact that crime is a phenomenon of normal sociology it does not follow that the criminal is a person normally constituted from the biological and psychological viewpoints. The two questions are independent of each other. This independence will be better understood when we have shown later the difference which exists between psychical and sociological facts.

[2]Calumny, insults, slander, deception, etc.

[3]We have ourselves committed the error of speaking of the criminal in this way through not having applied our rule (cf. *Division du travail social,* pp. 395, 396).

[4]But, although crime is a fact of normal sociology, it does not follow that we should not abhor it. Pain has likewise nothing desirable about it: the individual detests it just as society detests crime, and yet it is a normal physiological function. Not only does it necessarily derive from the very constitution of every living creature, but it plays a useful and irreplaceable role in life. Thus it would be a peculiar distortion to represent our thinking as an apologia for crime. We would not even have envisaged protesting against such an interpretation were we not aware of the strange accusations and misunderstandings to which one is exposed in undertaking to study moral facts objectively and to speak of them in language that is not commonly used.

◉ ◉ ◉

Questions

1. Why does Durkheim contend that crime is not only normal but necessary in society?

2. How does crime contribute to the development of, or a change in, society?

3. If Durkheim's view of crime is accurate, how effective can we expect social sanctions to be in deterring crime? How effective might various reform efforts be?

4. Think of specific crimes that occur on your campus. How would Durkheim explain the existence or prevalence of these crimes?

Social Structure and Anomie

ROBERT K. MERTON
Harvard University

This classic article by Robert Merton explains the role of social structure in generating anomie, or a sense of lawlessness and alienation, within individuals. Merton also discusses the intersection between one's adoption (or not) of culturally prescribed goals and one's adoption (or not) of accepted means of achieving those goals. Merton's resulting framework identifies particular responses to stress and anomie, including conformity, innovation, ritualism, retreatism, and rebellion.

*T*here persists a notable tendency in sociology theory to attribute the malfunctioning of social structure primarily to those of man's imperious biological drives which are not adequately restrained by social control. In this view, the social order is solely a device for "impulse management" and the "social processing" of tensions. These impulses which break through social control, be it noted, are held to be biologically derived. Nonconformity is assumed to be rooted in original nature.[1] Conformity is by implication the result of an utilitarian calculus or unreasoned conditioning. This point of view, whatever its other deficiencies, clearly begs one question. It provides no basis for determining the nonbiological conditions which induce deviations from prescribed patterns of conduct. In this paper, it will be suggested that certain phases of social structure generate the circumstances in which infringement of social codes constitutes a "normal" response.[2]

The conceptual scheme to be outlined is designed to provide a coherent, systematic approach to the study of socio-cultural sources of deviate behavior. Our primary aim lies in discovering how some social structures *exert a definite pressure* upon certain persons in the society to engage in nonconformist rather than conformist conduct. The many ramifications of

---

"Social Structure and Anomie," by Robert Merton, reprinted from *American Sociological Review*, vol. 3, 1938, pp. 672–682.

the scheme cannot all be discussed; the problems mentioned outnumber those explicitly treated.

Among the elements of social and cultural structure, two are important for our purposes. These are analytically separable although they merge imperceptibly in concrete situations. The first consists of culturally defined goals, purposes, and interests. It comprises a frame of aspirational reference. These goals are more or less integrated and involve varying degrees of prestige and sentiment. They constitute a basic, but not the exclusive, component of what Linton aptly has called "designs for group living." Some of these cultural aspirations are related to the original drives of man, but they are not determined by them. The second phase of the social structure defines, regulates, and controls the acceptable modes of achieving these goals. Every social group invariably couples its scale of desired ends with moral or institutional regulation of permissible and required procedures for attaining these ends. These regulatory norms and moral imperatives do not necessarily coincide with technical or efficiency norms. Many procedures which from the standpoint of *particular individuals* would be most efficient in securing desired values, e.g., illicit oil-stock schemes, theft, fraud, are ruled out of the institutional area of permitted conduct. The choice of expedients is limited by the institutional norms.

To say that these elements, culture goals and institutional norms, operate jointly is not to say that the ranges of alternative behaviors and aims bear some constant relation to one another. The emphasis upon certain goals may vary independently of the degree of emphasis upon institutional means. There may develop a disproportionate, at times, a virtually exclusive, stress upon the value of specific goals, involving relatively slight concern with the institutionally appropriate modes of attaining these goals. The limiting case in this direction is reached when the range of alternative procedures is limited only by technical rather than institutional considerations. Any and all devices which promise attainment of the all important goal would be permitted in this hypothetical polar case.[3] This constitutes one types of cultural malintegration. A second polar type is found in groups where activities originally conceived as instrumental are transmuted into ends in themselves. The original purposes are forgotten and ritualistic adherence to institutionally prescribed conduct becomes virtually obsessive.[4] Stability is largely ensured while change is flouted. The range of alternative behaviors is severely limited. There develops a tradition-bound, sacred society characterized by neophobia. The occupational psychosis of the bureaucrat may be cited as a case in point. Finally, there are the intermediate types of groups where a balance between culture goals and institutional means is maintained. These are the significantly integrated and relatively stable, though changing, groups.

An effective equilibrium between the two phases of the social structure is maintained as long as satisfactions accrue to individuals who conform to both constraints, viz., satisfactions from the achievement of the goals and satisfactions emerging directly from the institutionally canalized modes of striving to attain these ends. Success, in such equilibrated cases, is twofold. Success is reckoned in terms of the product and in terms of the process, in terms of the outcome and in terms of activities. Continuing satisfactions must derive from sheer *participation* in a competitive order as well as from eclipsing one's competitors if the order itself is to be sustained. The occasional sacrifices involved in institutionalized conduct must be compensated by socialized rewards. The distribution of statuses and roles through competition must be so organized that positive incentives for conformity to roles and adherence to status obligations are provided *for every position* within the distributive order. Aberrant conduct, therefore, may be viewed as a symptom of dissociation between culturally defined aspirations and socially structured means.

Of the types of groups which result from the independent variation of the two phases of the social structure, we shall be primarily concerned with the first, namely, that involving a disproportionate accent on goals. This statement must be recast in a proper perspective. In no group is there an absence of regulatory codes governing conduct, yet groups do vary in the degree to which these folkways, mores, and institutional controls are effectively integrated with the more diffuse goals which are part of the culture matrix. Emotional convictions may cluster about the complex of socially acclaimed ends, meanwhile shifting their support from the culturally defined implementation of these ends. As we shall see, certain aspects of the social structure may generate countermores and antisocial behavior precisely because of different emphases on goals and regulations. In the extreme case, the latter may be so vitiated by the goal emphasis that the range of behavior is limited only by considerations of technical expediency. The sole significant question then becomes, which available means is most efficient in netting the socially approved value.[5] The technically most feasible procedure, whether legitimate or not, is preferred to the institutionally prescribed conduct. As this process continues, the integration of the society becomes tenuous and anomie ensues.

Thus, in competitive athletics, when the aim of victory is shorn of its institutional trappings and success in contests becomes construed as "winning the game" rather than "winning through circumscribed modes of activity," a premium is implicitly set upon the use of illegitimate but technically efficient means. The star of the opposing football team is surreptitiously slugged; the wrestler furtively incapacitates his opponent through ingenious but illicit techniques; university alumni covertly subsidize "students" whose talents are largely confined to the athletic field. The emphasis on the goal has so attenuated the satisfactions deriving from sheer participation in the competitive activity that these satisfactions are virtually confined to a successful outcome. Through the same process, tension generated by the desire to win in a poker game is relieved by successfully dealing oneself four aces, or, when the cult of success has become completely dominant, by sagaciously shuffling the cards in a game of solitaire. The faint twinge of uneasiness in the last instance and the surreptious nature of public delicts indicate clearly that the institutional rules of the game *are known* to those who evade them, but that the emotional supports of these rules are largely vitiated by cultural exaggeration of the success goal.[6] They are microcosmic images of the social macrocosm.

Of course, this process is not restricted to the realm of sport. The process whereby exaltation of the end generates a *literal demoralization,* i.e., a deinstitutionalization, of the means is one which characterizes many[7] groups in which the two phases of the social structure are not highly integrated. The extreme emphasis upon the accumulation of wealth as a symbol of success[8] in our own society militates against the completely effective control of institutionally regulated modes of acquiring a fortune.[9] Fraud, corruption, vice, crime, in short, the entire catalogue of proscribed behavior, becomes increasingly common when the emphasis on the *culturally induced* success goal becomes divorced from a coordinated institutional emphasis. This observation of crucial theoretical importance in examining the doctrine that antisocial behavior most frequently derives from biological drives breaking through the restraints imposed by society. The difference is one between a strictly utilitarian interpretation which conceives man's ends as random and an analysis which finds these ends deriving from the basic values of the culture.[10]

Our analysis can scarcely stop at this juncture. We must turn to other aspects of the social structure if we are to deal with the social genesis of the varying rates and types of deviate behavior characteristic of different societies. Thus far, we have sketched three ideal types of social orders constituted by distinctive patterns of relations between cultural ends and means. Turning from these types of *culture patterning,* we find five logically possible, alternative modes of adjustment or adaptation *by individuals* within the culture-bearing society or groups.[11] These are schematically presented in the following table, where (+) signifies "acceptance," (-) signifies "elimination" and (±) signifies "rejection and substitution of new goals and standards."

	Culture and Goals	Institutionalized Means
I. Conformity	+	+
II. Innovation	+	-
III. Ritualism	-	+
IV. Retreatism	-	-
V. Rebellion[12]	±	±

Our discussion of the relation between these alternative responses and other phases of the social structure must be prefaced by the observation that persons may shift from one alternative to another as they engage in different social activities. These categories refer to role adjustments in specific situations, not to personality *in toto.* To treat the development of this process in various spheres of conduct would introduce a complexity unmanageable within the confines of this paper. For this reason, we shall be concerned primarily with economic activity in the broad sense, "the production, exchange, distribution and consumption of goods and services" in our competitive society, wherein wealth has taken on a highly symbolic cast. Our task is to search out some of the factors which exert pressure upon individuals to engage in certain of these logically possible alternative responses. This choice, as we shall see, is far from random.

In every society, Adaptation I (conformity to both culture goals and means) is the most common and widely diffused. Were this not so, the stability and continuity of society could not be maintained. The mesh of expectancies which constitutes every social order is sustained by the modal behavior of its members falling within the first category. Conventional role behavior oriented toward the basic values of the group is the rule rather than the exception. It is this fact alone which permits us to speak of a human aggregate as comprising a group or society.

Conversely, Adaptation IV (rejection of goals and means) is the least common. Persons who "adjust" (or maladjust) in this fashion are, strictly speaking, *in* the society if not *of* it. Sociologically, these constitute the true "aliens." Not sharing the common frame of orientation, they can be included within the societal population merely in a fictional sense. In this category are *some* of the activities of psychotics, psychoneurotics, chronic autists, pariahs, outcasts, vagrants, vagabonds, tramps, chronic drunkards and drug addicts.[13] These have relinquished, in certain spheres of activity, the culturally defined goals, involving complete aim-inhibition in the polar case, and their adjustments are not in accord with institutional norms. This is not to say that in some cases the source of their behavioral adjustments is not in part the very social structure which they have in effect repudiated nor that their very existence within a social area does not constitute a problem for the socialized population.

This mode of "adjustment" occurs, as far as structural sources are concerned, when both the culture goals and institutionalized procedures have been assimilated thoroughly by the individual and imbued with affect and high positive value, but where those institutionalized procedures which promise a measure of successful attainment of the goals are not available to the individual. In such instances, there results a twofold mental conflict insofar as the moral obligation for adopting institutional means conflicts with the pressure to resort to illegitimate means (which may attain the goal) and inasmuch as the individual is shut off from means which are both legitimate *and* effective. The competitive order is maintained, but the frustrated and handicapped individual who cannot cope with this order drops out. Defeatism, quietism and resignation are manifested in escape mechanisms which ultimately lead the individual to "escape" from the requirements of the society. It is an expedient which arises from continued failure to attain the goal by legitimate measures and from an inability to adopt the illegitimate route because of internalized prohibitions and institutionalized compulsives, *during which process the supreme value of the success-goal has as yet not been renounced.* The conflict is resolved by eliminating *both* precipitating elements, the goals and means. The escape is complete, the conflict is eliminated and the individual is a-socialized.

Be it noted that where frustration derives from the inaccessibility of effective institutional means for attaining economic or any other type of highly valued "success," that Adaptations II, III, and V (innovation, ritualism and rebellion) are also possible. The result will be determined by the particular personality, and thus, the *particular* cultural background, involved. Inadequate socialization will result in the innovation response whereby the conflict and frustration are eliminated by relinquishing the institutional means and retaining the success-aspiration; an extreme assimilation of institutional demands will lead to ritualism wherein the goal is dropped as beyond one's reach but conformity to the mores persists; and rebellion occurs when emancipation from the reigning standards, due to frustration or to marginalist perspectives, leads to the attempt to introduce a "new social order."

Our major concern is with the illegitimacy adjustment. This involves the use of conventionally proscribed but frequently effective means of attaining at least the simulacrum of culturally defined success—wealth, power, and the like. As we have seen, this adjustment occurs when the individual has assimilated the cultural emphasis on success without equally internalizing the morally prescribed norms governing means for its attainment. The question arises, While phases of our social structure predispose toward this mode of adjustment? We may examine a concrete instance, effectively analyzed by Lohman,[14] which provides a clue to the answer. Lohman has shown that specialized areas of vice in the near north side of Chicago constitute a "normal" response to a situation where the cultural emphasis upon pecuniary success has been absorbed, but where there is little access to conventional and legitimate means for attaining such success. The conventional occupational opportunities of persons in this area are almost completely limited to manual labor. Given our cultural stigmatization of manual labor, and its correlate, the prestige of white collar work, it is clear that the result is a strain toward innovational practices. The limitation of opportunity to unskilled labor and the resultant low income can not compete *in terms of conventional standards of achievement* with the high income from organized vice.

For our purposes, this situation involves two important features. First, such antisocial behavior is in a sense "called forth" by certain conventional values of the culture *and* by the class structure involving differential access to the approved opportunities for legitimate, prestige-bearing pursuit of the culture goals. The lack of high integration between the means-and-end elements of the cultural pattern and the particular class structure combine to favor a heightened frequency of antisocial conduct in such groups. The second consideration is of equal significance. Recourse to the first of the alternative responses, legitimate effort, is limited by the fact that actual advance toward desired success-symbols through conventional channels is, despite our persisting open-class ideology,[15] relatively rare and difficult for those handicapped by little formal education and few economic resources. The dominant pressure of group standards of success is, therefore, on the gradual attenuation of legitimate, but by and large ineffective, strivings and the increasing use of illegitimate, but more or less effective, expedients of vice and crime. The culture demands made on persons in this situation are incompatible. On the one hand, they are asked to orient their conduct toward the prospect of accumulating wealth and on the other, they are largely denied effective opportunities to do so institutionally. The consequences of such structural inconsistency are psychopathological personality, and/or antisocial conduct, and/or revolutionary activities. The equilibrium between culturally designated means and ends becomes highly unstable with the progressive emphasis on attaining the prestige-laden ends by any means whatsoever. Within this context, Capone represents the triumph of amoral intelligence over morally prescribed "failure," when the channels of vertical mobility are closed or narrowed[16] *in a society which places a high premium on economic affluence and social ascent for* all *its members.*[17]

This last qualification is of primary importance. It suggests that other phases of the social structure besides the extreme emphasis on pecuniary success, must be considered if we are to understand the social sources of antisocial behavior. A high frequency of deviate behavior is not generated simply by "lack of opportunity" or by this exaggerated pecuniary emphasis. A comparatively rigidified class structure, a feudalistic or caste order, may limit such opportunities far beyond the point which obtains in our society today. It is only when a system of cultural values extols, virtually above all else, certain *common* symbols of success *for the population at large* while its social structure rigorously restricts or completely eliminates access to approved modes of acquiring these symbols *for a considerable part of the same population,* that antisocial behavior ensues on a considerable scale. In other words, our egalitarian ideology denies by implication the existence of noncompeting groups and individuals in the pursuit of pecuniary success. The same body of success-symbols is held to be desirable for all. These goals are held to *transcend class lines,* not to be bounded by them, yet the actual social organization is such that there exist class differentials in the accessibility of these common success-symbols. Frustration and thwarted aspiration lead to the search for avenues of escape from a culturally induced intolerable situation; or unrelieved ambition may eventuate in illicit attempts to acquire the dominant values.[18] The American stress on pecuniary success and ambitiousness for all thus invites exaggerated anxieties, hostilities, neuroses and antisocial behavior.

This theoretical analysis may go far toward explaining the varying correlations between crime and poverty.[19] Poverty is not an isolated variable. It is one in a complex of interdependent social and cultural variables. When viewed in such a context, it represents quite different states of affairs. Poverty as such, and consequent limitations of opportunity, are not sufficient to induce a conspicuously high rate of criminal behavior. Even the often mentioned "poverty in the midst of plenty" will not necessarily lead to this result. Only insofar as poverty and associated disadvantages in competition for the culture values approved for *all* members of the society is linked with the assimilation of a cultural emphasis on monetary accumulation as a symbol of success is antisocial conduct a "normal" outcome. Thus, poverty is less highly correlated with crime in southeastern Europe than in the United States. The possibilities of vertical mobility in these European areas would seem to be fewer than in this country, so that neither poverty *per se* nor its association with limited opportunity is sufficient to account for the varying correlations. It is only when the full configuration is considered, poverty, limited opportunity and a commonly shared system of success symbols, that we can explain the higher association between poverty and crime in our society than in others where rigidified class structure is coupled with *differential class symbols of achievement*.

In societies such as our own, then, the pressure of prestige-bearing success tends to eliminate the effective social constraint over means employed to this end. "The-end-justifies-the-means" doctrine becomes a guiding tenet for action when the cultural structure unduly exalts the end and the social organization unduly limits possible recourse to approved means. Otherwise put, this notion and associated behavior reflect a lack of cultural coordination. In international relations, the effects of this lack of integration are notoriously apparent. An emphasis upon national power is not readily coordinated with an inept organization of legitimate, i.e., internationally defined and accepted, means for attaining this goal. The result is a tendency toward the abrogation of international law, treaties become scraps of paper, "undeclared warfare" serves as a technical evasion, the bombing of civilian populations is rationalized,[20] just as the same societal situation induces the same sway of illegitimacy among individuals.

The social order we have described necessarily produces this "strain toward dissolution." The pressure of such an order is upon outdoing one's competitors. The choice of means within the ambit of institutional control will persist as long as the sentiments supporting a competitive system, i.e., deriving from the possibility of outranking competitors and hence enjoying the favorable response of others, are distributed throughout the entire system of activities and are not confined merely to the final result. A stable social structure demands a balanced distribution of affect among its various segments. When there occurs a shift of emphasis from the satisfactions deriving from competition itself to almost exclusive concern with successful competition, the resultant stress leads to the breakdown of the regulatory structure.[21] With the resulting attenuation of the institutional imperatives, there occurs an approximation of the situation erroneously held by utilitarians to be typical of society generally wherein calculations of advantage and fear of punishment are the sole regulating agencies. In such situations, as Hobbes observed, force and fraud come to constitute the sole virtues in view of their relative efficiency in attaining goals,—which were for him, of course, not culturally derived.

It should be apparent that the foregoing discussion is not pitched on a moralistic plane. Whatever the sentiments of the writer or reader concerning the ethical desirability of coordinating the means and goals phases of the social structure, one must agree that lack of such coordination leads to anomie. Insofar as one of the most general functions of social organization is to provide a basis for calculability and regularity of behavior, it is increasingly limited in effectiveness as these elements of the structure become dissociated. At the extreme, predictability virtually disappears and what may be properly termed cultural chaos or anomie intervenes.

The statement, being brief, is also incomplete. It has not included an exhaustive treatment of the various structural elements which predispose toward one rather than another of the alternative responses open to individuals; it has neglected, but not denied the relevance of, the factors determining the specific incidence of these responses; it has not enumerated the various concrete responses which are constituted by combinations of specific values of the analytical variables; it has omitted, or included only by implication, any consideration of the social functions performed by illicit responses; it has not tested the full explanatory power of the analytical scheme by examining a large number of group variations in the frequency of deviate and conformist behavior; it has not adequately dealt with rebellious conduct which seeks to refashion the social framework radically; it has not examined the relevance of cultural conflict for an analysis of culture-goal and institutional-means malintegration. It is suggested that these and related problems may be profitably analyzed by this scheme.

ℰndnotes

[1] E.g., Ernest Jones, *Social Aspects of Psychoanalysis*, 28, London, 1924. If the Freudian notion is a variety of the "original sin" dogma, then the interpretation advanced in this paper may be called the doctrine of "socially derived sin."

[2] "Normal" in the sense of a culturally oriented, if not approved, response. This statement does not deny the relevance of biological and personality differences which may be significantly involved in the *incidence* of deviate conduct. Our focus of interest is the social and cultural matrix; hence we abstract from other factors. It is in this sense, I take it, that James S. Plant speaks of the "normal reaction of normal people to abnormal conditions." See his *Personality and the Cultural Pattern*, 248, New York, 1937.

[3] Contemporary American culture has been said to tend in this direction. See André Siegfried, *America Comes of Age*, 26–37, New York, 1927. The alleged extreme(?) emphasis on the goals of monetary success and material prosperity leads to dominant concern with technological and social instruments designed to produce the desired result, inasmuch as institutional controls become of secondary importance. In such a situation, innovation flourishes as the *range of means* employed is broadened. In a sense, then, there occurs the paradoxical emergence of "materialists" from an "idealistic" orientation. Cf. Durkheim's analysis of the cultural conditions which predispose toward crime and innovation, both of which are aimed toward efficiency, not moral norms. Durkheim was one of the first to see that "contrairement aux idées courantes le criminel n'apparait plus comme un être radicalement insociable, comme une sorte d'elément parasitaire, de corps étranger et inassimilable, introduit au sein de la société; c'est un agent régulier de la vie sociale." See *Les Régles de la Méthode Sociologique*, 86–89, Paris, 1927.

[4] Such ritualism may be associated with a mythology which rationalizes these actions so that they appear to retain their status as means, but the dominant pressure is in the direction of strict ritualistic conformity, irrespective of such rationalizations. In this sense, ritual has proceeded farthest when such rationalizations are not even called forth.

[5]In this connection, one may see the relevance of Elton Mayo's paraphrase of the title of Tawney's well known book. "Actually the problem *is not that of the sickness of an acquisitive society; it is that of the acquisitiveness of a sick society.*" *Human Problems of an Industrial Civilization*, 153, New York, 1933. Mayo deals with the process through which wealth comes to be a symbol of social achievement. He sees this as arising from a state of anomie. We are considering the unintegrated monetary-success goal as an element in producing anomie. A complete analysis would involve both phases of this system of interdependent variables.

[6]It is unlikely that interiorized norms are completely eliminated. Whatever residuum persists will induce personality tensions and conflict. The process involves a certain degree of ambivalence. A manifest rejection of the institutional norms is coupled with some latent retention of their emotional correlates. "Guilt feelings," "sense of sin," "pangs of conscience" are obvious manifestations of this unrelieved tension; symbolic adherence to the nominally repudiated values or rationalizations constitute a more subtle variety of tensional release.

[7]"Many," and not all, unintegrated groups, for the reason already mentioned. In groups where the primary emphasis shifts to institutional means, i.e., when the range of alternatives is very limited, the outcome is a type of ritualism rather than anomie.

[8]Money has several peculiarities which render it particularly apt to become a symbol of prestige divorced from institutional controls. As Simmel emphasized, money is highly abstract and impersonal. However acquired, through fraud or institutionally, it can be used to purchase the same goods and services. The anonymity of metropolitan culture, in conjunction with this peculiarity of money, permits wealth, the sources of which may be unknown to the community in which the plutocrat lives, to serve as a symbol of status.

[9]The emphasis upon wealth as a success symbol is possibly reflected in the use of the term "fortune" to refer to a stock of accumulated wealth. This meaning becomes common in the late sixteenth century (Spenser and Shakespeare). A similar usage of the Latin *fortuna* comes into prominence during the first century B.C. Both these periods were marked by the rise to prestige and power of the "bourgeosie."

[10]See Kingsley Davis, "Mental Hygiene and the Class Structure," *Psychiatry*, 1928, 1, esp. 62–63; Talcott Parsons, *The Structure of Social Action*, 59–60, New York, 1937.

[11]This is a level intermediate between the two planes distinguished by Edward Sapir, namely, culture patterns and personal habit systems. See his "Contribution of Psychiatry to an Understanding of Behavior in Society," *Amer. J. Sociol.*, 1937 42:862–70.

[12]This fifth alternative is on a plane clearly different from that of the others. It represents a *transitional* response which seeks to *institutionalize* new procedures oriented toward revamped cultural goals shared by the members of the society. It thus involves efforts to *change* the existing structure rather than to perform accomodative actions *within* this structure, and introduces additional problems with which we are not at the moment concerned.

[13]Obviously, this is an elliptical statement. These individuals may maintain some orientation to the values of their particular differentiated groupings within the larger society or, in part, of the conventional society itself. Insofar as they do so, their conduct cannot be classified in the "passive rejection" category (IV). Nels Anderson's description of the behavior and attitudes of the bum, for example, can readily be recast in terms of our analytical scheme. See *The Hobo,* 93–98, *et passim,* Chicago, 1923.

[14]Joseph D. Lohman, "The Participant Observer in Community Studies," *Amer. Sociol. Rev.,* 1937, 2:890–98.

[15]The shifting historical role of this ideology is a profitable subject for exploration. The "office-boy-to-president" stereotype was once in approximate accord with the facts. Such vertical mobility was probably more common then than now, when the class structure is more rigid. (See the following note.) The ideology largely persists, however, possibly because it still performs a useful function for maintaining the *status quo.* For insofar as it is accepted by the "masses," it constitutes a useful sop for those who might rebel against the entire structure, were this consoling hope removed. This ideology now serves to lessen the probability of Adaptation V. In short, the role of this notion has changed from that of an approximately valid empirical theorem to that of an ideology, in Mannheim's sense.

[16]There is a growing body of evidence, though none of it is clearly conclusive, to the effect that our class structure is becoming rigidified and that vertical mobility is declining. Taussig and Joslyn found that American business leaders are being *increasingly* recruited from the upper ranks of our society. The Lynds have also found a "diminished chance to get ahead" for the working classes in Middletown. Manifestly, these objective changes are not alone significant; the individual's subjective evaluation of the situation is a major determinant of the response. The extent to which this change in opportunity for social mobility has been recognized by the least advantaged classes is still conjectural, although the Lynds present some suggestive materials. The writer suggests that a case in point is the increasing frequency of cartoons which observe in a tragi-comic vein that "my old man says everybody can't be President. He says if ya can get three days a week steady on W.P.A. work ya ain't doin' so bad either." See F.

W. Taussig and C. S. Joslyn, *American Business Leaders,* New York, 1932; R. S. and H. M. Lynd, *Middletown in Transition,* 67 ff., chap. 12, New York 1937.

[17]The role of the Negro in this respect is of considerable theoretical interest. Certain elements of the Negro population have assimilated the dominant caste's values of pecuniary success and social advancement, but they also recognize that social ascent is at present restricted to their own caste almost exclusively. The pressures upon the Negro which would otherwise derive from the structural inconsistencies we have noticed are hence not identical with those upon lower-class whites. See Kingsley Davis, *op cit.,* 63; John Dollard, *Caste and Class in a Southern Town,* 66 ff., New Haven, 1936; Donald Young, *American Minority People,* 581, New York, 1932.

[18]The psychical coordinates of these processes have been partly established by the experimental evidence concerning *Aspruchsniveaus* and levels of performance. See Kurt Lewin, Vorsatz, Wille and Bedurfnis, Berlin, 1926; N. F. Hoppe, "Erfolg und Misserfolg," *Psychol. Forschung,* 1930, 14:1–63; Jerome D. Frank, "Individual Differences in Certain Aspects of the Level of Aspiration," *Amer. J. Psychol,* 1935, 47:119–28.

[19]Standard criminology texts summarize the data in this field. Our scheme of analysis may serve to resolve some of the theoretical contradictions which P. A. Sorokin indicates. For example, "not everywhere nor always do the poor show a greater proportion of crime . . . many poorer countries have had less crime than the richer countries. . . . The [economic] improvement in the second half of the nineteenth century, and the beginning of the twentieth, has not been followed by a decrease of crime." See his *Contemporary Sociological Theories* 560–61, New York, 1928. The crucial point is, however, that poverty has varying social significance in different social structures, as we shall see. Hence, one would not expect a linear correlation between crime and poverty.

[20]See M. W. Royce, *Aerial Bombardment and the International Regulation of War,* New York, 1928.

[21]Since our primary concern is with the socio-cultural aspects of this problem, the psychological correlates have been only implicitly considered. See Karen Horney, *The Neurotic Personality of Our Time,* New York, 1937, for a psychological discussion of this process.

❧ ❧ ❧

Questions

1. How is the intersection between goals and means relevant for generating deviant behavior?

2. How might you extend Merton's athletics analogy (that is, winning is the goal and "by all means necessary" is the strategy) to explain deviant behavior? Cite examples from the world of sport that fit each of Merton's five categories.

3. According to Merton, which of the following would have the greatest effect on the generation of deviant behavior: highly placed goals that may be unreasonable or unattainable *or* structurally blocked access to legitimate means of achieving the goals? Explain your reasoning.

4. Which type of deviant behavior does Merton's theoretical framework best describe? Does his theory work better for some subgroups than others? If so, which group's deviant behavior does the theory best explain?

5. To what degree does Merton's framework reflect society's motto of "by whatever means necessary" to achieve specific goals? With what type of behavior or action might you typically associate this statement?

The Rich Get Richer and the Poor Get Prison

JEFFREY H. REIMAN
American University

In the United States, poor people are more likely to be arrested, charged, and convicted than wealthy people. And if convicted, the poor are more likely to be sentenced to prison and to receive longer sentences. We find the same inequities when comparing African-Americans' and whites' experiences in the criminal-justice system—with whites receiving more favorable outcomes. In this selection, Jeffrey Reiman presents the supporting evidence for these findings, as well as potential explanations for the inequities.

. . .

For the same criminal behavior, the poor are more likely to be arrested; if arrested, they are more likely to be charged; if charged, more likely to be convicted; if convicted, more likely to be sentenced to prison; and if sentenced, more likely to be given longer prison terms than members of the middle and upper classes.[1] In other words, the image of the criminal population one sees in our nation's jails and prisons is distorted by the shape of the criminal justice system itself. It is the face of evil reflected in a carnival mirror, but it is no laughing matter.

The face in the criminal justice carnival mirror is also . . . very frequently a black face. Although blacks do not make up the majority of the inmates in our jails and prisons, they make up a proportion that far outstrips their proportion in the population.[2] Here, too, the image we see is distorted by the processes of the criminal justice system itself. Edwin Sutherland and Donald Cressey write in their widely used textbook *Criminology* that

> Numerous studies have shown that African-Americans are more likely to be arrested, indicted, convicted, and committed to an institution than are whites who commit the same offenses, and many other studies have shown

Excerpts from *The Rich Get Richer and The Poor Get Prison: Ideology, Class and Criminal Justice*, 5th ed. by Jeffrey H. Reiman, 1998. Copyright © 1998 by Jeffrey H. Reiman.

that blacks have a poorer chance than whites to receive probation, a suspended sentence, parole, commutation of a death sentence, or pardon.[3]

. . .

Curiously enough, statistics on differential treatment of races are available in greater abundance than are statistics on differential treatment of economic classes. For instance, although the FBI tabulates arrest rates by race (as well as by sex, age, and geographical area), it omits class or income. Similarly, both the President's Crime Commission Report and Sutherland and Cressey's *Criminology* have index entries for race or racial discrimination but none for class or income of offenders. It would seem that both independent and government data gatherers are more willing to own up to America's racism than to its class bias. Nevertheless, it does not pay to look at these as two independent forms of bias. It is my view that, at least as far as criminal justice is concerned, racism is simply one powerful form of economic bias. I use evidence on differential treatment of blacks as evidence of differential treatment of members of the lower classes. There are five reasons:

1. First and foremost, black Americans are disproportionately poor. In 1995, while one out of every eight white Americans received income below the poverty line, three out of every ten black Americans did.[4] The picture is even worse when we shift from income to wealth (property such as a home, land, stocks): In 1991, black households owned one-tenth the median net worth of white households.[5] Unemployment figures give a similarly dismal picture: In 1995, 4.9 percent of white workers were unemployed and 10.4 percent of blacks were. Among those in the crime-prone ages of 16 to 24, 15.6 percent of white youngsters (with no college) and 34.0 (more than one of every three) black youngsters (with no college) were jobless.[6]

2. The factors most likely to keep one out of trouble with the law and out of prison, such as a suburban living room instead of a tenement alley to gamble in or legal counsel able to devote time to one's case instead of an overburdened public defender, are the kinds of things that money can buy regardless of one's race, creed, or national origin. For example, as we shall see, arrests of blacks for illicit drug possession or dealing have skyrocketed in recent years, rising way out of proportion to drug

arrests for whites—though research shows no greater drug use among blacks than among whites. However, drug arrests are most easily made in "disorganized inner-city" areas, where drug sales are more likely to take place out of doors, and dealers are more willing to sell to strangers. Blacks are (proportionately) more likely than whites to live in such inner-city areas and thus more likely than whites to be arrested on drug charges.[7] But one very important reason that blacks are more likely than whites to live in disorganized inner-city areas is that a greater percentage of blacks than whites are poor and unemployed. What might at first look like a straightforward racial disparity turns out to reflect economic status.

3. Blacks who travel the full route of the criminal justice system and end up in jail or prison are close in economic condition to whites who do. In 1978, 53 percent of black jail inmates had pre-arrest incomes below $3,000, compared with 44 percent of whites.[8] 1983, the median pre-arrest income of black jail inmates was $4,067 and that of white jail inmates was $6,312. About half of blacks in jail were unemployed before arrest and 44 percent of whites were.[9] In 1991, 30 percent of whites in the prison population and 38 percent of blacks reported full- or part-time employment during the month before their arrest.[10]

4. Some studies suggest that race works to heighten the effects of economic condition on criminal justice outcomes, so that "being unemployed and black substantially increase[s] the chances of incarceration over those associated with being either unemployed or black."[11] This means that racism will produce a kind of selective economic bias, making a certain segment of the unemployed even more likely to end up behind bars.

5. Finally, it is my belief that the economic powers that be in America have sufficient power to end or drastically reduce racist bias in the criminal justice system. To the extent that they allow it to exist, it is not unreasonable to assume that it furthers their economic interests.

For all these reasons, racism will be treated here as either a form of economic bias or a tool that achieves the same end.

In the remainder of this [selection], I show how the criminal justice system functions to *weed out the wealthy* (meaning both middle- and upper-class offenders) at each stage of the process and thus produces a distorted image of the crime problem. Before entering into this discussion, three points are worth noting:

First, it is not my view that the poor are all innocent victims persecuted by the evil rich. The poor do commit crimes, and my own assumption is that the vast majority of the poor who are confined in our prisons are guilty of the crimes for which they were sentenced. In addition, there is good evidence that the poor do commit a greater portion of the crimes against person and property listed in the FBI Index than the middle- and upper classes do, relative to their numbers in the national population. What I have already tried to prove is that the crimes in the FBI Index are not the only acts that threaten us nor are they the acts that threaten us the most. What I will try to prove in what follows is that the poor are arrested and punished by the criminal justice system much more frequently than their contribution to the crime problem would warrant—thus the criminals who populate our prisons as well as the public's imagination are disproportionately poor.

Second, the following discussion has been divided into three sections that correspond to the major criminal justice decision points. . . . As always, such classifications are a bit neater than reality, and so they should not be taken as rigid compartments. Many of the distorting processes operate at all criminal justice decision points. So, for example, while I will primarily discuss the light-handed treatment of white-collar criminals in the section on charging and sentencing, it is also true that white-collar criminals are less likely to be arrested or convicted than are blue-collar criminals. The section in which a given issue is treated is a reflection of the point in the criminal justice process at which the disparities are the most striking. Suffice it to say, however, that the disparities between the treatment of the poor and the nonpoor are to be found at all points of the process.

Third, it must be borne in mind that the movement from arrest to sentencing is a funnelling process, so that discrimination that occurs at any early stage shapes the population that reaches later stages. Thus, for example, some recent studies find little economic bias in sentence length for people convicted of similar crimes.[12] When reading such studies, one should remember that the population that reaches the point of sentencing has already been subject to whatever discrimination exists at earlier stages. If, for example, among people with similar offenses and records, poor people are more likely to be charged and more likely to be convicted, then even if the sentencing of convicted criminals is evenhanded, it will reproduce the discrimination that occurred before.

❂ Arrest and Charging

The problem with most official records of who commits crime is that they are really statistics on who gets arrested and convicted. If, as I will show, the police are more likely to arrest some people than others, these official statistics may tell us more about police than about criminals. In any event, they give us little reliable data about those who commit crime and do not get caught. Some social scientists, suspicious of the bias built into official records, have tried to devise other methods of determining who has committed a crime. Most often, these methods involve an interview or questionnaire in which the respondent is assured of anonymity and asked to reveal whether he or she has committed any offenses for which he or she could be arrested and convicted. Techniques to check reliability of these self-reports also have been devised; however, if their reliability is still in doubt, common sense would dictate that they would understate rather than overstate the number of individuals who have committed crimes and never come to official notice. In light of this, the conclusions of these studies are rather astounding. It would seem that crime is the national pastime. The President's Crime Commission conducted a survey of 10,000 households and discovered that "91 percent of all Americans have violated laws that could have subjected them to a term of imprisonment at one time in their lives."[13]

A number of other studies support the conclusion that serious criminal behavior is widespread among middle- and upper-class individuals, although these individuals are rarely, if ever, arrested. Some of the studies show that there are no significant differences between economic classes in the incidence of criminal behavior.[14] The authors of a recent review of literature on class and delinquency conclude that "Research published since 1978, using both official and self-reported data suggests . . . that there is no pervasive relationship between SES [socioeconomic status] and delinquency."[15] This conclusion is echoed by Jensen and Thompson, who argue that

> The safest conclusion concerning class structure and delinquency is the same one that has been proposed for several decades: class, no matter how

defined, contributes little to explaining variation of self-reports of common delinquency.[16]

Others conclude that while lower-class individuals do commit more than their share of crime, arrest records overstate their share and understate that of the middle and upper classes.[17] Still other studies suggest that some forms of serious crime—forms usually associated with lower-class youth—show up *more frequently* among higher-class persons than among lower.[18] For instance, Empey and Erikson interviewed 180 white males aged 15 to 17 who were drawn from different economic strata. They found that "virtually all respondents reported having committed not one but a variety of different offenses." Although youngsters from the middle classes constituted 55 percent of the group interviewed, they admitted to 67 percent of the instances of breaking and entering, 70 percent of the instances of property destruction, and an astounding 87 percent of all armed robberies admitted to by the entire sample.[19] Williams and Gold studied a national sample of 847 males and females between the ages of 13 and 16.[20] Of these, 88 percent admitted to at least one delinquent offense.

Even those who conclude "that more lower status youngsters commit delinquent acts more frequently than do higher status youngsters"[21] also recognize that lower class youth are significantly overrepresented in official records. Gold writes that "about five times more lowest than highest status boys appear in the official records; if records were complete and unselective, we estimate that the ratio would be closer to 1.5:1."[22] The simple fact is that for the same offense, *a poor person is more likely to be arrested and, if arrested charged, than a middle- or upper-class person.*[23]

This means, first of all, that poor people are more likely to come to the attention of the police. Furthermore, even when apprehended, the police are more likely to formally charge a poor person and release a higher-class person *for the same offense.* Gold writes that

> boys who live in poorer parts of town and are apprehended by police for delinquency are four to five times more likely to appear in some official record than boys from wealthier sections who commit the same kinds of offenses. These same data show that, at each stage in the legal process from charging a boy with an offense to some sort of disposition in court, boys from different socioeconomic backgrounds are treated differently, so that those eventually incarcerated in public institutions, that site of most of the research on delinquency, are selectively poorer boys.[24]

From a study of self-reported delinquent behavior, Gold finds that when individuals were apprehended, "if the offender came from a higher status family, police were more likely to handle the matter themselves without referring it to the court."[25]

Terence Thornberry reached a similar conclusion in his study of 3,475 delinquent boys in Philadelphia. Thornberry found that among boys arrested *for equally serious offenses* and who had *similar prior offense records,* police were more likely to refer to lower-class youths than the more affluent ones to juvenile court. The police were more likely to deal with the wealthier youngsters informally, for example, by holding them in the station house until their parents came rather than instituting formal procedures. Of those referred to juvenile court, Thornberry found further that for *equally serious offenses* and with *similar prior records,* the poorer youngsters were more likely to be institutionalized than were the affluent ones. The wealthier youths were more likely to receive probation than the poorer ones. As might be expected, Thornberry found the same relationships when comparing the treatment of black and white youths apprehended for equally serious offenses.[26]

Recent studies continue to show similar effects. For example, Sampson found that, for the same crimes, juveniles in lower-class neighborhoods were more likely to have some police record than those in better-off neighborhoods. Again, for similar crimes, lower-class juveniles were more likely to be referred to court than better-off juveniles. If you think these differences are not so important because they are true only of young offenders, remember that this group accounts for much of the crime problem. Moreover, other studies not limited to the young tend to show the same economic bias. McCarthy found that, in metropolitan areas, for similar suspected crimes, unemployed people were more likely to be arrested than employed.[27]

As I indicated above, racial bias is but another form in which the bias against the poor works. And blacks are more likely to be suspected or arrested than whites. A 1988 *Harvard Law Review* overview of studies on race and the criminal process concludes that "most studies . . . reveal what many police officers freely admit: that police use race as an independently significant, if not determinative, factor in deciding whom to follow, detain, search, or arrest."[28] "A 1994 study of juvenile detention decisions found that African-American and Hispanic youths were more likely to be detained at each decision point, even after controlling for the influence of offense seriousness and social factors (e.g., single-parent home). Decisions by both police and the courts to detain a youngster were highly influenced by race."[29] The study states that, "[n]ot only were there direct effects of race, but indirectly, socioeconomic status was related to detention, thus putting youth of color again at risk for differential treatment."[30] Reporting the results of University of Missouri criminologist Kimberly Kempf's study of juvenile justice in fourteen Pennsylvania counties, Jerome Miller says that "Black teenagers were more likely to be detained, to be handled formally, to be waived to adult court, and to be adjudicated delinquent."[31] And the greater likelihood of arrest that minorities face is matched by a greater likelihood of being charged with a serious offense. For example, Huizinga and Elliott report that: "Minorities appear to be at greater risk for being charged with more serious offenses than whites when involved in comparable levels of delinquent behavior."[32] Bear in mind that once an individual has a criminal record, it becomes harder for that person to get employment thus increasing the likelihood of future criminal involvement and more serious criminal charges.

For reasons mentioned earlier, a disproportionately large percentage of the casualties in the recent War on Drugs are poor inner-city minority males. Michael Tonry writes that, "according to National Institute on Drug Abuse (1991) surveys of Americans' drug use, [Blacks] are not more likely than Whites ever to have used most drugs of abuse. Nonetheless, the . . . number of drug arrests of Blacks more than doubled between 1985 and 1989, whereas White drug arrests increased only by 27 percent."[33] A study conducted by the Sentencing Project, based mainly on Justice Department statistics, indicates that "Blacks make up 12 percent of the United States' population and constitute 13 percent of all monthly drug users . . . , but represent 35 percent of those arrested for drug possession, 55 percent of those convicted of drug possession and 74 percent of those sentenced to prison for drug possession."[34]

Numerous studies of police use of deadly force show that blacks are considerably more likely than whites or Hispanics to be shot by the police. For example, using data from Memphis, Tennessee, covering the years from 1969 through 1974, James Fyfe found that blacks were 10 times more likely than whites to have been shot at unsuccessfully by police, 18 times more likely to have been wounded, and 5 times more likely to have been killed."[35] A nation that has watched the brutal treatment meted out to Rodney King by California police officers will not find this surprising. Does anyone think this would have happened if King were a white man?

Any number of reasons can be offered to account for the differences in police treatment of poor versus well-off citizens. Some argue that they reflect that the poor have less privacy.[36] What others can do in their living rooms or backyards the poor do on the street. Others argue that a police officer's decision to book a poor youth and release a middle-class youth reflects either the officer's judgment that the higher-class youngster's family will be more likely and more able to discipline him or her than the lower-class youngster's, or differences in the degree to which poor and middle-class complainants demand arrest. Others argue that police training and police work condition police officers to be suspicious of certain kinds of people, such as lower-class youth, blacks, Mexicans, and so on,[37] a thus more likely to detect their criminality. Still others hold that police mainly arrest those with the least political clout,[38] those who are least able to focus public attention on police practices or bring political influence to bear, and these happen to be the members of the lowest social and economic classes.

Regardless of which view one takes, and probably all have some truth in them, one conclusion is inescapable. One of the reasons the offender "at the end of the road in prison is likely to be a member of the lowest social and economic groups in the country" is that the police officers who guard the access to the road to prison make sure that more poor people make the trip than well-to-do people.

Likewise for prosecutors. A recent study of prosecutors' decisions shows that lower-class individuals are more likely to have charges pressed against them than upper-class individuals.[39] Racial discrimination also characterizes prosecutors' decisions to charge. The *Harvard Law Review* overview of studies on race and the criminal process asserts, "Statistical studies indicate that prosecutors are more likely to pursue full prosecution, file more severe charges, and seek more stringent penalties in cases involving minority defendants than in cases involving nonminority defendants."[40] One study of whites, blacks, and Hispanics arrested in Los Angeles on suspicion of having committed a felony found that, among defendants with equally serious charges and prior records, 59 percent of whites had their charges dropped at the initial screening, compared with 40 percent of blacks and 37 percent of Hispanics.[41]

The *weeding out of the wealthy* starts at the very entrance to the criminal justice system: The decision about whom to investigate, arrest, or charge is not made simply on the basis of the offense committed or the danger posed.

It is a decision distorted by a systematic economic bias that works to the disadvantage of the poor.

This economic bias is a two-edged sword. Not only are the poor arrested and charged out of proportion to their numbers for the kinds of crimes poor people generally commit—burglary, robbery, assault, and so forth—but when we reach the kinds of crimes poor people almost never have the opportunity to commit, such as antitrust violations, industrial safety violations, embezzlement, and serious tax evasion, the criminal justice system shows an increasingly benign and merciful face. The more likely that a crime is the type committed by middle- and upper-class people, the less likely that it will be treated as a criminal offense. When it comes to crime in the streets, where the perpetrator is apt to be poor, he or she is even more likely to be arrested and formally charged. When it comes to crime in the suites, where the offender is apt to be affluent, the system is most likely to deal with the crime noncriminally, that is, by civil litigation or informal settlement. Where it does choose to proceed criminally, as we will see in the section on sentencing, it rarely goes beyond a slap on the wrist. Not only is the main entry to the road to prison held wide open to the poor but the access routes for the wealthy are largely sealed off. Once again, we should not be surprised at whom we find in our prisons.

• • •

◉ *C*onviction

Between arrest and imprisonment lies the crucial process that determines guilt or innocence. Studies of individuals accused of similar offenses and with similar prior records show that the poor defendant is more likely to be adjudicated guilty than is the wealthier defendant.[42] In the adjudication process the only thing that *should* count is whether the accused is guilty and whether the prosecution can prove it beyond a reasonable doubt. Unfortunately, at least two other factors that are irrelevant to the question of guilt or innocence significantly affect the outcome: One is the ability of the accused to be free on bail prior to trial; and the second is access to legal counsel able to devote adequate time and energy to the case. Because both bail and high-quality legal counsel cost money, it should come as no surprise that here as elsewhere the poor do poorly.

Being released on bail is important in several respects. First and fore-most is that those not released on bail are kept in jail like individuals who have been found guilty. They are thus punished while they are still legally innocent. "On June 30, 1995, an estimated 44 percent of the nation's adult jail inmates had been convicted on their current charge. An estimated 223,000 adult jail inmates were serving a sentence, awaiting sentencing, or serving time in jail for a probation or parole violation. Between 1985 and 1995 the number of convicted inmates rose by nearly 100,000—up from 13,409. During the same period, the number of convicted jail inmates, including those on trial or awaiting arraignment or trial, doubled (from 127,059 to an estimated 284,100)."[43] Beyond the obvious ugliness of punishing people before they are found guilty, confined defendants suffer from other disabilities. Specifically, they cannot actively aid in their own defense by seeking out witnesses and evidence. Several studies have shown that among defendants accused of the same offenses those who make bail are more likely to be acquitted than those who do not.[44] In a recent study of unemployment and punishment, Chiricos and Bales found that "after the effects of other factors [seriousness of crime, prior record, etc.] were controlled, an unemployed defendant was 3.2 times more like to be incar-cerated before trial than his employed counterpart."[45]

Furthermore, because the time spent in jail prior to adjudication of guilt may count as part of the sentence if one is found guilty, the accused are often placed in a ticklish position. Let us say the accused believes he or she is innocent, and let us say also that he or she has been in the slammer for two months awaiting trial. Along comes the prosecutor to offer a deal: If you plead guilty to such-and-such (usually a lesser offense than has been charged, say, possession of burglar's tools instead of burglary), the prosecu-tor promises to ask the judge to sentence you to two months. In other words, plead guilty and walk out of jail today (free, but with a criminal record that will make finding a job hard and insure a stiffer sentence next time around)—or maintain your innocence, stay in jail until trial, and then be tried for the full charge instead of the lesser offense! In fact, not only does the prosecutor threaten to prosecute for the full charge, but this is often accompanied by the implied but very real threat to press for the most severe penalty as well—for taking up the court's time.

Plea bargaining such as this is an everyday occurrence in the criminal justice system. Contrary to the Perry Mason image, the vast majority of crim-inal convictions in the United States are reached without a trial. It is estimated that between 70 and 95 percent of convictions are the result of a negotiated plea,[46] that is, a bargain in which the accused agrees to plead guilty (usually to a lesser offense than he or she is charged with or to one offense out of many he or she is charged with) in return for an informal promise of leniency from the prosecutor with the tacit consent of the judge. If you were the jailed defendant offered a deal like this, how would you choose? Suppose you were a poor black man not likely to be able to retain F. Lee Bailey or Edward Bennett Williams for your defense.

The advantages of access to adequate legal counsel during the adjudicative process are obvious but still worthy of mention. In 1963, the U.S. Supreme Court handed down the landmark *Gideon v. Wainwright* decision, holding that the states must provide legal counsel to the indigent in all felony cases. As a result, no person accused of a serious crime need face his or her accuser without a lawyer. However, the Supreme Court has not held that the Constitution entitles individuals to lawyers able to devote equal time and resources to their cases. Even though *Gideon* represents significant progress in making good on the constitutional promise of equal treatment before the law, we still are left with two transmission belts of justice: one for the poor and one for the affluent. There is an emerging body of case law on the right to effective assistance of counsel;[47] however, this is yet to have any serious impact on the assembly-line legal aid handed out to the poor.

Indigent defendants, those who cannot afford to retain their own lawyers, will be defended either by a public defender or by a private attorney assigned by the court. Because the public defender is a salaried attorney with a case load much larger than that of a private criminal lawyer,[48] and because court-assigned private attorneys are paid a fixed fee that is much lower than they charge their regular clients, neither is able or motivated to devote much time to the indigent defendant's defense. Both are strongly motivated to bring their cases to a close quickly by negotiating a plea of guilty. Because the public defender works in day-to-day contact with the prosecutor and the judge, the pressures on him or her to negotiate a plea as quickly as possible, instead of rocking the boat by threatening to go to trial,[49] are even greater than those that work on court-assigned counsel. In an essay aptly titled "Did You Have a Lawyer When You Went to Court? No, I Had a Public Defender," Jonathan Casper reports the perceptions of this process from the standpoint of the defendants:

> Most of the men spent very little time with their public defender. In the court in which they eventually plead guilty, they typically reported spend-

ing on the order of five to ten minutes with their public defender. These conversations usually took place in the bull-pen of the courthouse or in the hallway.

The brief conversations usually did not involved much discussion of the details surrounding the alleged crime, mitigating circumstances or the defendants' motives or backgrounds. Instead, they focused on the deal, the offer the prosecution was likely to make or had made in return for a cop out. Often the defendants reported that the first words the public defender spoke (or at least the first words the defendants recalled) were, "I can get you . . . , if you plead guilty."[50]

As might be expected, with less time and fewer resources to devote to the cause, public defenders and assigned lawyers cannot devote as much time and research to preparing the crucial pretrial motions that can often lead to dismissal of charges against the accused. A recent study of 28,315 felony defendants in various county and city jurisdictions in Tennessee, Virginia, and Kentucky shows that public defenders got cases dropped for 11.3 percent of their defendants, and private attorneys got dismissals for *48 percent of their defendants.* As also might be expected, the overall acquittal rate for privately retained counsel is considerably better than that for public defenders. The same study shows that public defenders achieved either dismissal of charges or a finding of not guilty in 11.4 percent of the indictments they handled, and private attorneys got their clients off the hook in *56 percent of their cases.* The superior record of private attorneys held good when comparisons were made among defendants accused of similar offenses and with similar prior records.[51] The picture that emerges from federal courts is not much different.[52]

The problem of adequate legal representation is particularly acute in capital cases. According to Robert Johnson, "Most attorneys in capital cases are provided by the state. Defendants, as good capitalists, routinely assume that they will get what they pay for: next to nothing." Their perceptions, he concludes, "may not be far from right." Indeed, Stephen Gettinger maintains that an inadequate defense was "the single outstanding characteristic" of the condemned persons he studied. The result: Capital defendants appeared in court as "creatures beyond comprehension, virtually gagged and masked in preparation for the execution chamber."[53] Writes Linda Williams in the *Wall Street Journal,*

The popular perception is that the system guarantees a condemned person a lawyer. But most states provide counsel only for the trial and the auto-

matic review of the sentence by the state appeals court. Indigent prisoners
—a description that applies to just about everybody on death row—who
seek further review must rely on the charity of a few private lawyers and
on cash-starved organizations like the Southern Prisoners Defense
Committee.[54]

A recent *Time* magazine article on this topic is entitled "You Don't Always
Get Perry Mason." Says the author, "Because the majority of murder defendants are . . . broke . . . , many of them get court-appointed lawyers who
lack the resources, experience or inclination to do their utmost. . . . Some
people go to traffic court with better prepared lawyers than many murder
defendants get."[55]

Needless to say, the distinct legal advantages that money can buy
become even more salient when we enter the realm of corporate and other
white-collar crime. Indeed, it is often precisely the time and cost involved in
bringing to court a large corporation with its army of legal eagles that is
offered as an excuse for the less formal and more genteel treatment accorded
to corporate crooks. This excuse is, of course, not equitably distributed to
all economic classes, any more than quality legal service is. This means that
regardless of actual innocence or guilt, one's chances of beating the rap
increase as one's income increases. Regardless of what fraction of crimes are
committed by the poor, the criminal justice system is distorted so that an
even greater fraction of those convicted will be poor. And with conviction
comes sentencing.

❧ Sentencing

On June 28, 1990, the House Subcommittee on Financial Institutions
Supervision, Regulation and Insurance met in the Rayburn House Office
Building to hold hearings on the prosecution of savings and loan criminals.
The chairman of the subcommittee, Congressman Frank Annunzio, called
the meeting to order and said:

> The American people are furious with the slow pace of prosecutions
> involving savings and loan criminals. These crooks are responsible for 1/3,
> 1/2, or maybe even more, of the savings and loan cost. The American
> taxpayer will be forced to pay $500 billion or more over the next 40 years,
> largely because of these crooks. For many Americans, this bill will not be
> paid until their grandchildren are old enough to retire.

We are here to get an answer to one question: "When are the S&L crooks going to jail?"

The answer from the administration seems to be: "probably never."

Frankly, I don't think the administration has the interest in pursuing Gucci-clad, white-collar criminals. These are hard and complicated cases, and the defendants often were rich, successful prominent members of their upper-class communities. It is far easier putting away a sneaker-clad high school dropout who tries to rob a bank of a thousand dollars with a stick-up note, than a smooth talking S&L executive who steals a million dollars with a fraudulent note.

Later in the hearing, Chairman Annunzio questioned the administration's representative:

You cited, Mr. Dennis, several examples in your testimony of successful convictions with stiff sentences, but the average sentence so far is actually about 2 years, compared to an average sentence of about 9 years for bank robbery. Why do we throw the book at people who rob a bank in broad daylight but we coddle people who . . . rob the bank secretly?[56]

The simple fact is that the criminal justice system reserves its harshest penalties for its lower-class clients and puts on kid gloves when confronted with a better class of crook.

We will come back to the soft treatment of the S&L crooks shortly. For the moment, note that the tendency to treat higher-class criminals more leniently than lower-class criminals has been with us for a long time. In 1972, the *New York Times* did a study on sentencing in state and federal courts. The *Times* stated that "crimes that tend to be committed by the poor get tougher sentences than those committed by the well-to-do," that federal "defendants who could not afford private counsel were sentenced nearly twice as severely as defendants with private or no counsel," and that a "study by the Vera Institute of Justice of courts in the Bronx indicates a similar pattern in the state courts."[57]

More recently, D'Alessio and Stolzenberg studied a random sample of 2,760 offenders committed to the custody of the Florida Department of Corrections during fiscal year 1985. Although they found no greater sentence severity for poor offenders found guilty of property crimes, they found that poor offenders did receive longer sentences for violent crimes, such as manslaughter, and for morals offenses, such as narcotics possession. Nor, by the way, did sentencing guidelines reduce this disparity.[58] A study of individuals convicted of drunk driving found that increased education (taken as an indicator of higher occupational status) "increase[d] the rate of movement from case filing to probation and decrease[d] the rate of movement to prison." And though when probation was given, more-educated offenders got longer probation, they also got shorter prison sentences, if sentenced to prison at all.[59]

Chiricos and Bales found that, for individuals guilty of similar offenses and with similar prior records, unemployed defendants were more likely to be incarcerated while awaiting trial, and for longer periods, than employed defendants. They were more than twice as likely as their employed counterparts to be incarcerated upon a finding of guilt. And defendants with public defenders experienced longer periods of jail time than those who could afford private attorneys.[60] McCarthy noted a similar link between unemployment and greater likelihood of incarceration.[61] In his study of 28,315 felony defendants in Tennessee, Virginia, and Kentucky, Champion also found that offenders who could afford private counsel had a greater likelihood of probation, and received shorter sentences when incarceration was imposed.[62] A study of the effects of implementing Minnesota's determinate sentencing program shows that socio-economic bias is "more subtle, but no less real" than before the new program.[63]

Tillman and Pontell examined the sentences received by individuals convicted of Medicaid provider fraud in California. Because such offenders normally have no prior arrests and are charged with grand theft, their sentences were compared with the sentences of other offenders convicted of grand theft and who also had no prior records. While 37.7 percent of the Medicaid defrauders were sentenced to some jail or prison time, 79.2 percent of the others convicted of grand theft were sentenced to jail or prison. This was so even though the median dollar loss due to the Medicaid frauds was $13,000, more than ten times the median loss due to the other grand thefts ($1,149). Tillman and Pontell point out that most of the Medicaid defrauders were health professionals, while most of the others convicted of grand theft had low-level jobs or were unemployed. They conclude that "differences in the sentences imposed on the two samples are indeed the result of the different social statuses of their members."[64]

As usual, data on racial discrimination in sentencing tell the same story of the treatment of those who cannot afford the going price of justice. A study of offender processing in New York State counties found that, for offenders with the same arrest charge and the same prior criminal records, minorities were incarcerated more often than comparably situated whites.[65] A study of sentencing in Miami concludes that when case-related attributes do not clearly point to a given sentence, sentencing disparities are more likely to be based on race.[66] Most striking perhaps is that, in 1993, 51 percent of inmates in state and federal prisons were black and 44 percent of inmates of jails were black, whereas blacks make up only 36.5 percent of those arrested for serious (FBI Index) crimes.[67] Furthermore, when we look only at federal prisons, where there is reason to believe that racial and economic discrimination is less prevalent than in state institutions, we find that in 1986, nonwhite inmates were sentenced, on average, 33 more months for burglary than white inmates and 22 more months for income tax evasion. In 1989, the average federal sentence for blacks found guilty of violent offenses was 10 months longer than for whites.[68]

Here must be mentioned the notorious "100-to-1" disparity between sentences for possession of cocaine in powder form (popular in the affluent suburbs) and in crack form (popular in poor inner-city neighborhoods). Federal laws require a mandatory five-year sentence for crimes involving 500 grams of powder cocaine or 5 grams of crack cocaine. This yields a sentence for first-time offenders (with no aggravating factors, such as possession of a weapon) that is higher than the sentence for kidnapping, and only slightly lower than the sentence for attempted murder![69] About 90 percent of those convicted of Federal crack offenses are black, about 4 percent are white. "As a result, the average prison sentence served by Black federal prisoners is 40 percent longer than the average sentence for Whites."[70] In 1995, the United States Sentencing Commission recommended ending the 100-to-1 disparity between powder and crack penalties, and, in an unusual display of bipartisanship, both the Republican Congress and the Democratic President rejected their recommendation.[71]

Sentencing disparities between the races are, of course, not new. An extensive study by the *Boston Globe* of 4,500 cases of armed robbery, aggravated assault, and rape found that "blacks convicted in the superior courts of Massachusetts receive harsher penalties than whites for the same crimes."[72] The authors of a study of almost 1,200 males sentenced to prison for armed robbery in a southeastern state found that "in 1977 whites incarcerated for armed robbery had a greater than average chance of receiving the least severe sentence, while nonwhites had a greater than average chance of receiving a moderately severe sentence."[73] A study of 229 adjudicated cases in a Florida judicial district yielded the finding that "whites have an 18 percent greater chance in the predicted probability of receiving probation than blacks when all other things are equal."[71] A recent study of criminal justice systems in California, Michigan, and Texas by Petersilia confirms the continuation of this trend. "Controlling for the factors most likely to influence sentencing and parole decisions," she writes, "the analysis still found that blacks and Hispanics are less likely to be given probation, more likely to receive *prison* sentences, more likely to receive longer sentences, and more likely to serve a greater portion of their original time."[75] Myers found that "harsher treatment of persons with fewer resources (e.g., female, unemployed, unmarried, black) is . . . pronounced in highly unequal counties."[76]

The federal government has introduced sentencing guidelines and minimum mandatory sentences that might be expected to eliminate discrimination, and many states have followed suit. The effect of this, however, has been not to eliminate discretion but to transfer it from those who sentence to those who decide what to charge—that is, from judges to prosecutors. Prosecutors can charge in a way that makes it likely that the offender will get less than the mandatory minimum sentence. Says U.S. District Judge J. Lawrence Irving of San Diego, "the system is run by the U.S. attorneys. When they decide how to indict, they fix the sentence."[77]

. . .

We have seen in this [selection] . . . that the criminl justice system is triply biased against the poor. First, there is the economic class bias *among harmful acts* as to which get labeled crimes and which are treated as regulatory matters . . . Second, there is economic class bias *among crimes* that we have already seen in this [selection]. The crimes that poor people are likely to commit carry harsher sentences than the "crimes in suites" committed by well-to-do- people. Third, *among defendants convicted of the same crimes*, the poor receive less probation and more years of confinement than well-off defendants, assuring us once again that the vast majority of those put behind bars are from the lowest social and economic classes in the nation. On either side of the law, the rich get richer . . .

❧ . . . and the *Poor Get Prison*

At 9:05 A.M. on the morning of Thursday, September 9, 1971, a group of inmates forced their way through a gate at the center of the prison, fatally injured a guard named William Quinn, and took 50 hostages. The Attica uprising had begun. It lasted four days, until 9:43 A.M. on the morning of Monday, September 13, when corrections officers and state troopers stormed the prison and killed 29 inmates and 10 hostages.[78] During those four days the nation saw the faces of its captives on television—the hard black faces of young men who had grown up on the streets of Harlem and other urban ghettos. Theirs were the faces of crime in America. The television viewers who saw them were not surprised. Here were faces of dangerous men who should be locked up. Nor were people outraged when the state launched its murderous attack on the prison, killing many more inmates and guards than did the prisoners themselves. Maybe they were shocked—but not outraged. Neither were they outraged when two grand juries refused to indict any of the attackers, nor when the mastermind of the attack, New York Gov. Nelson Rockefeller, was named to be vice president of the United States three years after the uprising and massacre.[79]

They were not outraged because the faces they saw on the TV screens fit and confirmed their beliefs about who is a deadly threat to American society and a deadly threat must be met with deadly force. How did those men get to Attica? How did Americans get their beliefs about who is a dangerous person? These questions are interwoven. People get their notions about who is a criminal at least in part from the occasional television or newspaper picture of who is inside our prisons. The individuals they see there have been put in prison because people believe certain kinds of individuals are dangerous and should be locked up.

I have argued in this [selection] that this is not a simple process of selecting the dangerous and the criminal from among the peace-loving and the law-abiding. It is also a process of *weeding out the wealthy* at every stage, so that the final picture—a picture like that that appeared on the TV screen on September 9, 1971—is not a true reflection of the real dangers in our society but a distorted image, the kind reflected in a carnival mirror.

It is not my view that the inmates in Attica were innocent of the crimes that sent them there. I assume they and just about all the individuals in prisons in America are probably guilty of the crime for which they were sentenced and maybe more. My point is that people who are equally or more dangerous, equally or more criminal, are not there; that the criminal justice system works systematically not to punish and confine the dangerous and the criminal *but to punish and confine the poor who are dangerous and criminal.*

It is successful at all levels. In 1973, there were 204,211 individuals in state and federal prisons, or 96 prisoners for every 100,000 individuals (of all ages) in the general population. By 1979, state and federal inmates numbered 301,470, or 133 per 100,000 Americans. By 1995, there were a total of 1,585,401 persons in state and federal prisons and in local jails, a staggering 600 for every 100,000 in the population. One in 167 U.S. residents (of all ages and both sexes) was behind bars by the end of 1995. However, of the 1,585,401 prisoners, more than a million are men, virtually all above the age of 18. Because the adult male population in the United States is about 93 million, *this means that more than one out of every 100 American adult men is behind bars.* [80] This enormous number of prisoners is, of course, predominantly from the bottom of society.

Of the estimated 711,643 people in state prisons in June 1991, 33 percent were not employed at all (full or part time) prior to their arrests. About half of these were looking for work and half were not. Another 12 percent had only part-time jobs before prison, making fully 45 percent who were without full-time employment prior to arrest. These statistics represent a general worsening compared with 1986, when 31 percent of state inmates had no pre-arrest employment at all, and 43 percent had no full-time pre-arrest employment. Of those 1991 state inmates who had been free at least a year before arrest, 19 percent had some pre-arrest annual income but less than $3,000 50 percent had some pre-arrest annual income but less than $10,000.[81]

To get an idea of what part of society is in prison, we should compare these figures with comparable figures for the general population. Because 95 percent of state inmates are male, we can look at employment and income figures for males in the general society in 1990. Statistics on employment and income for 1990 are close to those for 1988 and 1989, and so will give us a fair sense of the general population from which the current state inmates came.

In 1990, 5.6 percent of males, 16-years-old and above, in the labor force were unemployed and looking for work. This corresponds to half the state inmates who were unemployed before arrest, because the other half who were unemployed were not looking for work. Where 16 percent of state prisoners had been unemployed and still looking for work, only 5.6 percent of males in the general population were in this condition. Thus, prisoners were unemployed and looking for work at a rate three times that of males in the general population. But this doesn't give us the full picture, because it doesn't capture the unemployed prisoners who had not been seeking work. To capture that, let us assume that, as among the prisoners, the number of males in the general population who are unemployed and not looking is equal to the number in the labor force who are unemployed and looking. (Note that this assumption is high, but for present purposes conservative, as the higher it is the more it will decrease the relative difference between prisoners and general male population.) The 5.6 percent of males in the labor force represents approximately 3,799,000 persons. If we double it, we get 7,598,000 as an estimate of the total number of males in the general population who are unemployed, looking for work or not. As a percentage of the total noninstitutionalized population of males 16 and over, this is 8.5 percent. Compare this with the 33 percent of state inmates who were unemployed prior to being arrested. *Then, state prisoners were unemployed at a rate nearly four times that of males in the general population.*[82]

Where 19 percent of prisoners with any pre-arrest income at all earned less than $3,000 a year, 6.8 percent of males in the civilian labor force in 1990 earned between $1 and $2,499 a year, and 12.3 percent earned between $1 and $4,999. Fifty percent of the inmates had annual incomes between $1 and $10,000, while 25 percent of males in the general population earned in that range.[83]

Our prisoners are not a cross-section of America. They are considerably poorer and considerably less likely to be employed than the rest of Americans. Moreover, they are also less educated, which is to say less in possession of the means to improve their sorry situations. Of all U.S. prison inmates, 47 percent did not graduate from high school, compared to 21 percent of the U.S. adult population. Sixteen percent of prisoners said they had some college, compared to 43 percent of the U.S. adult population.[84]

The criminal justice system is sometimes thought of as a kind of sieve in which the innocent are progressively sifted out from the guilty, who end up behind bars. I have tried to show that the sieve works another way as well. It sifts the affluent out from the poor, so it is not merely the guilty who end up behind bars, but the *guilty poor.*

· · ·

*E*ndnotes

[1]Compare the statement, written more than half a century ago, by Professor Edwin H. Sutherland, one of the major luminaries of twentieth-century criminology:

First, the administrative processes are more favorable to persons in economic comfort than to those in poverty, so that if two persons on different economic levels are equally guilty of the same offense, the one on the lower level is more likely to be arrested, convicted, and committed to an institution. Second, the laws are written, administered, and implemented primarily with reference to the types of crimes committed by people of lower economic levels. [E. H. Sutherland, *Principles of Criminology* (Philadelphia: Lippincott, 1939), p.179].

[2]For example, in 1991, when blacks made up 12 percent of the national population, they accounted for 46 percent of the U.S. state prison population. BJS, *Survey of State Prison Inmates*, 1991, p. 3.

[3]Edwin H. Sutherland and Donald R. Cressey, *Criminology*, 9th ed. (Philadelphia: Lippincott, 1974), p. 133. The following studies are cited in support of this point (p. 133, note 4): Edwin M. Lemert and Judy Roseberg, "The Administration of Justice to Minority Groups in Los Angeles County," University of California Publications in Culture and Society 2, no. 1 (1948), pp. 1–28; Thorsten Sellin, "Race Prejudice in the Administration of Justice," American Journal of Sociology 41 (September 1935), pp. 212–217; Sidney Alexrad, "Negro and White Male Institutionalized Delinquents," *American Journal of Sociology* 57 (May 1952), pp. 569–74; Marvin E. Wolfgang, Arlene Kelly, and Hans C. Nolde, "Comparisons of the Executed and the Commuted Among Admissions to Death Row," *Journal of Criminal Law, Criminology, and Police Science* 53 (September 1962), pp. 301–11; Nathan Goldman, *The Differential Selection of Juvenile Offenders for Court Appearance* (New York National Council on Crime and Delinquency, 1963); Irving Piliavin and Scott Briar, "Police Encounters with Juveniles," *American Journal of Sociology* 70 (September 1964), pp. 206–14; Robert M. Terry, "The Screening of Juvenile Offenders," *Journal of Criminal Law, Criminology, and Police Science* 58 (June 1967), pp. 173–81. See also Ramsey Clark, *Crime in America* (New York: Simon and Schuster, 1970), p. 51: "Negroes are arrested more frequently and on less evidence than whites and are more often victims of mass or sweep arrests"; and Donald Taft, *Criminology*, 3d ed. (New York: Macmillan, 1956), p. 134:

Negroes are more likely to be suspected of crime than are whites. They are also more likely to be arrested. If the perpetrator of a crime is known to be a Negro the police may arrest all Negroes who were near the scene—a procedure they would rarely dare to follow with whites. After arrest Negroes are less likely to secure bail, and so are more liable to be counted in jail statistics. They are more liable than whites to be indicted and less likely to have their case nol prossed or otherwise dismissed. If tried, Negroes are more likely to be convicted. If convicted they are less likely to be given probation. For this reason they are more likely to be included in the count of prisoners. Negroes are also more likely than whites to be kept in prison for the full terms of their commitments and correspondingly less likely to be paroled.

[4]*StatAbst-1996*, p. 48, Table no. 49. See also Karen Pennar, "The Rich are Richer—and America May Be the Poorer," *Business Week*, November 18, 1991, pp. 85–88.

[5]*StatAbst-1994*, p. 482, Table no. 742. See also Carole Shammas, "A New Look at Long-Term Trends in Wealth Inequality in the United States," *American Historical Review* 98, no. 2 (April 1993), p. 422.

[6]*StatAbst-1996*, p. 48, Table no. 49; and p. 398, Table no. 623.

[7]Michael Tonry, "Racial Politics, Racial Disparities, and the War on Crime," *Crime & Delinquency* 40, no. 4 (October 1994), pp. 483, 485-86.

[8]*Sourcebook-1981*, p. 463.

[9]*StatAbst-1988*, p.175, Table no. 304.

[10]BJS, *Profile of Inmates in the United States and in England and Wales, 1991* (October 1994, NCJ-145863), p. 13.

[11]Theodore Chiricos and William Bales, "Unemployment and Punishment: An Empirical Assessment," *Criminology* 29, no. 4 (1991), p. 718.

[12]"An offender's socioeconomic status . . . did not impact sentence length for any of the property offenses." Stewart J. D'Alession and Lisa Stolzenberg, "Socioeconomic Status and the Sentencing of the Traditional Offender," *Journal of Criminal Justice* 21 (1993), p. 73. The same study did find lower economic status offenders received harsher sentences for violent and moral order crimes. Another study that finds no greater likelihood of incarceration based on socioeconomic status is Michael Benson and Esteban Walker, "Sentencing the White-Collar Offender," *American Sociological Review* 53 (April 1988), pp. 294–302. And yet another found higher-status offenders to be more likely to be incarcerated. David Weisburd, Elin Waring, and Stanton Wheeler, "Class, Status, and the Punishment of White Collar Criminals," *Law and Social Inquiry* 16 (1990), pp. 223–41. These last two studies are limited to offenders convicted of white-collar crimes, and so they deal with a sample that has already been subject to whatever discrimination exists in the arrest, charging, and conviction of white-collar offenders.

[13]Isidore Silver, "Introduction" to the Avon edition of *The Challenge of Crime in a Free Society* (New York: Avon, 1968), p. 31.

[14]This is the conclusion of Austin L. Porterfield, *Youth in Trouble* (Fort Worth: Leo Potishman Foundation, 1946); Fred J. Murphy, M. Shirley, and H.L. Witmer, "The Incidence of Hidden Delinquency," *American Journal of Orthopsychiatry* 16 (October 1946), pp. 686–96; James F. Short Jr., "A Report on the Incidence of Criminal Behavior, Arrests, and Convictions in Selected Groups," *Proceedings of the Pacific Sociological Society*, 1954, pp. 110–18, published as vol. 22, no. 2 of *Research Studies of the State College of Washington* (Pullman: State College of

Washington, 1954); F. Ivan Nye, James F Short Jr., and Virgil J. Olson, "Socioeconomic Status and Delinquent Behavior," *American Journal of Sociology* 63 (January 1958), pp. 381–89; Maynard L. Erickson and Lamar T. Empey, "Class Position, Peers and Delinquency," *Sociology and Social Research* 49 (April 1965), pp. 268–82; William J. Chambliss and Richard H. Nagasawa, "On the Validity of Official Statistics; A Comparative Study of White, Black, and Japanese High-School Boys," *Journal of Research in Crime and Delinquency* 6 (January 1969), pp. 71–77; Eugene Doleschal, "Hidden Crime," *Crime and Delinquency Literature* 2, no. 5 (October 1970), pp. 546–72; Nanci Koser Wilson, *Risk Ratios in Juvenile Delinquency* (Ann Arbor, Mich.: University Microfilms, 1972); and Maynard L. Erikson, "Group Violations, Socioeconomic Status, and Official Delinquency," *Social Forces* 52, no.1 (September 1973), pp. 41–52.

[15]Charles R. Tittle and Robert F Meier, "Specifying the SES/Delinquency Relationship," *Criminology* 28, no. 2 (1990), p. 292.

[16]Gary F. Jensen and Kevin Thompson, "What's Class Got to Do with It? A Further Examination of Power-Control Theory," *American Journal of Sociology* 95, no. 4 (January 1990) p.1021.

[17]This is the conclusion of Martin Gold, "Undetected Delinquent Behavior," *Journal of Research in Crime and Delinquency* 3, no. 1 (1966), pp. 27–46; and of Sutherland and Cressey, *Criminology*, pp. 137, 220.

[18]Cf. Larry Karacki and Jackson Toby, "The Uncommitted Adolescent: Candidate for Gang Socialization," *Sociological Inquiry* 32 (1962), pp. 203–15; William R. Arnold, "Continuities in Research—Scaling Delinquent Behavior," *Social Problems* 13, no. 1(1965), pp. 59–66; Harwin L. Voss, "Socio-economic Status and Reported Delinquent Behavior," *Social Problems*, 13, no. 3 (1966), pp. 314–24; LaMar Empey and Maynard L. Erikson, "Hidden Delinquency and Social Status," *Social Forces* 44, no. 4 (1966), pp. 546–54; Fred J. Shanley, "Middle-class Delinquency As a Social Problem," *Sociology and Social Research* 51(1967), pp. 185–98; Jay R. Williams and Martin Gold, "From Delinquent Behavior to Official Delinquency," *Social Problems* 20, no. 2 (1972), pp. 209–29.

[19]Empey and Erikson "Hidden Delinquency and Social Status," pp. 549, 551. Nye, Short, and Olson also found destruction of property to be committed most frequently by upper-class boys and girls, "Socioeconomic Status and Delinquent Behavior," p. 385.

[20]Williams and Gold, "From Delinquent Behavior to Official Delinquency," *Social Problems* 20, no. 2 (1972), pp. 209–29.

[21]Gold, "Undetected Delinquent Behavior," p. 37.

[22]Ibid., p. 44.

[23]Comparing socioeconomic status categories "scant evidence is found that would support the contention that group delinquency is more characteristic of the lower-status levels than other socioeconomic status levels. In fact, only arrests seem to be more characteristic of the low-status category than the other categories." Erikson, "Group Violations, Socioeconomic Status and Official Delinquency," p. 15.

[24]Gold, "Undetected Delinquent Behavior," p. 28 (emphasis added).

[25]Ibid., p. 38

[26]Terence P. Thornberry, "Race, Socioeconomic Status and Sentencing in the Juvenile Justice System," *Journal of Criminal Law and Criminology* 64, no. 1 (1973).

[27]Robert Sampson, "Effects of Socioeconomic Context on Official Reaction to Juvenile Delinquency," *American Sociological Review* 51 (December 1986), pp. 876–85; Belinda R. McCarthy, "Social Structure, Crime, and Social Control: An Examination of Factors Influencing Rates and Probabilities of Arrest," *Journal of Criminal Justice* 19, (1991), pp. 19–29.

[29]Jerome Miller, *Search and Destroy: African-American Males in the Criminal Justice System* (Cambridge: Cambridge University Press, 1996), p. 76. The study reported is M. Wordes, T. Bynum, and C. Corley, "Locking Up Youth: The Impact of Race on Detention Decision," *Journal of Research in Crime and Delinquency* 31, no. 2 (May 1994).

[30]M. Wordes et al., "Locking Up Youth," p. 164; quoted in Miller, *Search and Destroy*, pp. 76–77.

[31]Miller, *Search and Destroy*, p. 72. The study reported is Kimberly L. Kempf, *The Role of Race in Juvenile Justice Processing in Pennsylvania*, Study Grant #89–90/J/01/3615, Pennsylvania Commission on Crime and Delinquency, August 1992.

[32]David Huzinga and Delbert Elliott, "Juvenile Offenders: Prevalence, Offender Incidence and Arrest Rates by Race," paper presented at Meeting on Race and the Incarceration of Juveniles, Racine, Wisconsin, December 1986, University of Colorado, Boulder, Institute of Behavioral Science, National Youth Survey; reported in Miller, *Search and Destroy*, p. 73.

[33]Michael Tonry, "Racial Politics, Racial Disparities, and the War on Crime," *Crime & Delinquency* 40, no. 4 (October 1994), p. 483.

[34]Fox Butterfield, "More Blacks in Their 20's Have Trouble With the Law," *New York Times*, October 5, 1995, p. A8.

[35]James Fyfe, "Blind Justice: Police Shooting sin Memphis," *Journal of Criminal Law and Criminology* 73 (1982), pp. 707, 718–20.

³⁶See, for example, D. Chapman, "The Stereotype of the Criminal and the Social Consequences," *International Journal of Criminology and Penology* 1 (1973), p. 24.

³⁷This view is widely held, although the degree to which it functions as a self-fulfilling prophecy is less widely recognized. Versions of this view can be seen in *Challenge*, p. 79; Jerome Skolnick, *Justice Without Trial* (New York: Wiley, 1966), pp. 45–48, 217–218; and Jessica Mitford, *Kind and Usual Punishment*, p. 53. Piliavin and Briar write in "Police Encounters with Juveniles":

> *Compared to other youths, Negroes and boys whose appearance matched the delinquent stereotype were more frequently stopped and interrogated by patrolmen—often even in the absence of evidence that an offense had been committed—usually were given more severe dispositions for the same violations. Our data suggest, however, that these selective apprehension and disposition practices resulted not only from the intrusion of long-held prejudices of individual police officers but also from certain job-related experiences of law enforcement personnel. First, the tendency of police to give more severe dispositions to Negroes and to youths whose appearance correspond to that which police associated with delinquents partly reflected the fact, observed in this study, that these youths also were much more likely than were other types of boys to exhibit the sort of recalcitrant demeanor which police construed as a sign of the confirmed delinquent. Further, officers assumed, partly on the basis of departmental statistics that Negroes and juveniles who "look tough" (e.g. who wear chinos, leather jackets, boots, etc.) commit crimes more frequently than do other types of youths.* [p. 212]

Cf. Albert Reiss, *The Police and the Public* (New Haven, Conn.: Yale University Press, 1971). Reiss attributes the differences to the differences in the actions of complainants.

³⁸Richard J. Lundman, for example, found higher arrest rates to be associated with "offender powerlessness." "Routine Police Arrest Practices: A Commonweal Perspective," *Social Problems* 22, no. 1 (October 1974), pp. 127–41.

³⁹William Bales, "Race and Class Effects on Criminal Justice Prosecution and Punishment Decisions." (unpublished Ph.D. dissertation, Florida State University, 1987).

⁴⁰Note, "Developments in the Law-Race and the Criminal Process," *Harvard Law Review* 101 (1988), p. 1520.

⁴¹Spohn, Gruhl, and Welch, "The Impact of the Ethnicity and Gender of Defendants on the Decision to Reject or Dismiss Felony Charges," *Criminology* 25 (1987), pp. 175, 180, 185.

⁴²See, for example, Theodore G. Chiricos, Philip D. Jackson, and Gordon P. Waldo, "Inequality in the Imposition of a Criminal Label," *Social Problems* 19, no. 4 (Spring 1972), pp. 553–572.

[43]BJS, *Prison and Jail Inmates*, 195, p. 11.

[44]See, for example, C. E. Ares, A. Rankin, and J. H. Sturz, "The Manhattan Bail Project: An Interim Report on the Use of Pre-trial Parole," *NYU Law Review* 38 (1963), p. 67; C. Foote, "Compelling Appearances in Court-Administration of Bail in Philadelphia," *University of Pennsylvania Law Review* 102 (1954), pp. 10311079; and C. Foote, "A Study of the Administration of Bail in New York City," *University of Pennsylvania Law Review* 106 (1958), p. 693. For statistics on persons held in jail awaiting trial, see U.S. Bureau of the Census, *The Social and Economic Status of the Black Population in the U.S.*, 1974 (Washington, D.C.: U.S. Government Printing Office, 1975), p. 171; and USLEAA *Survey of Inmates in Local Jails—1972 Advance Report* (Washington, D.C.: U.S. Government Printing Office, 1974), pp. 5, 8.

[45]Theodore Chiricos and William Bales, "Unemployment and Punishment: An Empirical Assessment," *Criminology* 29, no. 4 (1991), p. 712.

[46]Blumberg, *Criminal Justice*, pp. 28–29; *Challenge*, p. 134; and Donald J. Newman, *Conviction: The Determination of Guilt or Innocence without Trial* (Boston: Little, Brown, 1966), p. 3.

[47]A good summary of these developments can be found in Joel Jay Finer, "Ineffective Assistance of Counsel," *Cornell Law Review* 58, no. 6 (July 1973), pp. 1077–1120.

[48]See, for example, Dallin H. Oaks and Warren Lehman, "Lawyers for the Poor," in *Law and Order. The Scales of Justice*, ed., A. Blumberg, pp. 92–93; also Jerome H. Skolnick, "Social Control in the Adversary System," in *Criminal Justice: Law and Politics*, ed., George Cole (Belmont, Calif.: Duxbury, 1972), pp. 266. "The National Legal Aid and Defender Association has suggested that experienced attorneys handle no more than 150 felony cases per year, rather than the case load of over 500 felony cases per attorney with which some public defender offices in major cities are burdened." Finer, "Ineffective Assistance of Counsel," p.1120.

[49]In several essays, Abraham S. Blumberg has described the role of the public defender as an officer of the court bureaucracy rather than as a defender of the accused. See his "Lawyers with Convictions," in *Law and Order: The Scales of Justice*, pp. 51–67; "The Practice of Law as Confidence Game: Organizational Cooptation of a Profession," in *Criminal Law in Action*, ed., William J. Chambliss (Santa Barbara, Calif: Hamilton, 1975), pp. 262–75; and his book *Criminal Justice* (Chicago: Quadrangle, 1967), especially pp. 13–115.

[50]Jonathan D. Casper, "Did You Have a Lawyer When You Went to Court? No, I Had a Public Defender," in *Criminal Justice: Law and Politics*, ed., Cole, pp. 239–40.

[51]Dean J. Champion, "Private Counsels and Public Defenders: A Look at Weak Cases, Prior Records, and Leniency in Plea Bargaining," *Journal of Criminal Justice* 17, no. 4 (1989), pp. 253–63.

[52]Of those defendants convicted in U.S. district courts in 1971, 46 percent had assigned lawyers (including public defenders); of those acquitted, 37.5 percent had assigned counsel; and of those dismissed, only 33.3 percent had assigned counsel. *Sourcebook-1974*, p. 388.

[53]Robert Johnson, *Condemned to Die: Life Under Sentence of Death* (New York: Elsevier, 1981), p. 138; Stephen Gettinger, *Sentenced to Die: The People, the Crimes and the Controversy* (New York: Macmillan, 1979), p. 261.

[54]"Death-Row Inmates Often Lack Help for Appeals, But Few Lawyers Want to Do Distasteful Work," *Wall Street Journal*, August 27, 1987, p. 48.

[55]Richard Lacayo, "You Don't Always Get Perry Mason," *Time*, June 1, 1992, pp. 38–39.

[56]"When Are the Savings and Loan Crooks Going to Jail?" *Hearing before the Subcommittee on Financial Institutions Supervision, Regulation and Insurance of the Committee on Banking, Finance and Urban Affairs, House of Representatives, 101st Congress, 2d Session, June 28, 1990* (Washington, D.C.: U.S. Government Printing Office, 1990), pp. 1, 21.

[57]Lesley Oelsner, "Wide Disparities Mark Sentences Here," *New York Times*, September 27, 1972, p.1.

[58]Stewart J. D'Alession and Lisa Stolzenberg, "Socioeconomic Status and the Sentencing of the Traditional Offender," *Journal of Criminal Justice* 21 (1993), pp. 71–74.

[59]Barbara C. Nienstedt, Marjorie Zatz, and Thomas Epperlein, "Court Processing and Sentencing of Drinking Drivers," *Journal of Quantitative Criminology* 4, no. 1 (1988), pp. 39–59.

[60]Theodore Chiricos and William Bales, "Unemployment and Punishment: An Empirical Assessment," *Criminology* 29, no. 4 (1991), pp. 701–24.

[61]Belinda R. McCarthy, "A Micro-Level Analysis of Social Control: Intrastate Use of Jail and Prison Confinement," *Justice Quarterly* 7, no. 2 (June 1990), pp. 334–35.

[62]Dean J. Champion, "Private Counsels and Public Defenders: A Look at Weak Cases, Prior Records, and Leniency in Plea Bargaining," p. 143.

[63]T. Miethe and C. Moore, "Socioeconomic Disparities Under Determinate Sentencing Systems: A Comparison of Preguideline and Postguideline Practices in Minnesota," *Criminology* 23, no. 2 (1985), p. 358.

[64]Robert Tillman and Henry Pontell, "Is Justice Collar-Blind?: Punishing Medicaid Provider Fraud," *Criminology* 30, no. 4 (1992), p. 547–73, quote from p. 560.

[65]James F. Nelson, "Hidden Disparities in Case Processing: New York State, 1985–1986," *Journal of Criminal Justice* 20 (1992), pp. 181–200.

[66]Unnever and Hembroff, "The Prediction of Racial/Ethnic Sentencing Disparities," *Journal of Research in Crime and Delinquency* 25 (1988), p. 53.

[67]BJS, *Prisoners in 1994*, August 1995 (NCJ-151654), p. 9; BJS, *Prison and Jail Inmates*, 1995, p.10; *Sourcebook-1994*, Table 4.11, p. 388.

[68]*Sourcebook-1987*, pp. 376, 491, 518; *Sourcebook-1992*, p. 492, Table no. 5.21.

[69]*Criminal Justice Newsletter*, March 1, 1995, p. 3; *Criminal Justice Newsletter*, April 17, 1995, p. 5.

[70]McDonald, Douglas and Ken Carlson, *Sentencing in the Federal Courts: Does Race Matter?* (Washington, D.C.: BJS, 1993), cited in Tonry, "Racial Politics, Racial Disparities, and the War on Crime," *Crime & Delinquency* 40, no. 4 (October 1994), p. 487.

[71]Ronald Smothers, "Wave of Prison Uprisings Provokes Debate on Crack," *New York Times*, October 24, 1995, p. A12.

[72]"Blacks Receive Stiffer Sentences," *Boston Globe*, April 4, 1979, pp. 1, 50f.

[73]Randall Thomson and Matthew Zingraff, "Detecting Sentencing Disparity: Some Problems and Evidence," *American Journal of Sociology* 86, no. 4 (1981), pp. 869–80, especially p. 875.

[74]J. Unnever, C. Frazier, and J. Henretta, "Race Differences in Criminal Sentencing," *Sociological Quarterly* 21 (Spring 1980), pp. 197–205, especially p. 204.

[75]J. Petersilia, "Racial Disparities in the Criminal Justice System: A Summary," *Crime & Delinquency* 31, no. 1 (1985), p. 28. See also G. Bridges and R. Crutchfield, "Law, Social Standing and Racial Disparities in Imprisonment," *Social Forces* 66, no. 3 (1988), pp. 699–724.

[76]M. Myers, "Economic Inequality and Discrimination in Sentencing," *Social Forces* 65, no. 3 (1987), p. 761.

[77]Mary Pat Flaherty and Joan Biskupic, "Rules Often Impose Toughest Penalties on Poor, Minorities," *Washington Post*, October 9, 1996, p. A26.

[78]Tom Wicker, *A Time to Die* (New York: Quadrangle, 1975), pp. 311, 314.

[79]Ibid, p. 310.

[80]*Sourcebook-1987*, p. 486, BJS, *Correctional Populations in the United States, 1985*, p.10, Table no. 2.6; *StatAbst-1988*, p. 13, Table no. 13; BJS, *Prison and Jail Inmates*, 1995, pp. 2 and 5.

[81]BJS, *Survey of State Prison Inmates, 1991*, p. 3.

[82]*StatAbst-1992*, p. 383, Table no. 612.

[83]*StatAbst-1992*, p. 453, Table no. 711.

[84]BJS, *Profile of Inmates in the United States and in England and Wales*, 1991 (October 1994, NCJ-145863), p. 14.

☙ ☙ ☙

Questions

1. How does the criminal-justice system favor the wealthy in terms of conviction and sentencing?

2. How different are the rates of conviction between the poor and the wealthy? How much does being assigned a public defender or a court-appointed defender affect these rates?

3. Do the inequities built into the criminal-justice system penalize impoverished persons or minorities? To what degree can you separate poverty and minority status and draw a definitive conclusion?

4. Cite examples illustrating that sentencing is inequitably distributed to the poor. What type(s) of differences in sentencing are given out for the same crime? What type(s) of differences in sentencing are there for different crimes of a similar nature (for instance, embezzlement/fraud versus theft)?

5. In your opinion, is inequity by social class and race or ethnicity inherent in the U.S. criminal-justice system? If so, why? If not, what reforms might correct some of the inequity? What barriers and forms of resistance would your proposed reforms encounter, and how could you surmount them?

Lower Class Culture as a Generating Milieu of Gang Delinquency

WALTER B. MILLER

Why do gangs form? This is a central question for anyone who studies gangs. In this classic article, Walter Miller claims that gangs form in response to the cultural conditions of the lower classes, not from the characteristics of the gang members themselves. Miller makes his case by presenting several core values of lower-class culture and tracing these values' expression in youth gangs.

*T*he etiology of delinquency has long been a controversial issue, and is particularly so at present. As new frames of reference for explaining human behavior have been added to traditional theories, some authors have adopted the practice of citing the major postulates of each school of thought as they pertain to delinquency, and going on to state that causality must be conceived in terms of the dynamic interaction of a complex combination of variables on many levels. "The major sets of etiological factors currently adduced to explain delinquency are, in simplified terms, the physiological (delinquency results from organic pathology), the psychodynamic (delinquency is a "behavioral disorder" resulting primarily from emotional disturbance generated by a defective mother-child relationship), and the environmental (delinquency is the product of disruptive forces, "disorganization," in the actor's physical or social environment).

This paper selects one particular kind of "delinquency"—law-violating acts committed by members of adolescent street corner groups in lower class communities—and attempts to show that the dominant component of motivation underlying these acts consists in a directed attempt by the actor to adhere to forms of behavior, and to achieve standards of value as they are

"Lower Class Culture as a Generating Milieu of Gang Delinquency," by Walter B. Miller, reprinted from *Journal of Social Issues*, vol. 14, 1959, pp. 5–19.

defined within that community. It takes as a premise that the motivation of behavior in this situation can be approached most productively by attempting to understand the nature of cultural forces impinging on the acting individual as they are perceived *by the actor himself*—although by no means only that segment of these forces of which the actor is consciously aware—rather than as they are perceived and evaluated from the reference position of another cultural system. In the case of "gang" delinquency, the cultural system which exerts the most direct influence on behavior is that of the lower class community itself—a long-established, distinctively patterned tradition with an integrity of its own—rather than a so-called "delinquent subculture" which has arisen through conflict with middle class culture and is oriented to the deliberate violation of middle class norms.

The bulk of the substantive data on which the following material is based was collected in connection with a service-research project in the control of gang delinquency. During the service aspect of the project, which lasted for three years, seven trained social workers maintained contact with twenty-one corner group units in a "slum" district of a large eastern city of periods of time ranging from ten to thirty months. Groups were Negro and white, male and female, and in early, middle, and late adolescence. Over eight thousand pages of direct observational data on behavior patterns of group members and other community residents were collected; almost daily contact was maintained for a total time period of about thirteen worker years. Data include workers' contact reports, participant observation reports by the writer—a cultural anthropologist—and direct tape recordings of group activities and discussions.

● Focal Concerns of Lower Class Culture

There is a substantial segment of present-day American society whose way of life, values, and characteristic patterns of behavior are the product of a distinctive cultural system which may be termed "lower class." Evidence indicates that this cultural system is becoming increasingly distinctive, and that the size of the group which shares this tradition is increasing. The lower class way of life, in common with that of all distinctive cultural groups, is characterized by a set of focal concerns—areas or issues which command widespread and persistent attention and a high degree of emotional involvement. The specific concerns cited here, while by no means confined to the American lower classes, constitute a distinctive *patterning* of concerns which differs significantly, both in rank order and weighting from that of American middle class culture. The following chart presents a highly schematic and simplified listing of six of the major concerns of lower class culture. Each is conceived as a "dimension" within which a fairly wide and varied range of alternative behavior patterns may be followed by different individuals under different situations. They are listed roughly in order of the degree of *explicit* attention accorded each, and, in this sense represent a weighted ranking of concerns. The "perceived alternatives" represent polar positions which define certain parameters within each dimension. As will be explained in more detail, it is necessary in relating the influence of these "concerns" to the motivation of delinquent behavior to specify *which* of its aspects is oriented to, whether orientation is *overt* or *covert, positive* (conforming to or seeking the aspect), or *negative* (rejecting or seeking to avoid the aspect).

The concept "focal concern" is used here in preference to the concept "value" for several interrelated reasons: (1) It is more readily derivable from direct field observation. (2) It is descriptively neutral—permitting independent consideration of positive and negative valences as varying under different conditions, whereas "value" carries a built-in positive valence. (3) It makes possible more refined analysis of subcultural differences, since it reflects actual behavior, whereas "value" tends to wash out intracultural differences since it is colored by notions of the "official" ideal.

Trouble: Concern over "trouble" is a dominant feature of lower class culture. The concept has various shades of meaning; "trouble" in one of its aspects represents a situation or a kind of behavior which results in unwelcome or complicating involvement with official authorities or agencies of middle class society. "Getting into trouble" and "staying out of trouble" represent major issues for male and female, adults and children. For men, "trouble" frequently involves fighting or sexual adventures while drinking; for women, sexual involvement with disadvantageous consequences. Expressed desire to avoid behavior which violates moral or legal norms is often based less on an explicit commitment to "official" moral or legal standards than on a desire to avoid "getting into trouble," e.g., the complicating consequences of the action.

The dominant concern over "trouble" involves a distinction of critical importance for the lower class community—that between "law-abiding" and

CHART 1 *Focal Concerns of Lower Class Culture*

Area	Perceived Alternatives (state, quality, condition)	
1. *Trouble:*	law-abiding behavior	law-violating behavior
2. *Toughness:*	physical prowess, skill; "masculinity"; fearlessness, bravery, daring	weakness, ineptitude; effeminacy; timidity, cowardice, caution
3. *Smartness:*	ability to outsmart, dupe, "con"; gaining money by "wits"; shrewdness, adroitness in repartee	gullibility, "con-ability"; gaining money by hard work; slowness, dull-wittedness, verbal maladroitness
4. *Excitement:*	thrill; risk, danger; change, activity	boredom; "deadness," safeness; sameness, passivity
5. *Fate:*	favored by fortune, being "lucky"	ill-omened, being "unlucky"
6. *Autonomy:*	freedom from external constraint; freedom from superordinate authority; independence	presence of external constraint; presence of strong authority; dependency, being "cared for"

"non-law-abiding" behavior. There is a high degree of sensitivity as to where each person stands in relation to these two classes of activity. Whereas in the middle class community a major dimension for evaluating a person's status is "achievement" and its external symbols, in the lower class, personal status is very frequently gauged along the law-abiding-non-law-abiding dimension. A mother will evaluate the suitability of her daughter's boyfriend less on the basis of his achievement potential than on the basis of his innate "trouble" potential. This sensitive awareness of the opposition of "trouble-producing" and "non-trouble-producing" behavior represents both a major basis for deriving status distinctions, and an internalized conflict potential for the individual.

As in the case of other focal concerns, which of two perceived alternatives—"law abiding" or "non-law-abiding"—is valued varies according to the individual and the circumstances; in many instances there is an overt commitment to the "law-abiding" alternative, but a covert commitment to the "non-law abiding." In certain situations, "getting into trouble" is overtly recognized as prestige-conferring; for example, membership in certain adult and adolescent primary groupings ("gangs") is contingent on having demonstrated an explicit commitment to the law-violating alternative. It is most important to note that the choice between "law-abiding" and "non-law-abiding" behavior is still a choice *within* lower class culture; the distinction between the policeman and the criminal, the outlaw and the sheriff, involves primarily this one dimension; in other respects they have a high community of interests. Not infrequently brothers raised in an identical cultural milieu will become police and criminals respectively.

For a substantial segment of the lower class population "getting into trouble" is not in itself overtly defined as prestige-conferring, but is implicitly recognized as a means to other valued ends, e.g., the covertly valued desire to be "cared for" and subject to external constraint, or the overtly valued state of excitement or risk. Very frequently "getting into trouble" is multi-functional and achieves several sets of valued ends.

Toughness: The concept of "toughness" in lower class culture represents a compound combination of qualities or states. Among its most important components are physical prowess, evidenced both by demonstrated possession of strength and endurance and athletic skill; "masculinity," symbolized by a distinctive complex of acts and avoidances (bodily tattooing; absence of sentimentality; non-concern with "art," "literature," conceptualization of women as conquest objects, etc.); and bravery in the face of physical threat. The model of the "tough guy"—hard, fearless, undemonstrative, skilled in physical combat—is represented by the movie gangster of the thirties, the "private-eye," and the movie cowboy.

The genesis of the intense concern over "toughness" in lower class culture is probably related to the fact that a significant proportion of lower class males are reared in a predominantly female household, and lack a consistently present male figure with whom to identify and from whom to learn essential components of a "male" role. Since women serve as a primary object of identification during pre-adolescent years, the almost obsessive lower class concern with "masculinity" probably resembles a type of compulsive reaction-formation. A concern over homosexuality runs like a persistent thread through lower class culture. This is manifested by the institutionalized practice of baiting "queers," often accompanied by violent physical attacks, an expressed contempt for "softness" or frills, and the use of the local term for "homosexual" as a generalized pejorative epithet (e.g., higher class individuals or upwardly mobile peers are frequently characterized as "fags" or "queers"). The distinction between "overt" and "covert" orientation to aspects of an area of concern is especially important in regard to "toughness." A positive overt evaluation of behavior defined as "effeminate" would be out of the question for a lower class male; however, built into lower class culture is a range of devices which permit men to adopt behaviors and concerns which in other cultural milieux fall within the province of women, and at the same time to be defined as "tough" and manly. For example, lower class men can be professional short-order cooks in a diner and still be regarded as "tough." The highly intimate circumstances of the secret corner gang involve the recurrent expression of strongly affectionate feelings towards other men. Such expressions, however, are disguised as their opposite, taking the form of ostensibly aggressive verbal and physical interaction (kidding, "ranking," roughhousing, etc.).

Smartness: "Smartness," as conceptualized in lower class culture, involves the capacity to outsmart, outfox, outwit, dupe, "take," "con" another or others, and the concomitant capacity to avoid being outwitted, "taken," or duped oneself. In its essence, smartness involves the capacity to achieve a valued entity—material goods, personal status—through a maximum use of mental agility and a minimum use of physical effort. This capacity has an extremely long tradition in lower class culture, and is highly valued. Lower class culture can be characterized as "non-intellectual" only if intellectualism is defined specifically in terms of control over a particular body of formally learned knowledge involving "culture" (art, literature, "good" music, etc.), a generalized perspective on the past and present conditions of our own and other societies, and other areas of knowledge imparted by formal educational institutions. This particular type of mental attainment is, in general, overtly disvalued and frequently associated with effeminacy; "smartness" in the lower class sense, however, is highly valued.

The lower class child learns and practices the use of this skill in the street corner situation. Individuals continually practice duping and outwitting one another through recurrent card games and other forms of gambling, mutual exchanges of insults, and "testing" for mutual "compatibility." Those who demonstrate competence in this skill are accorded considerable prestige. Leadership roles in the corner group are frequently allocated according to demonstrated capacity in the two areas of "smartness" and "toughness"; the ideal leader combines both, but the "smart" leader is often accorded more prestige than the "tough" one—reflecting a general lower class respect for "brains" in the "smartness" sense.

The model of the "smart" person is represented in popular media by the card shark, the professional gambler, the "con" artist, the promoter. A conceptual distinction is made between two kinds of people: "suckers," targets of exploitation; and sharp operators, the "brainy" ones, who live by their wits and "getting" from the suckers by mental adroitness.

Involved in the syndrome of capacities related to "smartness" is a dominant emphasis in lower class culture on ingenious aggressive repartee. This skill, learned and practiced in the context of the corner group, ranges in form from the widely prevalent semi-ritualized teasing, kidding, razzing, "ranking," so characteristic of male peer group interaction, to the highly ritualized type of mutual insult interchange known as "the dirty dozens," "the dozens," "playing house," and other terms. This highly patterned cultural form is practiced on its most advanced level in adult male Negro society, but less polished variants are found throughout lower class culture—practiced, for example, by white children, male and female, as young as four or five. In essence, "doin' the dozens" involves two antagonists who vie with each other in the exchange of increasingly inflammatory insults, with incestuous and perverted sexual relations with the mother a dominant theme. In this form of insult interchange, as well as on other less ritualized occasions for joking, semi-serious, and serious mutual invective, a very high premium is placed on ingenuity, hair-trigger responsiveness, inventiveness, and the acute exercise of mental faculties.

Excitement: For many lower class individuals the rhythm of life fluctuates between periods of relatively routine or repetitive activity and sought situations of great emotional stimulation. Many of the most characteristic features of lower class life are related to the search for excitement or "thrill." Involved here are the prevalent use of alcohol by both sexes and the widespread use of gambling of all kinds—playing the numbers, betting on horse races, dice, cards. The quest for excitement finds what is perhaps its most vivid expression in the highly patterned practice of the recurrent "night on the town." This practice, designated by various terms in different areas ("honky-tonkin'"; "goin' out on the town"; "bar hoppin'"), involves a patterned set of activities in which alcohol, music, and sexual adventuring are major components. A group or individual sets out to "make the rounds" of various bars or night clubs. Drinking continues progressively throughout the evening. Men seek to "pick up" women, and women play the risky game of entertaining sexual advances. Fights between men involving women, gambling, and claims of physical prowess, in various combinations, are frequent consequences of a night of making the rounds. The explosive potential of this type of adventuring with sex and aggression, frequently leading to "trouble," is semi-explicitly sought by the individual. Since there is always a good likelihood that being out on the town will eventuate in fights, etc., the practice involves elements of sought risk and desired danger.

Counterbalancing the "flirting with danger" aspect of the "excitement" concern is the prevalence in lower class culture of other well established patterns of activity which involve long periods of relative inaction, or passivity. The term "hanging out" in lower class culture refers to extended periods of standing around, often with peer mates, doing what is defined as "nothing," "shooting the breeze," etc. A definite periodicity exists in the pattern of activity relating to the two aspects of the "excitement" dimension. For many lower class individuals the venture into the high risk world of alcohol, sex, and fighting occurs regularly once a week, with interim periods devoted to accommodating to possible consequences of these periods, along with recurrent resolves not to become so involved again.

Fate: Related to the quest for excitement is the concern with fate, fortune, or luck. Here also a distinction is made between two states—being "lucky" or "in luck," and being unlucky or jinxed. Many lower class individuals feel that their lives are subject to a set of forces over which they have relatively little control. These are not directly equated with the supernatural forces of formally organized religion, but relate more to a concept of "destiny," or man as a pawn of magical powers. Not infrequently this often implicit world view is associated with a conception of the ultimate futility of directed effort towards a goal: if the cards are right, or the dice good to you, or if your lucky number comes up, things will go your way; if luck is against you, it's not worth trying. The concept of performing semi-magical rituals so that one's "luck will change" is prevalent; one hopes that, as a result he will move from the state of being "unlucky" to that of being "lucky." The element of fantasy plays an important part in this area. Related to and complementing the notion that "only suckers work" (Smartness) is the idea that once things start going your way, relatively independent of your own effort, all good things will come to you. Achieving great material rewards (big cars, big houses, a roll of cash to flash in a fancy night club), valued in lower class is well as in other parts of American culture, is a recurrent theme in lower class fantasy and folk lore; the cocaine dreams of Willie the Weeper or Minnie the Moocher present the components of this fantasy in vivid detail.

The prevalence in the lower class community of many forms of gambling, mentioned in connection with the "excitement" dimension, is also relevant here. Through cards and pool which involve skill, and thus both "toughness" and "smartness"; or through race horse betting, involving "smartness"; or through playing the numbers, involving predominantly "lucky," one may make a big killing with a minimum of directed and persistent effort within conventional occupational channels. Gambling in its many forms illustrates the fact that many of the persistent features of lower class culture are multi-functional—serving a range of desired ends at the same time. Describing some of the incentives behind gambling has involved mention of all of the focal concerns cited so far—Toughness, Smartness, and Excitement, in addition to Fate.

Autonomy: The extent and nature of control over the behavior of the individual—an important concern in most cultures—has a special significance and is distinctively patterned in lower class culture. The discrepancy between what is overtly valued and what is covertly sought is particularly striking in this area. On the overt level there is a strong and frequently expressed resentment of the idea of external controls, restrictions on behavior, and unjust or coercive authority. "No one's gonna push *me* around," or "I'm gonna tell him he can take the job and shove it . . ." are commonly expressed sentiments. Similar explicit attitudes are maintained to systems of behavior-restricting rules, insofar as these are perceived as representing the injunctions, and bearing the sanctions of superordinate authority. In addition, in lower class culture a close conceptual connection is made between "authority" and "nurturance." To be restrictively or firmly controlled is to be cared for. Thus the overtly negative evaluation of superordinate authority frequently extends as well to nurturance, care, or protection. The desire for personal independence is often expressed in such terms as "I don't need *nobody* to take care of me. I can take care of myself!" Actual patterns of behavior, however, reveal a marked discrepancy between expressed sentiment and what is covertly valued. Many lower class people appear to seek out highly restrictive social environments wherein stringent external controls are maintained over their behavior. Such institutions as the armed forces, the mental hospital, the disciplinary school, the prison or correctional institution, provide environments which incorporate a strict and detailed set of rules defining and limiting behavior, and enforced by an authority system which controls and applies coercive sanctions for deviance from these rules. While under the jurisdiction of such systems, the lower class person generally expresses to his peers continual resentment of the coercive, unjust, and arbitrary exercise of authority. Having been released, or having escaped from these milieux, however, he will often act in such a way as to insure recommitment, or choose recommitment voluntarily after a temporary period of "freedom."

Lower class patients in mental hospitals will exercise considerable ingenuity to insure continued commitment while voicing the desire to get out; delinquent boys will frequently "run" from a correctional institution to activate efforts to return them; to be caught and returned means that one is cared for. Since "being controlled" is equated with "being cared for," attempts are frequently made to "test," the severity and strictness of superordinate authority to see if it remains firm. If intended or executed rebellion reduces swift and firm punitive sanctions, the individual is reassured, at the same time that he is complaining bitterly at the injustice of being caught and punished. Some environmental milieux, having been tested in this fashion for the "firmness" of their coercive sanctions, are rejected, ostensibly for being too strict, actually for not being strict enough. This is frequently so in the case of "problematic" behavior by lower class youngsters in the public schools, which generally cannot command the coercive controls implicitly sought by the individual.

A similar discrepancy between what is overtly and covertly desired is found in the area of dependence-independence. The pose of tough rebellious independence often assumed by the lower class person frequently conceals powerful dependency cravings. These are manifested primarily by obliquely expressed resentment when "care" is not forthcoming rather than by expressed satisfaction when it is. The concern over autonomy-dependency is related both to "trouble" and "fate." Insofar as the lower class individual feels that his behavior is controlled by forces which often propel him into "trouble" in the face of in explicit determination to avoid it, there is an implied appeal to "save me from myself." A solution appears to lie in arranging things so that his behavior will he coercively restricted by an externally imposed set of controls strong enough to forcibly restrain his inexplicable inclination to get in trouble. The periodicity observed in connection with the "excitement" dimension is also relevant here; after involvement in trouble-producing behavior (assault, sexual adventure, a "drunk"), the individual will actively seek a locus of imposed control (his wife, prison, a restrictive job); after a given period of subjection to this control, resentment against it mounts, leading to a "break away" and a search for involvement in further "trouble."

❧ Focal Concerns of the Lower Class Adolescent Street Corner Group

The one-sex peer group is a highly prevalent and significant structural form in the lower-class community. There is a strong probability that the prevalence and stability of this type of unit is directly related to the prevalence of a stabilized type of lower class child-rearing unit—the "female-based" household. This is a nuclear kin unit in which a male parent is either absent from the household, present only sporadically, or, when present, only minimally or inconsistently involved in the support and rearing of children. This unit usually consists of one or more females of child-bearing age and their offspring. The females are frequently related to one another by blood or marriage ties, and the unit often includes two or more generations of women, e.g., the mother and/or aunt of the principal child-bearing female.

The nature of social groupings in the lower class community may be clarified if we make the assumption that it is the *one-sex peer unit* rather than the two-parent family unit which presents the most significant relational unit for both sexes in lower class communities. Lower class society may be pictured comprising a set of age-graded one-sex groups which constitute the major psychic focus and reference group for those over twelve or thirteen. Men and women of mating age leave these groups periodically to form temporary marital alliances, but these lack stability, and after varying periods of "trying out" the two-sex family arrangement, gravitate back to the more "comfortable" one-sex grouping, whose members exert strong pressure on the individual *not* to disrupt the group by adopting a two-sex household pattern in life. Membership in a stable and solidary peer unit is vital to the lower class individual precisely to the extent to which a range of essential functions—psychological, educational, and others, are not provided by the "family" unit.

The adolescent street corner group represents the adolescent variant of this lower class structural form. What has been called the "delinquent gang" is one subtype of this form, defined on the basis of frequency of participation in law-violating activity; this subtype should not be considered a legitimate unit of study per se, but rather as one particular variant of the adolescent street corner group. The "hanging" peer group is a unit of particular importance for the adolescent male. In many cases it is the most stable and solidery primary group he has ever belonged to; for boys reared in female-based households the corner group provides the first real opportunity to learn essential aspects of the male role in the context of peers facing similar problems of sex-role identification.

The form and function of the adolescent corner group operate as a selective mechanism in recruiting members. The activity patterns of the group require a high level of inter-group solidarity; individual members must possess a good capacity for subordinating individual desires to general group interests as well as the capacity for intimate and persisting interaction. Thus highly "disturbed" individuals, or those who cannot tolerate consistently imposed sanctions on "deviant" behavior cannot remain accepted members; the group itself will extrude those whose behavior exceeds limits defined as "normal." This selective process produces a type of group whose members possess to an unusually high degree both the *capacity* and *motivation* to conform to perceived cultural norms, so that the nature of the system of norms and values oriented to is a particularly influential component of motivation.

Focal concerns of the male adolescent corner group are those of the general cultural milieu in which it functions. As would be expected, the relative weighting and importance of these concerns pattern somewhat different for adolescents than for adults. The nature of this patterning centers around two additional "concerns" of particular importance to this group—concern with "belonging" and with "status." These may be conceptualized as being on a higher level of abstraction than concerns previously cited, since "status" and "belonging" are achieved *via* cited concern areas of Toughness, etc.

Belonging: Since the corner group fulfills essential functions for the individual, being a member in good standing of the group is of vital importance for its members. A continuing concern over who is "in" and who is not involves the citation and detailed discussion of highly refined criteria for "in-group" membership. The phrase "he hangs with us" means "he is accepted as a member in good standing by current consensus"; conversely, "he don't hang with us" means he is not so accepted. One achieves "belonging" primarily by demonstrating knowledge of and a determination to adhere to the system of standards and valued qualities defined by the group. One maintains membership by acting in conformity with valued aspects of Toughness, Smartness, Autonomy, etc. In those instances where conforming to norms of this reference group at the same time violates norms of other reference groups (e.g., middle class adults, institutional "officials"), immediate reference group norms are much more compelling since violation risks invoking the group's most powerful sanction: exclusion.

Status: In common with most adolescents in American society, the lower class corner group manifests a dominant concern with "status." What differentiates this type of group from others, however, is the particular set of criteria and weighting thereof by which "status" is defined. In general, status is achieved and maintained by demonstrated possession of the valued qualities of lower class culture—Toughness, Smartness, expressed resistance to authority, daring, etc. It is important to stress once more that the individual orients to these concerns *as they are defined within lower class society;* e.g., the status-conferring potential of "smartness" in the sense of scholastic achievement generally ranges from negligible to negative.

The concern with "status" is manifested in a variety of ways. Intra-group status is a continued concern, and is derived and tested constantly by means of a set of status-ranking activities; the intra-group "pecking order" is constantly at issue. One gains status within the group by demonstrated superiority in Toughness (physical prowess, bravery, skill in athletics and games such as pool and cards), Smartness (skill in repartee, capacity to "dupe" fellow group members), and the like. The term "ranking," used to refer to the pattern of intra-group aggressive repartee, indicates awareness of the fact that this is one device for establishing the intra-group status hierarchy.

The concern over status in the adolescent corner group involves in particular the component of "adultness," the intense desire to be seen as "grown up," and a corresponding aversion to "kid stuff." "Adult" status is defined less in terms of the assumption of "adult" responsibility than in terms of certain external symbols of adult status—a car, ready cash, and in particular, a perceived "freedom" to drink, smoke, and gamble as one wishes and to come and go without external restrictions. The desire to be seen as "adult" is often a more significant component of much involvement in illegal drinking, gambling, and automobile driving than the explicit enjoyment of these acts as such.

The intensity of the corner group member's desire to be seen as "adult" is sufficiently great that he feels called upon to demonstrate qualities associated with adultness (Toughness, Smartness, Autonomy) to a much greater degree than a lower class adult. This means that he will seek out and utilize those avenues to these qualities which he perceives as available with greater intensity than an adult and less regard for their "legitimacy." In this sense the adolescent variant of lower class culture represents a maximization or an intensified manifestation of many of its most characteristic features.

Concern over status is also manifested in reference to other street corner groups. The term "rep" used in this regard is especially significant, and has broad connotations. In its most frequent and explicit connotation, "rep" refers to the "toughness" of the corner group as a whole relative to that of other groups; a "pecking order" also exists among the several corner groups in a given interactional area, and there is a common perception that the safety or security of the group and all its members depends on maintaining a solid "rep" for toughness vis-a-vis other groups. This motive is most frequently advanced as a reason for involvement in gang fights: "We *can't* chicken out on this fight; our rep would be shot!"; this implies that the group would be relegated to the bottom of the status ladder and become a helpless and recurrent target of external attack.

On the other hand, there is implicit in the concept of "rep" the recognition that "rep" has or may have a dual basis—corresponding to the two aspects of the "trouble" dimension. It is recognized that group as well as individual status can be based on both "law-abiding' and "law-violating" behavior. The situational resolution of the persisting conflict between the "law-abiding" and "law-violating" bases of status comprises a vital set of dynamics in determining whether a "delinquent" mode of behavior will be adopted by a group, under what circumstances, and how persistently. The determinants of this choice are evidently highly complex and fluid, and rest on a range of factors including the presence and perceptual immediacy of different community reference-group loci (e.g., professional criminals, police, clergy, teachers, settlement house workers), the personality structures and "needs" of group members, the presence in the community of social work, recreation, or educational programs which can facilitate utilization of the "law-abiding" basis of status, and so on.

What remains constant is the critical importance of "status" both for the members of the group as individuals and for the group as a whole insofar as members perceive their individual destinies as linked to the destiny of the group, and the fact that action geared to attain status is much more acutely oriented to the fact of status itself than to the legality or illegality, morality or immorality of the means used to achieve it.

◉ Lower Class Culture and the Motivation of Delinquent Behavior

The customary set of activities of the adolescent street corner group includes activities which are in violation of laws and ordinances of the legal code. Most of these center around assault and theft of various types (the gang fight; auto theft; assault on an individual; petty pilfering and shoplifting; "mugging"; pocketbook theft). Members of street corner gangs are well aware of the law-violating nature of these acts; they are not psychopaths, nor physically or mentally "defective"; in fact, since the corner group supports and enforces a rigorous set of standards which demand a high degree of fitness and personal competence, it tends to recruit from the most "able" members of the community.

Why, then, is the commission of crimes a customary feature of gang activity? The most general answer is that the commission of crimes by members of adolescent street corner groups is motivated primarily by the attempt to achieve ends, states, or conditions which are valued, and to avoid those that are disvalued within their most meaningful cultural milieu through those culturally available avenues which appear as the most feasible means of attaining those ends.

The operation of these influences is well illustrated by the gang fight—a prevalent and characteristic type of corner group delinquency. This type of activity comprises a highly stylized and culturally patterned set of sequences. Although details vary under different circumstances, the following events are generally included. A member or several members of group A "trespass" on the claimed territory of group B. While there they commit an act or acts which group B defines is a violation of its rightful privileges, an affront to their honor, or a challenge to their "rep." Frequently this act involves advances to a girl associated with group B; it may occur at a dance or party; sometimes the mere act of "trespass" is seen as deliberate provocation. Members of group B then assault members of group A, if they are caught while still in B's territory. Assaulted members of group A return to their "home" territory and recount to members of their group details of the incident, stressing the insufficient nature of the provocation ("I just *looked* at her! Hardly even said anything!"), and the unfair circumstances of the assault ("About *twenty* guys jumped just the *two* of us!"). The highly colored account is acutely inflammatory; group A, perceiving its honor violated and its "rep" threatened, feels obligated to retaliate in force. Sessions of detailed planning now occur; allies are recruited if the size of group A and its potential allies appears to necessitate larger numbers; strategy is plotted, and messengers dispatched. Since the prospect of a gang fight is frightening to even the "toughest" group members, a constant rehearsal of the provocative incident or incidents and the essentially evil nature of the opponents accompanies the planning process to bolster possibly weakening motivation to fight. The excursion into "enemy" territory sometimes results in a full scale fight; more often group B cannot be found, or the police appear and stop the fight, "tipped off" by an anonymous informant. When this occurs, group members express disgust and disappointment; secretly there is much relief;

their honor has been avenged without incurring injury; often the anony-mous tipster is a member of one of the involved groups.

The basic elements of this type of delinquency are sufficiently stabilized and recurrent as to constitute an essentially ritualized pattern, resembling both in structure and expressed motives for action classic forms such as the European "duel," the American Indian tribal war, and the Celtic clan feud. Although the arousing and "acting out" of individual aggressive emotions are inevitably involved in the gang fight, neither its form nor motivational dynamics can be adequately handled within a predominantly personality-focused frame of reference.

It would be possible to develop in considerable detail the processes by which the commission of a range of illegal acts is either explicitly supported by, implicitly demanded by, or not materially inhibited by factors relating to the focal concerns of lower class culture. In place of such a development, the following three statements condense in general terms the operation of these processes:

1. *Following cultural practices which comprise essential elements of the total life pattern of lower class culture automatically violates certain legal norms.*

2. *In instances where alternate avenues to similar objectives are available, the non-law abiding avenue frequently provides a relatively greater and more immediate return for a relatively smaller investment of energy.*

3. *The "demanded" response to certain situations recurrently engendered within lower class culture involves the commission of illegal acts.*

The primary thesis of this paper is that the dominant component of the motivation of "delinquent" behavior engaged in by members of lower class corner groups involves a positive effort to achieve states, conditions, or qual-ities valued within the actor's most significant cultural milieu. If "conformity to immediate reference group values" is the major component of motivation of "delinquent" behavior by gang members, why is such behavior frequently referred to as negativistic, malicious, or rebellious? Albert Cohen, for exam-ple, in *Delinquent Boys* (Glencoe: Free Press, 1955) describes behavior which violates school rules as comprising elements of "active spite and malice, contempt and ridicule, challenge and defiance." He ascribes to the gang "keen delight in terrorizing 'good' children, and in general making them-selves obnoxious to the virtuous." A recent national conference on social work with "hard-to-reach" groups characterized lower class corner groups as "youth groups in conflict with the culture of their (*sic*) communities." Such characterizations are obviously the result of taking the middle class community and its institutions as an implicit point of reference.

A large body of systematically interrelated attitudes, practices, behaviors, and values characteristic of lower class culture are designed to support and maintain the basic features of the lower class way of life. In areas where these differ from features of middle class culture, action oriented to the achievement and maintenance of the lower class system may violate norms of middle class culture and be perceived as deliberately non-conforming or malicious by an observer strongly cathected to middle class norms. This does not mean, however, that violation of the middle class norm is the dominant component of motivation; it is a by-product of action primarily oriented to the lower class system. The standards of lower class culture cannot be seen merely as a reverse function of middle class culture—as middle class standards "turned upside down"; lower class culture is a distinctive tradition many centuries old with an integrity of its own.

From the viewpoint of the acting individual, functioning within a field of well-structured cultural forces, the relative impact of "conforming" and "rejective" elements in the motivation of gang delinquency is weighted preponderantly on the conforming side. Rejective or rebellious elements are inevitably involved, but their influence during the actual commission of delinquent acts is relatively small compared to the influence of pressures to achieve what is valued by the actor's most immediate reference groups. Expressed awareness by the actor of the element of rebellion often represents only that aspect of motivation of which he is explicitly conscious; the deepest and most compelling components of motivation—adherence to highly meaningful group standards of Toughness, Smartness, Excitement, etc.—are often unconsciously patterned. No cultural pattern as well-established as the practice of illegal acts by members of lower class corner groups could persist if buttressed primarily by negative, hostile, or rejective motives; its principal motivational support, as in the case of any persisting cultural tradition, derives from a positive effort to achieve what is valued within that tradition, and to conform to its explicit and implicit norms.

● ● ●

Questions

1. What are the focal concerns of lower-class culture?

2. What are the focal concerns of youth gangs?

3. According to Miller, why do youth gangs commit crimes?

4. This article was written in 1959. Do you think that the lower social classes in the United States still have the same focal concerns now? Explain.

5. If all members of the lower classes share the same values, how come young men tend to form gangs? Why not women? Why not older people?

Social Support as an Organizing Concept for Criminology

Francis T. Cullen
University of Cincinnati

In this article, Francis Cullen explores the role of social support in criminal behavior. Social support can take many different forms; for example, both social and emotional support. Cullen argues that boosting this kind of support has various social benefits that in turn reduce crime—at the national, community, and family levels. This kind of support also encourages criminals to turn away from crime, and it increases the effectiveness of correctional treatment.

Chicago strikes me as a particularly appropriate gathering place for criminologists, since so many of our intellectual roots extend to the scholars who explored the lives of offenders earlier in this century and mapped the distribution of their crimes. As Kurtz (1984:72) observes in his analysis of the contributions of the Chicago schools, "[E]xcept for strain models of deviance, delinquency theory originated at the University of Chicago" (also see Kornhauser 1978).

In preparing this address, it thus seemed appropriate to revisit the writings of these early Chicago school theorists—such as Frederick Thrasher and Clifford Shaw and Henry McKay—as well as those of prominent social reformers, such as Jane Addams, who influenced the development of this school (Bulmer 1984:23—24). I was reminded of their enduring influence on our understandings of the origins of crime. Most notably, their research on social disorganization laid the foundation for ecological studies and for control theories, and their investigations of the cultural transmission of

"Social Support as an Organizing Concept for Criminology," by Francis T. Cullen, reprinted from *JusticeQuarterly*, vol. 11, no. 4, 1994, pp. 527–559.

criminal values and skills gave rise to work on gangs, subcultural theory, and illegitimate opportunity structures.

The theoretical legacy has been cataloged by numerous criminological texts—including my own (Cullen 1984; Lilly, Cullen, and Ball 1989; Sykes and Cullen 1992)—and we now pass on stock summaries of the Chicago school to our students, as do I each year. My purpose is not to argue that past accounts of the Chicago school are incorrect or need revision. But I suggest that we are missing something important when we reduce these theorists' perspectives to the sterile interplay of the concepts of disorganization, control, and cultural values. The underlying humanity of their criminology and (I believe) their insights on the importance of social support are overlooked.

Perhaps because I was reading with a different lens, the landscape appeared to have changed on my latest excursion through the Chicago school's writings. I saw depictions of how the powerful social forces that tore apart communities and families left youths to fend for themselves in an inhospitable environment. In Thrasher's ([1927] 1963:32) view, for example, "gangs represent the spontaneous efforts of boys to create a society for themselves where none adequate for their needs exists"; invariably, he noted, a delinquent's family "fails to hold the boy's interest, neglects him, or actually forces him into the street" ([1927] 1963:340). Shaw's life histories of Stanley, the "jack-roller," and of Sidney's "natural delinquent career" similarly document the inordinate neglect that many youths experienced ([1930] 1966, [1931] 1976).

In short, the writings of The Chicago School suggest that a lack of social support—not simply exposure to criminal cultures or a lack of control—is implicated in crime. Not surprisingly, the Chicago school's policy prescriptions embodied the view that support, not punishment, was integral to reducing crime. In retrospect we may see their policies as misguided, naïve, and shaped by class interests (Platt 1969; Rothman 1980). But we should not take this revisionism too far; to do so would be to miss the humanity, decency, and caring that informed these reform efforts (see Garland 1990). Settlement houses in the slums, the saving of youths in the juvenile court, the Chicago Area Project's attempt to help residents reconstruct their neighborhoods—all contrast sharply with contemporary discourse on crime, which has ranged in the past two presidencies from "Willie Horton" to "three strikes and you're out." Further, on a more personal dimension, members of the Chicago school moved beyond scientific analysis to helping others (Addams 1910). As Snodgrass (1982:146) points out in *The Jack-Roller at Seventy*, Stanley, the offender interviewed by Clifford Shaw, "attributes his turning from a life in crime and his personal ontology in no small measure to Shaw's kindness and support."

I do not mean to single out the Chicago school as the only source of insights on social support; quite the opposite. My intention is to argue that notions of social support appear in diverse criminological writings. In some works, the concept is used explicitly (Agnew 1992; Astin, Lawrence, and Foy 1993; Brownfield and Sorenson 1991). In others, such as feminist and peacemaking/humanist writings that focus on caring, connectedness, and responsiveness, allusions to social support can be detected easily (Braswell 1989, 1990; McDermott 1994; Pepinsky and Quinney 1991). In still others, social support can be recognized by considering the reverse of the central theoretical concept of stigmatization (Braithwaite 1989) or of Regoli and Hewitt's (1994) concept of "differential social oppression." Finally, in many other works, I suspect that valuable insights on social support can be uncovered with some mining.

What is lacking, however, is an attempt to integrate these diverse insights on social support into a coherent criminological paradigm. In the sociology of mental illness, for example, considerable progress has been made in this direction (Lin, Dean, and Ensel 1986; Vaux 1988). But in criminology the insights linking social support to crime remaining disparate, and are not systemized so far as to direct theoretical and empirical investigation. Indeed, I can offer one (nonetheless significant) indicator of the latency of this concept: virtually no introductory or theoretical textbook lists "social support" in its index (see, for example, Akers 1994; Barlow 1993; Beirne and Messerschmidt 1991; Empey 1982; Lilly et al. 1989; Pfohl 1985; Sheley 1991; Sutherland, Cressey, and Luckenbill 1992; Vito and Holmes 1994; Vold and Bernard 1986).

My goal, then, is to argue that social support, if approached systematically, can be an important organizing concept for criminology. In the pages ahead, I will discuss propositions that might form the parameters, in a preliminary way, for a criminological paradigm, which draws on existing knowledge to illuminate new research vistas.

☉ *What is Social Support?*

As a prelude to this discussion, let me comment on the concept of social support. Since detailed analyses of the concept are readily available (House 1981; Lin et al. 1986; Vaux 1988), I will sketch out only the major dimensions.

Lin (1986:18) defines social support as "the perceived or actual instrumental and/or expressive provisions supplied by the community, social networks, and confiding partners." Dissection of this definition reveals three major dimensions of support. The first is the distinction between the objective delivery and the perception of support. Taking perceptions into account is important because it leads to the insight that people do not receive support in a mechanical way but interpret, appraise, and anticipate it in the context of social situations (see Matsueda 1992).

Second, although different typologies exist, social support is usually divided into two broad rubrics: instrumental and expressive. According to Lin (1986:20), "the instrumental dimension involves the use of the relationship as a means to a goal, such as seeking a job, getting a loan, or finding someone to babysit." Vaux (1988:21) suggests that "instrumental functions may be served through the provision of goods or money (material aid or financial assistance) and through providing information, making suggestions, and clarifying issues (advice and guidance)."

The expressive dimension, again according to Lin (1986:20), "involves the use of the relationship as an end as well as a means. It is the activity of sharing sentiments, ventilating frustrations, reaching an understanding on issues and problems, and affirming one's own as well as the other's worth and dignity." Vaux (1988:21) notes that the "affective functions" of support "include meeting the needs for love and affection, esteem and identity, and belonging and companionship. These needs are met respectively through emotional support, feedback and social reinforcement, and socializing."

Third, Lin's definition indicates that support occurs on different social levels. Micro-level support can be delivered by a confiding individual, such as a spouse or a best friend. But social support also can be viewed as a property of social networks and of communities and larger ecological units in which individuals are enmeshed.[1]

A fourth dimension, not discussed by Lin, must be added: whether the support is delivered by a formal agency or through informal relations (Vaux 1988). Informal social support would occur through social relationships with others who lack any official status relative to the individual. Formal social support might be provided by schools, governmental assistance programs, and—perhaps most interesting to us—the criminal justice system.[2]

◉ The Ecology of Social Support

In the past decade, scholars have shown a renewed interest in studying the social ecology of crime, as did Shaw and McKay (1942) (Bursik and Grasmick 1993a; Byrne and Sampson 1986; Reiss and Tonry 1986). This research has shown that crime rates vary across nations and, within a single nation, across communities. It is noteworthy, if unsurprising, that the United States has higher rates of serious crime, especially violent offenses, than other Western industrialized nations (Adler 1983; Archer and Gartner 1984; Currie 1985; Messner and Rosenfeld 1994; also see Lynch 1995). This finding prompts my first proposition:

1. *America has higher rates of serious crime than other industrialized nations because it is a less supportive society.*

I am not claiming that Americans, as individuals, are ungenerous in giving their money to charity or their time to voluntary organizations; quite the opposite appears to be the case (Wuthnow 1991). Even so, I assert that American society is not *organized,* structurally or culturally, to be socially supportive. This conclusion receives confirmation from several sources, which make interrelated or complementary points.

First, Braithwaite (1989:100) observes that societies differ in their "communitarian" quality—that is, in the extent to which "individuals are densely enmeshed in interdependencies which have the special qualities of *mutual help and trust*" (emphasis added). With a mobile, heterogeneous, urban population, the United States is low in communitarianism. Accordingly the structural basis for creating and sustaining supportive social relations is weak.

Second, numerous commentators—often referred to as communitarians—have documented the corrosive effects of America's culture of excessive individualism (Bellah et al. 1985, 1991; Coles 1993; Etzioni 1993; Reich 1988; Wuthnow 1991). In the influential *Habits of the Heart,* Bellah et al. (1985) decry in particular "utilitarian individualism"—the dominance of individual self-interest in the pursuit of desired, usually material ends (also see Messner and Rosenfeld 1994). "We have committed," say Bellah et al. (1985:285), "what to the republican founders of our nation was the cardinal sin: we have put our own good, as individuals, as groups, as a nation, above the common good." Building a "good society," in which concern for community and mutuality of support dominate, awaits a fundamental "transformation of American culture" (Bellah et al. 1985:275–96, 1991).

Wuthnow (1991) notes that even compassion is "bounded" by the culture of individualism. Compassionate behavior is managed by being segmented into limited roles (e.g., a few hours of volunteer work). If pursued so extensively that it interferes with a person's self-interest, such behavior is regarded as an unhealthy obsession (1991:191–220). As a result, while "some of the work—the work that can be divided up into limited commitments—is accomplished, much of it remains to be done" (1991:220). Wuthnow expresses this point nicely:

> Although millions of hours are donated to volunteer activities each year, this effort falls far short of what is needed. I mentioned earlier that two-thirds of American people have visited someone in the hospital in the past year and a quarter have taken care of someone seriously ill in their homes. But thousands of people have no one to care for them. Substantial numbers in our society fear they could not count on anyone for help if they or a member of their family became seriously ill. Nearly four in ten (37 percent) feel that they could not count on their immediate neighbors. . . . One person in three doubts it would be possible to count on relatives outside the immediate family. . . . Half the population think volunteers in their community could not be counted on for help; two people in three think this about social welfare agencies.
>
> As a society we pay lip service to altruistic values, but these values must be seen in the context of other pursuits, the majority of which focus on ourselves rather than others (1991:11).

In short, Wuthnow suggests that the demand for support in America exceeds the supply. This observation leads to a corollary to the first proposition: *The more a society is deficient in the support needed, the higher its crime rate will be.*[3]

Third, Currie (1985, 1989, 1993) makes perhaps the most compelling case that support is low in America and is linked inextricably to the country's high violent crime rate. As Currie points out, America's past and recent economic development has disrupted the traditional "private cushions" provided by networks of social support. Unlike other Western nations, however, America's welfare state has been stingy, if not mean-spirited, in the support it offers to the casualties of the social dislocation and wide inequalities bred by this development (also see Block et al. 1987). The cost of undermining the delivery of support, argues Currie, is an inordinately high rate of violent crime:

> It isn't accidental, then, that among developed countries, the United States is afflicted simultaneously with the worst rates of violent crime, the widest spread in income inequality, and the most severe public policies toward the disadvantaged. The industrial societies that have escaped our extremes of criminal violence tend either to have highly developed public sectors with fairly generous systems of income support, relatively well-developed employment policies, and other cushions against the "forces of the market," or (like Japan) to accomplish much the same ends through private institutions backed by an ethos of social obligation and mutual responsibility (1985:171–72).

Currie also challenges attempts to relate America's high crime rate to a weakness in control. Because other Western nations are more socially integrated, the argument goes, they are better able to exercise informal controls over their citizens (Adler 1983; Bayley 1976). Although this view may have merit, it overlooks the role of support in reducing crime. Japan offers an instructive example. Currie (1985:46) notes that previous analyses have neglected "the ways in which Japanese society is more *supportive* than ours, not simply more 'controlling'" (author's emphasis). In particular, he points both to Japan's "private mechanisms of social obligation" and to Japan's efforts to limit inequality and to provide lifetime job security to most workers (also see Beirne and Messerschmidt 1991:608–609).[4]

As I will discuss again later, the broader point here is that criminologists often confound the effects of informal control with those of social support. These concepts are not necessarily rivals in explaining criminal behavior; in reality, support and control may be mutually reinforcing in reducing crime. Still, the distinction between the two is important both for achieving theoretical precision and because their policy implications can differ dramatically. In a similar vein, a social support perspective leads us to reconsider the connection to crimes of inequality, which research indicates is a salient predictor of cross-cultural variations in violent offenses (Braithwaite 1979; Braithwaite and Braithwaite 1980; Currie 1985; Messner 1980). This relationship often is interpreted from a strain theory perspective: inequality breeds feelings of relative deprivation and, in turn, criminal involvement

(Bailey 1984; Blau and Blau 1982: Rosenfeld 1986). As stated by Currie (1985), however, economic inequality can generate crime not only by exposing people to relative deprivation but also by eviscerating and inhibiting the development of social support networks.[5]

The social ecology of support and crime varies not only across but also within nations (Currie 1985). Thus I offer a second proposition:

2. *The less social support there is in a community, the higher the crime rate will be.*

This thesis is buttressed by several pieces of evidence. Admittedly, quantitative research on communities and crime has not systematically explored the relationship of social support to crime (Bursik and Grasmick 1993a; Byrne and Sampson 1986; Reiss and Tonry 1986; but see Zuravin 1989). Nonetheless, variables employed in various studies may be viewed as operationalizing the concept of support.

First, there is evidence that governmental assistance to the poor tends to lessen violent crime across ecological units (DeFronzo 1983; Messner 1986; see Rosenfeld 1986). Thus, contrary to conservatives' claims that welfare corrodes individual initiative and fosters irresponsibility, including lawlessness (Murray 1984; but see Block et al. 1987; Ellwood 1988), it appears that state support buffers against criminogenic forces (also see Currie 1985, 1989, 1993).

Second, research reveals that crime rates are higher in communities characterized by family disruption, weak friendship networks, and low participation in local voluntary organizations (Sampson 1986a, 1986b; Sampson and Groves 1989). Sampson interprets these findings as an indication that such communities are unable to exert informal social control over their residents (also see Bursik and Grasmick 1993b). Although this perspective may have merit, it is unclear why these variables are measures of control and not of support. It is telling that the mental illness literature uses neighborhood interaction and participation in voluntary organizations to assess "community and network support" (Lin, Dumin, and Woelfel 1986). Further, high rates of family disruption may operationalize not only adults' ability to exert surveillance over youths but also the availability to youths of both adult support networks and the opportunity to develop intimate relations. In short, existing ecological studies can be interpreted as containing measures of social support and, in turn, as showing that support reduces rates of criminal involvement.

Zuravin's (1989) study on the "ecology of child abuse and neglect" across Baltimore neighborhoods provides a useful example of this line of inquiry. "High-risk neighborhoods," she theorizes, "are characterized by demographic, social, and physical characteristics that negatively impact on family and individual stress levels by decreasing the availability as well as the adequacy of support systems" (1989:102). In contrast, families in low-risk neighborhoods are "embedded in informal helping networks," a situation which, in turn, reduces stress and "protects against child maltreatment" (1989:102). Incorporating ecological measures of "inadequate support" into her analysis, Zuravin presents preliminary data suggesting that child maltreatment is related inversely to the ecology of support.

Quantitative and ethnographic research on the "underclass" or the "truly disadvantaged" also is relevant to the social ecology of crime and support. This research documents the powerful social forces—deindustrialization, joblessness, persisting racial segregation, migration to the suburbs—that have created socially and economically isolated inner-city enclaves (Devine and Wright 1993; Jencks and Peterson 1991; Lemann 1991; Massey and Denton 1993; Sullivan 1989; Wilson 1987). This trend, which has been described as a continuing process of social and cultural "disinvestment" in these neighborhoods, has enormous social consequences (Hagan 1993a; Short 1990, 1991).

The literature essentially documents the erosion of community social institutions and of their ability to provide social support. Wilson (1987:144) notes, for example, that the departure of many middle-class families from inner-city neighborhoods reduced the "social buffer" or human capital needed to "absorb the shock or cushion the effect of uneven economic growth and periodic recessions." Similarly, in his review of Anderson's (1990) *Street Wise,* an ethnography of the Philadelphia neighborhood of "Northton," Hagan (1993a:329) shows how "structural and cultural disinvestment" has frayed the supportive relations between adults and youths that previously protected youths against crime. In the past, writes Hagan of Northton,

> The mentor and protégé relationship between old heads and young boys was . . . a defining feature of the social organization of Northton. The old heads were respected older women and men of the community who, as *guides* and role models, *encouraged* youth to invest in conventional culture. However, as structural investment in Northton and other such neighborhoods declined, the moral authority of the old heads and their emphasis

on "honesty, independence, hard work, and family values" diminished...
The result is a form of cultural disinvestment, *as old heads and young boys
go their separate ways, each losing the opportunity of investment from the other*
(1993a:329, emphasis added; also see Duneier 1992:59–62).[6]

Sullivan's (1989) *"Getting Paid"* illuminates how differences in support
structures across neighborhoods either divert youths from a criminal life
course or set them on such a course (also see Hagan 1993b:471–73).
Sullivan studied Latino, African-American, and white youths in three
Brooklyn neighborhoods. In contrast to the more impoverished minority
youths, whose access to support was structurally limited, white juveniles
from the working-class area of "Hamilton Park" were able to mobilize social
networks to provide the resources they needed to escape being deeply
embedded in a criminal role. Thus they avoided legal sanctions through
"personal connections. . . . When in trouble, many of them went immediately to relatives on the police force or in the courts for advice and aid"
(1989:197). Even more telling, they were able to join the legitimate work-
force because their family ties provided entry into "extensive labor market
networks" (1989:218; also see Kasinitz 1993). Accordingly, observes
Sullivan,

> The Hamilton Park youths found a relatively plentiful supply of temporary,
> part-time, almost always off-the-books work through relatives, friends and
> local employers during their middle teens, most of it in the local vicinity.
> As these youths reached their late teens, they employed these same
> networks to gain access to a substantial if diminishing supply of desirable
> blue-collar jobs characterized by high pay, strong unions, and job protec-
> tion. The minority youths suffered during both periods from their lack of
> comparable job networks (1989:103).

In short, my thesis is that both across nations and across communities,
crime rates vary inversely with the level of social support. The social ecolo-
gists of crime have largely overlooked this possibility, but (as I hope I have
revealed) their work contains evidence favoring the social support thesis and
offers important clues for future investigation. In the next section I explore
ways in which the presence or absence of support is implicated in individuals' involvement in crime.

◉ Support and Crime

Since the inception of American criminology, interest in the criminogenic effects of family life has ebbed and flowed (Wilkinson 1974). Over the past decade, attention has increased once again, in part because of the American family's beleaguered status (Sykes and Cullen 1992) and in part because of the emergence of salient criminological findings showing that the pathway to serious adult criminality begins in childhood (Loeber and Le Blanc 1990; Nagin and Farrington 1992; Nagin and Paternoster 1991; Sampson and Laub 1993).

This renewed interest has prompted not only numerous empirical studies on family correlates of crime (Loeber and Stouthamer-Loeber 1986; Wells and Rankin 1991) but also widely read theoretical frameworks. Although these theories differ fundamentally, they emphasize the criminogenic role that the family plays by the way it exercises or instills *control* (Colvin and Pauly 1983; Gottfredson and Hirschi 1990; Hagan 1989; Regoli and Hewitt 1994; Wilson and Herrnstein 1985). These perspectives are earning a measure of empirical confirmation (see, for example, Akers 1994; Burton et al. 1994; Grasmick et al. 1993; Hagan 1989; Hagan, Gillis, and Simpson 1990; Messner and Krohn 1990); thus I will not argue against their value. At the same time, as a result of criminologists' emphasis on control, virtually no theoretical attention has been paid to how family-related social support, or its absence, is involved in crime causation. Accordingly I offer my third proposition:

3. *The more support a family provides, the less likely it is that a person will engage in crime.*

We have considerable evidence that parental expressive support diminishes children's risk of criminal involvement. Glueck and Glueck (1950:113–15, 125), for example, found that in comparison with nondelinquents, delinquents had less "warm" relations with their parents, were less likely to engage in family activities, and came from families that were less "cohesive, that is, evincing strong emotional ties among the members, joint interests, pride in their home, and a 'we' feeling in general." Similarly, Alexander (1973) reported that "supportive" as opposed to "defensive" communication was present more often in nondelinquents' than delinquents' families. More recently, Walsh and Petee's (1987) study revealed that "love deprivation" was an important predictor of violence in a sample of juvenile probationers.

The firmest empirical evidence, however, can be drawn from Loeber and Stouthamer-Loeber's (1986) comprehensive meta-analysis of family correlates of delinquency: factors indicating a lack of parental support clearly increase delinquent involvement. (Also see Feldman's [1993:196] discussion of "positive parenting.") Loeber and Stouthamer-Loeber conclude that delinquency is related inversely to "child-parent involvement, such as the amount of intimate communication, confiding, sharing of activities, and seeking help" (1986:42). Similarly, their analysis indicates that measures of parental rejection of children, such as "rejection, not warm, lack of love, lack of affection, less affectionate," were "consistently related to delinquency and aggression" (1986:54; also see Sampson and Laub 1993:119). These "support" elements, moreover, were among the most powerful family factors related to delinquency; their effects exceeded those of parental criminality, marital discord, parental absence, parental health, and family size (1993:120–23).[7]

Also relevant are criminological studies of the social bond theory concept of "attachment to parents." Research reveals that attachment is generally, though not uniformly, related inversely to delinquency (Burton 1991; Mawhorr 1992). As Mawhorr points out, interpreting this relationship is difficult because attachment has been conceptualized and operationalized in diverse ways. Notably, measures of attachment often confound "indirect control," bonds that make youths not wish to disappoint parents by getting into trouble (Rankin and Wells 1990), with youths' perceptions of parental support, such as expressing love, being nurturant, and providing a confiding relationship. Although the results are not fully consistent (Mawhorr 1992) and the concept of support has not been measured systematically, at least some evidence exists to suggest that perceived parental support mitigates delinquency (Van Voorhis et al. 1988; also see Barnes 1984).

In contrast to expressive support, criminological research contains few empirical studies on the impact of instrumental family support on crime (see, for example, Loeber and Stouthamer-Loeber 1986). It is premature to conclude that instrumental support is as salient as expressive support, and possibly these forms of support vary in their effects across the life cycle. In any case, the literature contains some clues as to the importance of instrumental family support. Thus, if we revisit Glueck and Glueck (1950:129–30), we discover that delinquents were more likely than nondelinquents to have parents who "had not given any thought to the boys' futures." Further, as noted above, family-based networks are an important source of entry into the job market; this, in turn, can undermine continued involvement in crime (Sullivan 1989; also see Curtis 1989:155).

Finally, any discussion of families and crime must be careful to avoid what Currie (1985:185) calls the "fallacy of autonomy—the belief that what goes on inside the family can usefully be separated from the forces that affect it from the outside: the larger social context in which families are embedded for better or for worse." Indeed, large social forces have transformed many American families in ways that often have reduced their capacity to support children (see, for example, Hewlett 1991; Wilson 1987). For example, adolescents today are much less likely than in the past to eat evening meals with parents or to spend time at home (Felson 1994:104; Messner and Rosenfeld 1994:103); the potential time that parents have to spend with children is declining (Hewlett 1991:90–92); and "less than 5 percent of all families have another adult (e.g., grandparent) living in the home, compared to 50 percent two generations ago. This reduces the backup support that might otherwise be available to working parents" (Panel on High-Risk Youth 1993:56).

Most disconcerting, however, is the concentration of forces that have ripped apart families of the underclass, or the "truly disadvantaged" (Devine and Wright 1993; Wilson 1987), and have made inner-city youths vulnerable to crime, drugs, and an array of unhealthy behaviors (Currie 1985, 1993; Panel on High-Risk Youth 1993). The Panel on High-Risk Youth states,

> Perhaps the most serious risk facing adolescents in high risk settings is isolation from the nurturance, safety, and guidance that comes from sustained relationships with adults. Parents are the best source of support, but for many adolescents, parents are not positively involved in their lives. In some cases, parents are absent or abusive. In many more cases, parents strive to be good parents, but lack the capacity or opportunity to be so (1993:213).

Accordingly I offer this as a corollary to my third proposition: *The more support is given to families, the less crime will occur.* As Rivara and Farrington (forthcoming) observe, "increased social support to families can take the form of information (e.g., parenting programs), emotional support (e.g., home visitors), provision of material needs (e.g., food stamps, housing) or instrumental help (e.g., day care)." They also note that the "most successful interventions appear to be those which offer more than one type of social support service, thereby affecting a number of risk factors for the development of delinquency and violence" (forthcoming; also see Farrington 1994). Echoing this theme, Currie (1989:18–19, 1993:310–17) argues persuasively that the government should institute a "genuinely supportive national family policy," including, for example, child care, family leaves, and special programs for families at risk for mistreating children.

Currie's (1985, 1989, 1993) analyses and the above discussion on changing levels of support within the American family lead to a second corollary: *Changes in levels of support for and by families have contributed since the 1960s to increases in crime and to the concentration of serious violence in high-risk inner-city neighborhoods.* This statement contradicts the thinking of Murray (1984), who blames the "generous revolution" of the Great Society programs for eroding individual responsibility and for fostering criminal and other deviant behaviors (see Lemann 1991; Lupo 1994).

Beyond the family, Krohn (1986) contends that social networks may provide a "web of conformity" (also see Sampson and Laub 1993). Krohn emphasizes how dimensions of networks operate to control behavior; scholars in the sociology of mental illness study how these characteristics of networks are an important source of social support (Lin et al. 1986; Vaux 1988). In short, the web of conformity involves not only constraints but also supports (Sullivan 1989; also see Zuravin 1989). This point leads to my fourth proposition:

4. *The more social support in a person's social network, the less crime will occur.*

Social support theorists have examined most extensively how supports mitigate the effects of strain or "stress." The relationships are complex, but social supports can prevent stresses from arising or can lessen negative consequences if stresses should emerge (House 1981; Vaux 1988). These findings are important in light of the recent revitalization of strain theory, particularly empirical research linking strain to criminal behavior (Agnew 1985a, 1989; Agnew and White 1992; Burton and Cullen 1992; Farnworth and Leiber 1989; McCarthy and Hagan 1992; Vaux and Ruggiero 1983).

Most important is Agnew's (1992) attempt to lay the foundation for a "general strain theory." Agnew argues that in focusing almost exclusively on the Mertonian or status frustration version of strain theory, criminologists have conceptualized criminogenic strain too narrowly. In addition to the blockage of desired (success) goals emphasized by the Mertonian tradition, Agnew demarcates two other general categories of strain: removal of positively valued stimuli, and the presentation of noxious stimuli (also see Agnew 1985a, 1989; Agnew and White 1992; McCarthy and Hagan 1992, Vaux and Ruggiero 1983).

The remaining issue, largely ignored by strain theorists (Cullen 1984), is how people respond to this range of stressful conditions. Building on the social support literature (e.g., Vaux 1988), Agnew (1992) suggests that the ability to cope with criminogenic strains is contingent on access to supports. "Adolescents with conventional social support," he observes, "should be better able to respond to objective strains in a nondelinquent manner" (1992:72). This contention suggests my fifth proposition:

5. *Social support lessens the effects of exposure to criminogenic strains.*

In their important reassessment of Glueck and Glueck's longitudinal data, Sampson and Laub (1993) study not only sources of the stability of crime across the life course but also the "turning points" at which offenders depart from the criminal "pathway." Their analysis shows that during adulthood, job stability and attachments to spouse contribute to desistance from crime. They interpret these findings as indicating that "adult social bonds" provide offenders with social capital which subjects them to "informal social controls" (1993:140–43). "Adult social ties," they observe, "create interdependent systems of obligation and restraint that impose significant costs for translating criminal propensities into action" (1993:141).

I will not take issue with the control theory set forth by Sampson and Laub, but I observe that their *Crime in the Making* also contains insights on the salience of adult *social supports. Thus* Sampson and Laub (1993:141) take note of the "social capital invested by employers and spouses," not simply that invested by offenders. With regard to marriage, for example, life histories on offenders in Glueck and Glueck's sample reveal that this investment took the form of wives' providing "material and emotional *support"* (Sampson and Laub 1993:205, 220, emphasis added; also see Vaux 1988:173).[8] Two points follow from this observation.

First, marital and employment "social supports" may reduce crime by increasing social capital and thus expanding the basis for informal social controls. Second, these social supports may exert independent (main) effects on crime not by facilitating control but by reducing other sources of crime (e.g., lessening emotional difficulties, relieving strains, transforming deviant identities). More broadly, I offer my sixth proposition:

6. *Across the life cycle, social support increases the likelihood that offenders will turn away from a criminal pathway.*

I do not mean to confine this proposition to the role of adult social supports in crime desistance. In particular, accounts of at-risk youths suggest that supports can trigger their turning away from crime (see also Dubow and Reid 1994). Such supports may involve a youth's special informal relationship with an adult (e.g., teacher, coach), participation in a mentorship program (Kuznik 1994; Panel on High-Risk Youth 1993:213–14), or placement in a community program (Curtis 1989:154–60).

Commentary on impoverished juveniles at risk for crime also frequently emphasizes the sense of isolation felt by these youths. The Panel on High-Risk Youth (1993:217), for example, notes that "young people from high-risk settings" often "confront the emotional pain and feelings of hope-lessness that can interfere with positive development." Echoing this theme, Curtis (1989:158) observes that inner-city minority youths think "the cards are stacked hopelessly against them. These youths believe that fate will not permit them to 'make it' in any legitimate form."

This isolation might be viewed as a detachment from social bonds that lessens control and increases criminal involvement, but another process also may be operating: These youths may perceive that they will always lack the instrumental and expressive supports needed to change the circumstances in which they are enmeshed.[9] This possibility leads to my seventh proposition:

7. *Anticipation of a lack of social support increases criminal involvement.*

Thus far I have concentrated on how *receiving* support diminishes crim-inality, but it also seems important to consider how *giving* support affects involvement in crime. The logic of writings from the peacemaking/human-ist and feminist perspectives suggests that providing support should reduce criminal propensities (McDermott 1994). Pepinsky (1988), in fact, regards crime as the opposite of "responsiveness" to others. Further, in *The Call of Service,* Coles (1993) tells how the experience of supporting others can transform selves, inculcate idealism, foster moral purpose, and create long-standing interconnections—all of which would seem anticriminogenic.

I know of no systematic empirical investigation of the link between giving support and crime, but some insights can be gleaned from the research. Sampson and Laub (1993:219–20), for example, note that the offenders in their study were likely to desist from crime when they were devoted to their spouses and children, and were "financially responsible not only to their spouses, but also to parents and siblings if the need arose." That is, as offenders assumed a role as providers of expressive and instrumental support, their involvement in crime ceased.

Ward's (1988) research on "urban adolescents' conceptions of violence" also is relevant. Youths were asked to describe a violent event they had witnessed and whether those involved were "right or wrong in what they did." Of the youths who interpreted the episode with a "care" as opposed to a "justice" logic,[10] "none found violence justifiable in any way . . . care calls for an injunction *against* hurt" (1988:193; author's emphasis). There is a clear distinction, of course, between caring behavior and caring attitudes, but these results at least indicate that a caring or supportive orientation toward others facilitates connectedness and makes victimization incongruous (see McCord 1992).

Lynne Goodstein (personal communication, January 2, 1994) offers another pertinent insight: "Women's traditional responsibility for the delivery of social support and nurturance to others (children, elders, partners) and the dramatically lower crime rates for women is an interesting association." Although this association is open to differing interpretations,[11] it suggests that the experience of providing support creates sentiments (e.g., compassion), identities, role expectations, and problem-solving skills that are generally incompatible with the "seductions of crime" (Katz 1988; also see Gilligan, Ward, and Taylor 1988).

In any event, these various considerations lead to my eighth proposition:

8. *Giving social support lessens involvement in crime.*

Finally, Albert Cohen (personal communication, January 29, 1994) has alerted me to the need to consider the broader concept of "differential social support."[12] To this point, I have largely explored the role of supports in making conformity possible. Cohen, however, observes

> that social support is equally important to non-conformity, to crime. Indeed, the burden of much of the literature on causation is that associations, the situation of company, provide much of the support that makes it possible to break the law, more effectively to thwart the justice process and reduce the "hurtfulness" and other consequences of punishment.

Indeed, insights on support for crime are evident in the literature on peers and co-offending (Reiss 1988), on the acquisition and performance of criminal roles (Cloward 1959; Steffensmeier 1983), and on the organizational conditions that make corporate crime possible (Hills 1987; Sutherland 1949). Differential social support also might operate in situational contexts. As shown by Richard Felson (1982; Felson and Tedeschi 1993), "third parties" to interpersonal conflict can support the escalation of violence or can mediate tensions and diminish subsequent aggression. These observations lead to my ninth proposition:

> 9. *Crime is less likely when social support for conformity exceeds social support for crime.*

In a related vein, Ronald Akers (personal communication, January 1994) has cautioned that social supports are likely to be most effective when they are linked to "conformity-inducing outcomes." The *source* of the support may be particularly important. For instance, support from conformist sources may not only address criminal risk factors (e.g., strain) but also provide an opportunity for prosocial modeling (Andrews and Bonta 1994:202–205). Conversely, support from criminal friends (e.g., comfort in the face of a stressful life event) may be counteracted if these associations also expose youths to criminogenic influences.

On this point, the research on the effects of marriage provides relevant data. Although the findings are not fully consistent (Sampson and Laub 1993), we find some evidence that marriage—conceptualized here as a social support—reduces crime only if spouses are not themselves deviant or criminal (Farrington, Ohlin, and Wilson 1986:56; West 1982:100–104). Thus I offer this corollary to Proposition 9: *Social support from conformist sources is most likely to reduce criminal involvement.*

❧ Support and Control

As stated earlier, recent advances in criminological theory have been dominated by attempts to link control with crime. I have tried to show that these perspectives overlook social support and potentially confound the effects of control and with the effects of support. Now I wish to make a different, but related, argument, which is set forth in my tenth proposition:

> 10. *Social support often is a precondition for effective social control.*

The criminological literature contains numerous illustrations of this proposition. Braithwaite's (1989) influential theory of "reintegrative shaming," however, is perhaps the most noteworthy example (also see Braithwaite and Mugford 1994; Makkai and Braithwaite 1994). In brief, Braithwaite contends that legal violations often evoke formal and informal attempts at "shaming," which he defines as "all processes of expressing disapproval which have the intention or effect of invoking remorse in the person being shamed and/or condemnation by others who become aware of the shaming" (1989:9). Braithwaite observes, however, that shaming takes two general forms. Disintegrative shaming is criminogenic; as labeling theory would predict, it stigmatizes, excludes, and ensures the exposure of offenders to criminogenic conditions. Reintegrative shaming, in contrast, achieves conformity. After the act is condemned, attempts are made "to reintegrate the offender back into the community of law-abiding or respectable citizens through words or gestures of forgiveness or ceremonies to decertify the offender as deviant" (1989:100–101). Even if repeated efforts are required, the goal is to avoid exclusion and thus to embed the offender in conventional, accepting relationships (Braithwaite and Mugford 1994).

In the language of the social support paradigm, Braithwaite is asserting that control can be effective only in the context of support (see Sherman 1992). Further, the very likelihood that reintegrative shaming will be used depends on the extent to which the larger society is supportive or, as Braithwaite puts its, "communitarian." Not surprisingly, shaming in the United States tends to be disintegrative (also see Benson 1990).

A related insight can be gained from the correctional literature. It appears that family support of offenders during and after incarceration improves chances of successful completion of parole supervision (Farrington et al. 1986:147; Wright and Wright 1992:54). In short, control with support is more effective than control by itself.

The family socialization literature also offers useful information. Wilson and Herrnstein (1985:237–40) argue that "restrictive" parenting is important in detecting and discouraging rule transgressions and thus in teaching that behavior has consequences. But restrictiveness is most effective when coupled with parental warmth. "A warm parent," they state, "is approving and supportive of the child, frequently employs praise as a reinforcement for good behavior, and explains the reasons for rules" (1985:237). In this case, warmth (support) empowers restrictiveness (control): when children care

about their parents, obedience is rewarding and disobedience is unrewarding (1985:239). As Maccoby puts it,

> A common theme in these various findings seems to be that parental
> warmth binds children to their parents in a positive way—it makes chil-
> dren responsive and more willing to accept guidance. If the parent-child
> relationship is close and affectionate, parents can exercise what control is
> needed without having to apply heavy disciplinary pressure. It is as if
> parents' responsiveness, affection, and obvious commitment to their chil-
> dren's welfare gave them the right to make demands and exercise control
> (cited in Braithwaite 1989:166–67).

These observations suggest a broader conclusion about the correction of
crime:

11. A supportive correctional system lessens crime.

Braithwaite's (1989) theoretical work on reintegrative shaming suggests
this proposition (also see Braithwaite and Mugford 1994). Experiences in
the United States, however, offer additional, substantive confirmatory
evidence. Over the past two decades, American policy makers have engaged
in what Clear (1994) calls an experiment in "penal harm," largely on the
assumption that inflicting pain on offenders rather than supporting them
will lessen the crime problem (also see Currie 1989). Policy makers have
attempted to increase the scale of imprisonment (Zimring and Hawkins
1991) and to replace community *corrections* with intermediate *punishments*
(Byrne, Lurigio, and Petersilia 1992). This experiment in reducing crime
through nonsupport must be termed a failure: America's crime rates have
stubbornly resisted the intended effects of penal harm (Clear 1994; Cullen
and Wright forthcoming; Currie 1985; Irwin and Austin 1994; Petersilia
1992; Steffensmeier and Harer 1993; Visher 1987; Zimring and Hawkins
1991; but see Wright 1994).

Evaluations of correctional interventions also are instructive. It is rather
clear that punishment-oriented programs have virtually no effect on recidivism—indeed, they may actually increase it (Andrews and Bonta 1994;
Byrne and Pattavina 1992; Cullen, Wright, and Applegate 1993; Petersilia
and Turner 1993). In contrast, meta-analyses show clearly that rehabilitation programs reduce recidivism across programs by 10 to 12 percent
(Palmer 1992:158), and by about 50 percent when interventions are based
on principles of effective treatment (Andrews and Bonta 1994; also see
Lipsey 1992).

These findings are important for two reasons. First, although rehabilitation is often criticized for justifying coercive practices (Cullen and Gilbert 1982), it represents a correctional philosophy that embodies sentiments of "doing good." It implies a genuine concern for protecting the social order, but with the understanding that this goal is best achieved by addressing offenders' criminogenic needs and assisting their reintegration into conventional roles. In short, rehabilitation is a supportive, not a punitive, correctional approach (Cullen and Gilbert 1982; Cullen and Wright forthcoming).

Second, as Andrews and Bonta (1994) point out, support is an integral part of effective correctional treatment programs. In behavioral programs, for example, they note that counselors should "give at least four positive supportive statements for every punishing one" (1994:205). They also observe the importance of "high quality relationships" characterized by "mutual liking, respect and caring . . . openness, warmth and understanding" (1994:203–204). These supportive relationships, contend Andrews and Bonta (1994:204–205), provide a basis for effective modeling and for increasing the chances that expressions of disapproval will matter to offenders.[13]

Although the evidence for this point is less highly developed, I speculate in my twelfth proposition that support also is integral to law enforcement:

12. *Social support leads to more effective policing.*

This proposition reflects the belief that law enforcement works more effectively—to reduce crime, to serve community needs—when police and citizens are involved in a mutually supportive relationship. In this case, the goal is to encourage the "co-production" of order by police and citizens acting in concert.

The "community-policing" movement is the most obvious example of mutually supportive policing (see Bayley 1976). Traditional policing emphasizes largely impersonal, reactive, centralized law enforcement. In contrast, community policing views officers as located in the community, where they can interact with and listen to local residents; as building personal, trusting relationships with citizens; and as attempting proactively to work with citizens to solve community problems related to crime (Skolnick and Bayley 1988; Sparrow 1988; Wycoff 1988).

It is premature to conclude that supportive policing ventures will reap the anticipated benefits, especially if they are implemented with unrealistic expectations and without program integrity (Mastrofski 1988). Still, initial results show some promise: community-policing ventures appear to reduce citizens' crime-related fears and perceptions of disorder (Spelman and Eck 1987; Wycoff 1988). Further, although solid evaluations are lacking, it seems reasonable to anticipate that community-oriented policing which actually delivers meaningful support to the community will diminish crime rates (National Institute of Justice 1992; Skolnick and Bayley 1988; Spelman and Eck 1987; but see Bowers and Hirsch 1987). As Thurman concludes:

> Co-producing solutions to crime and related social problems seems the best means at hand for bringing human resources together with the police for mutual benefit, while at the same time engendering respect for the ability of residents within communities to make an important contribution to community-based problem-solving (1993:22).

In connection with this point, Guarino-Ghezzi (1994) argues that the police could become more effective in reducing juvenile lawlessness by participating in a "model of reintegrative surveillance" (see Braithwaite 1989). Drawing on the results from "model programs for juveniles"—"pockets of innovation that involve aggressive outreach efforts by police" (1994:146)—Guarino-Ghezzi illuminates the benefits that accrue when officers are involved more fully in the lives of community members, especially youthful offenders. By building interpersonal bonds and increasing their understanding of urban youths, officers can 1) exercise more consistent surveillance over, and impose graduated sanctions on, problem youths and 2) foster the reintegration of offenders through caring responses and the provision of services—that is, by delivering social supports. "In short," observes Guarino-Ghezzi (1994:149), "the police role needs to be reexamined as an important *resource* for juvenile offender reintegration and crime prevention, particularly in high-crime neighborhoods where *other vital supports are lacking* and disorder is prevalent" (emphasis added; also see Myers and Chiang 1993).

❧ Support and Victimization

My general thesis is that social support, both ecologically and in individuals' lives, reduces the number of persons motivated to break the law. A reduction in persons with criminal propensities should limit the crime rate and, by implication, should decrease victimization in society. This point leads into my thirteenth proposition:

13. Social support lessens criminal victimization.

As Cohen and Felson (1979:589) point out, however, the presence of "motivated offenders" is only one of the elements necessary for victimization; there also must be a "suitable target" and "the absence of capable guardians against a violation" (also see Garofalo 1987). Although it is speculative, I offer the following corollary to my proposition: *Social support reduces victimization by decreasing suitable targets and by increasing guardianship.*

I contend that the provision of social support potentially builds connectedness among community members; in particular, it fosters bonds of reciprocity and intimacy. Under these conditions, "targets" become less attractive for two reasons. First, if a motivated offender previously received support from a potential target, a victimization would violate reciprocity norms and would exact a psychic cost. Second, intimacy creates the possibility that a target could identify an offender; again, the target's attractiveness would be decreased by increasing the costs of a victimization (see Felson 1986).

In the same vein, the more widespread the provision of social support and thus of interpersonal knowledge in an area, the greater the overall level of guardianship. Because of investments in relationships, high levels of social support provide the social capital for guardianship. Further, interpersonal knowledge stemming from support creates a larger pool of potential "informants" (Felson 1986), who are available to report those who otherwise might contemplate victimizing others. "A tight community—where people know people, property, and their linkages," observes Felson (1986:123), "offers little opportunity for common exploitive crime."

Finally, I offer another corollary: *A more supportive society reduces exposure to victimization.* Here I draw on Maume's (1989) research revealing that "one of the hidden costs of inequality is that some people are constrained to live risk-prone lifestyles," which make their victimization more likely (also see Cao and Maume 1993; Carroll, personal communication, December 29, 1993; Carroll and Jackson 1983). A supportive society, which presumably would diminish racial and economic inequalities (Currie 1985), thus would provide disadvantaged citizens with resources to follow less risky lifestyles and to commensurately reduce their exposure to victimization.[14]

There also is evidence that social support mitigates the effects of crime victimization. As Agnew (1985b:234) notes, "[D]ata indicate that fear of crime is lower when social support is high." Although relationships are often complex, other studies suggest that social support improves victims' psychological adjustment (Astin et al. 1993; Testa et al. 1992). Support to victims can be expressive, as in providing comfort and helping to neutralize self-blame, or instrumental, as in supplying information on how to avoid future victimizations or providing the resources to escape the threat of continuing abuse (e.g., shelters for battered women) (Agnew 1985b; Saunders and Azar 1989:494–508; also see Nurius, Furrey, and Berliner 1992). These considerations lead to my final proposition:

14. Social support lessens the pains of criminal victimization.

● Next Steps

I have outlined only the broad parameters suggesting how social support might serve as an organizing concept for criminology. If a social support paradigm is to bear fruit, I suspect that my initial ideas will warrant empirical scrutiny, revision, and perhaps reversal. Here I want to identify three steps that might be taken by criminologists interested in advancing the paradigm of social support and crime.

First, scholars must conceptualize and study which forms of social support are implicated most deeply in diminishing criminal involvement. Social support is a multifaceted concept (see Vaux 1988), which undoubtedly has a complex relationship to crime. Although my thesis is that social support generally reduces lawbreaking, we must learn to recognize when the provision of various types of support, and by whom, has no effect or has the unanticipated consequence of increasing criminal involvement (e.g., when support is of poor quality or comes from a source enmeshed in crime).

Second, I have stopped far short of developing a formal theory of social support and crime—in part because my thinking has not progressed to that point and in part because I suspect that social support operates as a general protective factor across a variety of criminogenic risk factors. Even so, the theoretical task is still the identification of the precise mechanisms by which social support does, or does not, decrease criminal behavior.

I hope I have provided reasonable clues about the nature of these mechanisms. Thus, among other proposals, I have suggested that the provision of social supports reduces criminogenic strains, fosters effective parenting and a nurturing family life, supplies the human and social capital needed to desist from crime, creates opportunities for prosocial modeling, strengthens efforts at informal and formal control, and reduces opportunities for victimization. Research must discern which of these hunches have merit, and to what degree.

Third, to advance the social support paradigm, criminologists must incorporate measures of support into their research designs. With secondary data sets, the challenge is to reexamine questions on surveys and other variables (e.g., census data) while considering how these data operationalize various dimensions of social support. In collecting new data, the challenge is to devise measures of support—with considerable help from the existing sociological literature on social support (Cleary 1988; Lin et al. 1986; Vaux 1988)—and to incorporate them into empirical studies of crime causation and into tests of rival criminological theories.

◉ Good Criminology and the Good Society

Over the past decade, an increasing number of voices have joined in a national conversation about the requirements for what Robert Bellah and his colleagues call the "Good Society" (Bellah et al. 1991; also see Bellah et al. 1985; Coles 1993; Etzioni 1993; Reich 1988; Wuthnow 1991). Fundamental to this ongoing conversation is a critique of the excessive individualism in the United States, which too often degenerates into a politics justifying either the crass pursuit of rights or materialistic self-aggrandizement. In this context, there is a lack of attention to the public good, service to others, and an appreciation for our need for connectedness. Accordingly there is a call to revitalize our common bonds and to build a society supportive of all its citizens.

I realize the risk in linking one's criminology to a larger social agenda: regardless of how crime is affected, attempts to build a Good Society certainly should stand or fall on their own merits (Felson 1994:12–13). Still, it is equally misguided to assume that criminological ideas have no consequences (Bohm 1993; Lilly et al. 1989). A criminology that emphasizes the need for social supports thus may have the potential to make a difference.

Indeed, if the social supports paradigm proves to be "Good Criminology," it will provide empirical grounds for suggesting that an important key to solving the crime problem is the construction of a support-ive social order—the Good Society. Accordingly this paradigm may present an opportunity to challenge the current hegemony of punitive policy in criminal justice. It may prompt us to consider that the cost of a nonsup-portive society, exacerbated by mean-spirited or neglectful public policies, is a disgraceful level of crime and violence (Currie 1985). And, hopefully, it may provide the basis for criminal justice and public policies which help to create a society that is more supportive and hence safer for its citizens.

Endnotes

[1]Social support is not identical to social networks, social integration, or social ties. The distinctive quality of social support is not the mere existence of social rela-tionships but the extent to which such relations deliver instrumental and expressive assistance.

[2]Again, this discussion presents only the bare bones of the concept of social support. Thus other dimensions of social support could be introduced: consistency, quality, depth, source, and the difference between chronic and situational.

[3]The limits of compassion are evident in the recent discussions of Americans' "compassion fatigue" regarding the homeless. Further, Link et al. (1992) ques-tion the assumption of compassion fatigue, largely on the grounds that Americans never showed unmixed compassion toward the homeless in the first place.

[4]In a related issue, Currie (1985) disputes the conservatives' claim that permissive-ness accounts for America's high crime rate. Currie observes that many Western nations are more permissive than the United States, both culturally and in their criminal justice systems, and he reasserts that the distinctive quality of American social policy is the grudging nature of its support for the impover-ished. Also see Beirne and Messerschmidt (1991).

[5]The relationship of relative deprivation to crime is problematic. Within the United States, support for a relationship between relative deprivation and crime is inconsistent for both individual-level studies (Burton et al. 1994; Burton and Dunaway 1994) and macro-level studies (see, for example, Bailey 1984). Further, it is not clear that inequality causes crime by deprivation, through other processes such as routine activities (Cao and Maume 1993; Carroll and

Jackson 1983; Maume 1989), or (as I suggest) by undermining social support networks.

[6]A risk of emphasizing the deteriorating conditions of inner cities is that the existence and importance of social support networks in these areas are often overlooked. See, in particular, *Slim's Table* (Duneier 1992). This sometimes touching ethnography not only reveals supports among African-American men but also challenges stereotypes about ghetto males by making working-class blacks and their respectability visible.

[7]Evidence suggesting the harmful effects of nonsupportive parents also is present in research linking physical abuse to delinquency and adult violence. See, for example, Regoli and Hewitt (1994), Straus (1990), and Widom (1989).

[8]Criminological research paints a complicated picture of the relationship of marriage to criminal involvement (see, for example, Farrington, Ohlin, and Wilson 1986:56; Rand 1987; Wright and Wright 1992). A weakness in this research is the shortage of studies measuring marital quality and, in particular, the personal characteristics and behavior of spouses in the relationship. In the social support literature, marriage is often used as a proxy measure for support (as opposed to control). Even in this research, however, the quality of marital support has not been explored extensively. As Vault (1988:200) points out, "marriage often provides individuals with a readily accessible source of each important mode of support in the context of a long-standing relationship based on love, mutual obligation, and intimate knowledge." At the same time, continues Vaux (1988:200), "many marriages survive for a lifetime but perform these support functions poorly. Many others prove so unrewarding or aversive that they are terminated."

[9]These perceptions would be classified as "appraisals of support" (Vaux 1988). Here, however, the focus is on appraising not only current support but future support as well. On the potential importance of anticipations of support and rejection, see Link et al. (1989).

[10]This distinction in moral orientations has been made by Gilligan (1982; Gilligan and Attanucci 1988), who argues that moral issues tend to be viewed by males in terms of "justice" (an emphasis on rules, reciprocity, and fair treatment) and by females in terms of "care" (an emphasis on interconnections and on responsiveness to others' needs) (also see McDermott 1994).

[11]For example, Hagan's (1989) power-control theory might suggest that females confined to supportive, domestic roles are subjected to greater control and thus are involved in less crime.

[12]Ronald Akers (personal communication, January 1994) has made a similar observation.

[13]For a compelling statement of the value of a supportive correctional system, see Miller (1991).

[14]Although this idea is not developed here systematically, I would propose that opportunities for victimization would be related inversely to ecological and individual-level measures of support (especially of social networks).

References

Addams, J. (1910) *Twenty Years at Hull House*. New York: Signet.

Adler, F. (1983) *Nations Not Obsessed with Crime*. Littleton, CO: Rothman.

Agnew, R. (1985a) "A Revised Strain Theory of Delinquency." *Social Forces* 64:15167.

_____. (1985b) "Neutralizing the Impact of Crime." *Criminal Justice and Behavior* 12:221–39.

_____. (1989) "A Longitudinal Test of Revised Strain Theory." *Journal of Quantitative Criminology* 5:373–87.

_____. (1992) "Foundation for a General Strain Theory of Crime and Delinquency." *Criminology* 30:47–86.

Agnew, R. and H. R. White (1992) "An Empirical Test of General Strain Theory." *Criminology* 30:475–99.

Akers, R. L. (1994) *Criminological Theories: Introduction and Evaluation*. Los Angeles: Roxbury.

Alexander, J. F. (1973) "Defensive and Supportive Communications in Normal and Deviant Families." *Journal of Consulting and Clinical Psychology* 40:223–31.

Anderson, E. (1990) *Street Wise: Race, Class, and Change in an Urban Community*. Chicago: University of Chicago Press.

Andrews, D. A. and J. Bonta (1994) *The Psychology of Criminal Conduct*. Cincinnati: Anderson.

Archer, D. and R. Gartner (1984) *Violence and Crime in Cross-National Perspective*. New Haven: Yale University Press.

Astin, M. C., K. J. Lawrence, and D. W. Foy (1993) "Posttraumatic Stress Disorder among Battered Women: Risk and Resiliency Factors." *Violence and Victims* 8:17–28.

Bailey, W. C. (1984) "Poverty, Inequality, and City Homicide Rates." *Criminology* 22:531–50.

Barlow, H. D. (1993) *Introduction to Criminology*. 6th ed. New York: HarperCollins.

Barnes, G. M. (1984) "Adolescent Alcohol Abuse and Other Problem Behaviors: Their Relationships and Common Parental Influences." *Journal of Youth and Adolescence* 13:329–47.

Bayley, D. H. (1976) *Forces of Order: Police Behavior in Japan and the United States.* Berkeley: University of California Press.

Beirne, P. and J. Messerschmidt (1991) *Criminology.* San Diego: Harcourt Brace Jovanovich.

Bellah, R. N., R. Madsen, W. M. Sullivan, A. Swidler, and S. M. Tipton (1985) *Habits of the Heart: Individualism and Commitment in American Life.* Berkeley: University of California Press.

_____. (1991) *The Good Society.* New York: Knopf.

Benson, M. L. (1990) "Emotions and Adjudication: Status Degradation among White-Collar Criminals." *Justice Quarterly* 7:515–28.

Blau, J. R. and P. M. Blau (1982) "The Cost of Inequality: Metropolitan Structure and Violent Crime." *American Sociological Review* 47:114–29.

Block, F., R. A. Cloward, B. Ehrenreich, and F. F. Piven (1987) *The Mean Season: The Attack on the Welfare State.* New York: Pantheon.

Bohm, R. M. (1993) "On the State of Criminal Justice: 1993 Presidential Address to the Academy of Criminal Justice Sciences." *Justice Quarterly* 10:529–40.

Bowers, W. J. and J. H. Hirsch (1987) "The Impact of Foot Patrol Staffing on Crime and Disorder in Boston: An Unmet Promise." *American Journal of Police* 6:17–44.

Braithwaite, J. (1979) *Inequality, Crime and Public Policy.* London: Routledge and Kegan Paul.

_____. (1989) *Crime, Shame and Reintegration.* Cambridge, UK: Cambridge University Press.

Braithwaite, J. and V. Braithwaite (1980) "The Effect of Income Inequality and Social Democracy on Homicide." *British Journal of Criminology* 20:45–53.

Braithwaite, J. and S. Mugford (1994) "Conditions of Successful Reintegration Ceremonies: Dealing with Juvenile Offenders." *British Journal of Criminology* 34:139–71.

Braswell, M. C. (1989) "Correctional Treatment and the Human Spirit: A Focus on Relationship." *Federal Probation* 53 (June): 49–60.

_____. (1990) "Peacemaking: A Missing Link in Criminology." *The Criminologist* 15 (May–June): 1, 3–5.

Brownfield, D. and A. M. Sorenson (1991) "Religion and Drug Use among Adolescents: A Social Support Conceptualization and Interpretation." *Deviant Behavior* 12:2 (59–76).

Bulmer, M. (1984) *The Chicago School of Sociology: Institutionalization, Diversity, and the Rise of Sociological Research.* Chicago: University of Chicago Press.

Bursik, R. J., Jr. and H. G. Grasmick (1993a) *Neighborhoods and Crime: The Dimensions of Effective Community Control.* New York: Lexington Books.

———. (1993b) "Economic Deprivation and Neighborhood Crime Rates, 1960–1980." *Law and Society Review* 27:263–83.

Burton, V. S., Jr. (1991) "Explaining Adult Criminality: Testing Strain, Differential Association, and Control Theories." Doctoral dissertation, University of Cincinnati.

Burton, V. S., Jr. and F. T. Cullen (1992) "The Empirical Status of Strain Theory." *Journal of Crime and Justice* 15 (2):1–30.

Burton, V. S., Jr., F. T. Cullen, T. D. Evans, and R. G. Dunaway (1994) "Reconsidering Strain Theory: Operationalization, Rival Theories, and Adult Criminality." *Journal of Quantitative Criminology* 10:213–39.

Burton, V. S., Jr. and R. G. Dunaway (1994) "Strain, Relative Deprivation, and Middle-Class Delinquency." In G. Barak (ed.), *Varieties of Criminology: Readings from a Dynamic Discipline,* pp. 79–96. Westport, CT: Praeger.

Byrne, J. M., A. J. Lurigio, and J. Petersilia, eds. (1992) *Smart Sentencing: The Emergence of Intermediate Sanctions.* Newbury Park, CA: Sage.

Byrne, J. M. and A. Pattavina (1992) "The Effectiveness Issue: Assessing What Works in the Adult Community Corrections System." In J. M. Byrne, A. J. Lurigio, and J. Petersilia (eds.), *Smart Sentencing: The Emergence of Intermediate Sanctions,* pp. 281–303. Newbury Park, CA: Sage.

Byrne, J. M. and R. J. Sampson, eds. (1986) *The Social Ecology of Crime.* New York: Springer-Verlag.

Cao, L. and D. J. Maume Jr. (1993) "Urbanization, Inequality, Lifestyles and Robbery: A Comprehensive Model." *Sociological Focus* 26:11–26.

Carroll, L. and P. I. Jackson (1983) "Inequality, Opportunity, and Crime Rates in Central Cities." *Criminology* 21:178–94.

Clear, T. R. (1994) *Harm in American Penology: Offenders, Victims, and Their Communities.* Albany: SUNY Press.

Cleary, P. D. (1988) "Social Support: Conceptualization and Measurement." In H. B. Weis and F. H. Jacobs (eds.), *Evaluating Family Programs,* pp. 195–216. New York: Aldine.

Cloward, R. A. (1959) "Illegitimate Means, Anomie, and Deviant Behavior." *American Sociological Review* 24:164–76.

Cohen, L. E. and M. Felson (1979) "Social Change and Crime Rate Trends: A Routine Activity Approach." *American Sociological Review* 44:588–608.

Coles, R. (1993) *The Call of Service: A Witness to Idealism.* New York: Houghton Mifflin.

Colvin, M. and J. Pauly (1983) "A Critique of Criminology: Toward an Integrated Structural-Marxist Theory of Delinquency Production." *American Journal of Sociology* 89:513–51.

Cullen, F. T. (1984) *Rethinking Crime and Deviance Theory: The Emergence of a Structuring Tradition.* Totowa, NJ: Rowman and Allenheld.

Cullen, F. T. and K E. Gilbert (1982) *Reaffirming Rehabilitation.* Cincinnati: Anderson.

Cullen, F. T. and J. P. Wright (forthcoming) "The Future of Corrections." In B. Maguire and P. Radosh (eds.), *The Past, Present, and Future of American Criminal Justice.* New York: General Hall.

Cullen, F. T., J. P. Wright, and B. K Applegate (1993) "Control in the Community: The Limits of Reform?" Paper presented at the annual meeting of the International Association of Residential and Community Alternatives, Philadelphia.

Currie, E. (1985) *Confronting Crime: An American Challenge.* New York: Pantheon.

_____. (1989) "Confronting Crime: Looking toward the Twenty-First Century." *Justice Quarterly* 6:5–25.

_____. (1993) *Reckoning: Drugs, the Cities, and the American Future.* New York: Hill and Wang.

Curtis, L. A. (1989) "Race and Violent Crime: Toward a New Policy." In N. A. Weiner and M. E. Wolfgang (eds.), *Violent Crime, Violent Criminals,* pp. 139–70. Newbury Park, CA: Sage.

DeFronzo, J. (1983) "Economic Assistance to Impoverished Americans: Relationship to Incidence of Crime." *Criminology* 21:119–36.

Devine, J. A. and J. D. Wright (1993) *The Greatest of Evils: Urban Poverty and the American Underclass.* New York: Aldine.

Dubow, E. F. and G. J. Reid (1994) "Risk and Resource Variables in Children's Aggressive Behavior: A Two-Year Longitudinal Study." In L. R. Huesmann (ed.), *Aggressive Behavior: Current Perspectives,* pp. 187–211. New York: Plenum.

Duneier, M. (1992) *Slim's Table: Race, Respectability, and Masculinity.* Chicago: University of Chicago Press.

Ellwood, D. T. (1988). *Poor Support: Poverty in the American Family.* New York: Basic Books.

Empey, L. T. (1982) *American Delinquency: Its Meaning and Construction.* 2nd ed. Homewood, IL: Dorsey.

Etzioni, A. (1993) *The Spirit of Community: Rights, Responsibilities, and the Communitarian Agenda.* New York: Crown.

Farnworth, M. and M. J. Leiber (1989) "Strain Theory Revisited: Economic Goals, Educational Means, and Delinquency." *American Sociological Review* 54:263–74.

Farrington, D. P. (1994) "Delinquency Prevention in the First Few Years of Life." Plenary address presented at the Fourth European Conference on Law and Psychology, Barcelona.

Farrington, D. P., L. E. Ohlin, and J. Q. Wilson (1986) *Understanding and Controlling Crime: Toward a New Research Strategy.* New York: Springer-Verlag.

Feldman, P. (1993) *The Psychology of Crime: A Social Science Textbook.* Cambridge, UK: Cambridge University Press.

Felson, M. (1986) "Linking Criminal Choices, Routine Activities, Informal Control, and Criminal Outcomes." In D. B. Cornish and R. V. Clarke (eds.), *The Reasoning Criminal: Rational Choice Perspectives on Offending,* pp. 119–28. New York: Springer-Verlag.

_____. (1994) *Crime and Everyday Life: Insight and Implications for Society.* Thousand Oaks, CA: Pine Forge Press.

Felson, R. B. (1982) "Impression Management and the Escalation of Aggression and Violence." *Social Psychology Quarterly* 45:245–54.

Felson, R. B. and J. T. Tedeschi (1993) "A Social Interactionist Approach to Violence: Cross-Cultural Applications." *Violence and Victims* 8:295–310.

Garland, D. (1990) *Punishment and Modern Society: A Study in Social Theory.* Chicago: University of Chicago Press.

Garofalo, J. (1987) "Reassessing the Lifestyle Model of Criminal Victimization." In M. R. Gottfredson and T. Hirschi (eds.), *Positive Criminology,* pp. 23–42. Newbury Park, CA: Sage.

Gilligan, C. (1982) *In a Different Voice: Psychological Theory and Women's Development.* Cambridge, MA: Harvard University Press.

Gilligan, C. and J. Attanucci (1988) "Two Moral Orientations." In C. Gilligan, J. V. Ward, and J. M. Taylor (eds.), with B. Bardige, *Mapping the Moral Domain: A Contribution of Women's Thinking to Psychological Theory and Education,* pp. 73–86. Cambridge, MA: Harvard University Press.

Gilligan, C., J. V. Ward, and J. M. Taylor (eds.) with B. Bardige (1988), *Mapping the Moral Domain: A Contribution of Women's Thinking to Psychological Theory and Education.* Cambridge, MA: Harvard University Press.

Glueck, S. and E. Glueck (1950) *Unraveling Juvenile Delinquency.* Cambridge, MA: Harvard University Press.

Gottfredson, M. R. and T. Hirschi (1990) *A General Theory of Crime.* Stanford: Stanford University Press.

Grasmick, H. G., C. R. Tittle, R. J. Bursik Jr., and B. J. Arneklev (1993) "Testing the Core Empirical Implications of Gottfredson and Hirschi's General Theory of Crime." *Journal of Research in Crime and Delinquency* 30:5–29.

Guarino-Ghezzi, S. (1994) "Reintegrative Police Surveillance of Juvenile Offenders: Forging an Urban Model." *Crime and Delinquency* 40:131–53.

Hagan, J. (1989) *Structural Criminology.* New Brunswick: Rutgers University Press.

_____. (1993a) "Structural and Cultural Disinvestment and the New Ethnographies of Poverty and Crime." *Contemporary Sociology* 22:327–32.

_____. (1993b) "The Social Embeddedness of Crime and Unemployment." *Criminology* 31:465–91.

Hagan, J., A. R. Gillis, and J. Simpson (1990) "Clarifying and Extending Power-Control Theory." *American Journal of Sociology* 95:1024–37.

Hewlett, S. A. (1991) *When the Bough Breaks: The Cost of Neglecting Our Children.* New York: HarperColhns.

Hills, S. L., ed. (1987) *Corporate Violence: Injury and Death for Profit.* Totowa, NJ: Rowman and Littlefield.

House, J. L. (1981) *Work Stress and Social Support.* Reading, MA: Addison-Wesley.

Irwin, J. and J. Austin (1994) *It's About Time: America's Prison Binge.* Belmont, CA: Wadsworth.

Jencks, C. and P. E. Peterson, eds. (1991) *The Urban Underclass.* Washington, DC: Brookings Institution.

Kasinitz, P. (1993) "The Real Jobs Problem." *Wall Street Journal,* November 26, p. A-6.

Katz, J. (1988) *Seductions of Crime: Moral and Sensual Attractions of Doing Evil.* New York: Basic Books.

Kornhauser, R. R. (1978) *Social Sources of Delinquency: An Appraisal of Analytic Models.* Chicago: University of Chicago Press.

Krohn, M. D. (1986) "The Web of Conformity: A Network Approach to the Explanation of Delinquent Behavior." *Social Problems* 33:581–93.

Kurtz, L. R. (1984) *Evaluating Chicago Sociology: A Guide to the Literature with an Annotated Bibliography.* Chicago: University of Chicago Press.

Kuznik, F. (1994) "An Uncommon Bond." *USA Weekend,* January 14–16, pp. 4–5.

Lemann, N. (1991) *The Promised Land: The Great Black Migration and How It Changed America*. New York: Knopf.

Lilly, J. R., F. T. Cullen, and R. A. Ball (1989) *Criminological Theory: Context and Consequences*. Newbury Park, CA: Sage.

Lin, N. (1986) "Conceptualizing Social Support." In N. Lin, A. Dean, and W. Edsel (eds.), *Social Support, Life Events, and Depression*, pp. 17–30. Orlando: Academic Press.

Lin, N., A. Dean, and W. Ensel, eds. (1986) *Social Support, Life Events, and Depression*. Orlando: Academic Press.

Lin, N., M. Y. Dumin, and M. Woelfel (1986) "Measuring Community and Network Support." In N. Lin, A. Dean, and W. Ensel (eds.), *Social Support, Life Events, and Depression*, pp. 153–70. Orlando: Academic Press.

Link, B. G., F. T. Cullen, E. Struening, P. E. Shrout, and B. G. Dohrenwend (1989) "A Modified Labeling Theory Approach to Mental Disorders: An Empirical Assessment." *American Sociological Review* 54:400–23.

Link, B. G., S. Schwartz, R. E. Moore, J. Phelan, E. L. Struening, C. A. Stueve, and M. E. Colton (1992) "Public Knowledge, Attitudes, and Beliefs toward Homeless People: Evidence for Compassion Fatigue?" Paper presented at the annual meeting of the American Public Health Association, Washington, DC.

Lipsey, M. W. (1992) "Juvenile Delinquency Treatment: A Meta-Analytic Inquiry into the Variability of Effects." In T. D. Cook, H. Cooper, D. S. Cordray, H. Hartmann, L. V. Hedges, R. J. Light, T. A. Louis, and F. Mosteller (eds.), *Meta Analysis for Explanation: A Casebook*, pp. 83–127. New York: Russell Sage.

Loeber, R. and M. Le Blanc (1990) "Toward a Developmental Criminology." In M. Tonry and N. Morris (eds.), *Crime and Justice: A Review of Research*, vol. 12, pp. 375–473. Chicago: University of Chicago Press.

Loeber, R. and M. Stouthamer-Loeber (1986) "Family Factors as Correlates and Predictors of Juvenile Conduct Problems and Delinquency." In M. Tonry and N. Morris (eds.), *Crime and Justice: An Annual Review of Research*, vol. 7, pp. 291–49. Chicago: University of Chicago Press.

Lupo, A. (1994) "Still Yearning for the Great Society." *Boston Globe*, January 30, p. 66.

Lynch, J. (1995) "Crime in International Perspective." In J. Q. Wilson and J. Petersilia (eds.), *Crime*, pp. 11–38. San Francisco: ICS Press.

Makkai, T. and J. Braithwaite (1994) "Reintegrative Shaming and Compliance with Regulatory Standards." *Criminology* 32:361–85.

Massey, D. S. and N. A. Denton (1993) *American Apartheid: Segregation and the Making of the Underclass*. Cambridge, MA: Harvard University Press.

Mastrofski, S. D. (1988) "Community Policing as Reform: A Cautionary Tale." In J. D. Greene and S. D. Mastrofski (eds.), *Community Policing: Rhetoric or Reality,* pp. 47–68. New York: Praeger.

Matsueda, R. L. (1992) "Reflected Appraisals, Parental Labeling, and Delinquency: Specifying a Symbolic Interactionist Theory." *American Journal of Sociology* 6:1577–1611.

Maume, D. J., Jr. (1989) "Inequality and Metropolitan Rape Rates: A Routine Activity Approach." *Justice Quarterly* 6:513–27.

Mawhorr, T. L. (1992) "Unraveling the Attachment-Delinquency Link." Doctoral dissertation, Bowling Green State University.

McCarthy, B. and J. Hagan (1992) "Mean Streets: The Theoretical Significance of Situational Delinquency among Homeless Youths." *American Journal of Sociology* 98:597–627.

McCord, J. (1992) "Understanding Motivations: Considering Altruism and Aggression." In J. McCord (ed.), *Facts, Frameworks, and Forecasts: Advances in Criminological Theory,* vol. 3. New Brunswick, NJ: Transaction.

McDermott, M. J. (1994) "Criminology as Peacemaking, Feminist Ethics and the Victimization of Women." *Women and Criminal Justice* 5 (2):21–44.

Messner, S. F. (1980) "Income Inequality and Murder Rates: Some Cross-National Findings." *Comparative Social Research* 3:185–98.

_____. (1986) "Geographical Mobility, Governmental Assistance to the Poor, and Rates of Urban Crime." *Journal of Crime and Justice* 9:1–18.

Messner, S. F. and M. D. Krohn (1990) "Class, Compliance Structures, and Delinquency: Assessing Integrated Structural-Marxist Theory." *American Journal of Sociology* 96:300–28.

Messner, S. F. and R. Rosenfeld (1994) *Crime and the American Dream.* Belmont, CA: Wadsworth.

Miller, J. G. (1991) *Last One Over the Wall: The Massachusetts Experiment in Closing Reform Schools.* Columbus: Ohio State University Press.

Murray, C. (1984) *Losing Ground: American Social Policy, 1950–1980.* New York: Basic Books.

Myers, L. B. and C. P. Chiang (1993) "Law Enforcement Officer and Peace Officer: Reconciliation Using the Feminine Approach." *Journal of Crime and Justice* 16 (2):31–41.

Nagin, D. S. and D. P. Farrington (1992) "The Stability of Criminal Potential from Childhood to Adulthood." *Criminology* 30:235–60.

Nagin, D. S. and R. Paternoster (1991) "On the Relationship of Past to Future Participation in Delinquency." *Criminology* 29:163–89.

National Institute of Justice (1992) *Community Policing in Seattle: A Model Partnership between Citizens and Police.* Washington, DC: National Institute of Justice.

Nurius, P. S., M. Furrey, and L. Berliner (1992) "Coping Capacity among Women with Abusive Partners." *Violence and Victims* 7:229–43.

Palmer, T. (1992) *The Re-Emergence of Correctional Intervention.* Newbury Park, CA: Sage.

Panel of High-Risk Youth (1993) *Losing Generations: Adolescents in High-Risk Settings.* Washington, DC: National Academy Press.

Pepinsky, H. E. (1988) "Violence as Unresponsiveness: Toward a New Conception of Crime." *Justice Quarterly* 4:539–63.

Pepinsky, H. E. and R. Quinney, eds. (1991) *Criminology as Peacemaking.* Bloomington: Indiana University Press.

Petersilia, J. (1992) "California's Prison Policy: Causes, Costs, and Consequences." *The Prison Journal* 72:8–36.

Petersilia, J. and S. Turner (1993) "Intensive Probation and Parole." In M. Tonry (ed.), *Crime and Justice: A Review of Research,* vol. 17, pp. 281–335. Chicago: University of Chicago Press.

Pfohl, S. J. (1985) *Images of Deviance and Social Control: A Sociological History.* New York: McGraw-Hill.

Platt, A. M. (1969) *The Child Savers: The Invention of Delinquency.* Chicago: University of Chicago Press.

Rand, A. (1987) "Transitional Life Events and Desistance from Delinquency and Crime." In M. E. Wolfgang, T. P. Thornberry, and R. M. Figlio (eds.), *From Boy to Man, from Delinquency to Crime,* pp. 134–62. Chicago: University of Chicago Press.

Rankin, J. H. and E. L. Wells (1990) "The Effect of Parental Attachments and Direct Controls on Delinquency." *Journal of Research in Crime and Delinquency* 27:140–65.

Regoli, R. M. and J. D. Hewitt (1994) *Delinquency in Society.* 2nd ed. New York: McGraw-Hill.

Reich, R. B., ed. (1988) *The Power of Public Ideas.* Cambridge, MA: Harvard University Press.

Reiss, A. J., Jr. (1988) "Co-Offending and Criminal Careers." In M. Tonry and N. Morris (eds.), *Crime and Justice: An Annual Review of Research,* vol. 10, pp. 117–70. Chicago: University of Chicago Press.

Reiss, A. J., Jr. and M. Tonry, eds. (1986) *Communities and Crime.* Chicago: University of Chicago Press.

Rivara, F. P. and D. P. Farrington (forthcoming) "Prevention of Violence: Role of the Pediatrician." *Archives of Pediatrics and Adolescent Medicine.*

Rosenfeld, R. (1986) "Urban Crime Rates: Effects of Inequality, Welfare Dependency, Region, and Race." In J. M. Byrne and R. J. Sampson (eds.), *The Social Ecology of Crime,* pp. 116–30. New York: Springer-Verlag.

Rothman, D. J. (1980) *Conscience and Convenience: The Asylum and Its Alternatives in Progressive America.* Boston: Little, Brown.

Sampson, R. J. (1986a) "Neighborhood Family Structure and the Risk of Personal Victimization." In J. M. Byrne and R. J. Sampson (eds.), *The Social Ecology of Crime,* pp. 25–46. New York: Springer-Verlag.

_____. (1986b) "Crime in Cities: The Effects of Formal and Informal Social Control." In A J. Reiss Jr. and M. Tonry (eds.), *Communities and Crime,* pp. 271–311. Chicago: University of Chicago Press.

Sampson, R. J. and W. B. Groves (1989) "Community Structure and Crime: Testing Social-Disorganization Theory." *American Journal of Sociology* 94:774–802.

Sampson, R. J. and J. H. Laub (1993) *Crime in the Making: Pathways and Turning Points through Life.* Cambridge, MA: Harvard University Press.

Saunders, D. G. and S. T. Azar (1989) "Treatment Programs for Family Violence." In L. Ohlin and M. Tonry (eds.), *Family Violence,* pp. 481–546. Chicago: University of Chicago Press.

Shaw, C. R. ([1930] 1966) *The Jack-Roller: A Delinquent Boy's Own Story.* Chicago: University of Chicago Press.

Shaw, C. R., with M. E. Moore ([1931] 1976) *The Natural History of a Delinquent Career.* Chichago: University of Chicago Press.

Shaw, C. R. and H. D. McKay (1942) *Juvenile Delinquency and Urban Areas.* Chicago: University of Chicago Press.

Sheley, J. F., ed. (1991) *Criminology: A Contemporary Handbook.* Belmont, CA: Wadsworth.

Sherman, L. W., with J: D. Schmidt and D. P. Rogan (1992) *Policing Domestic Violence: Experiments and Dilemmas.* New York: Free Press.

Short, J. F., Jr. (1990) "Cities, Gangs, and Delinquency." *Sociological Forum* 5:657–68.

_____. (1991) "Poverty, Ethnicity; and Crime: Change and Continuity in U.S. Cities." *Journal of Research in Crime and Delinquency* 28:501–18.

Skolnick, J. H. and D. H. Bayley (1988) "Theme and Variation in Community Policing." In M. Tonry and N. Morris. (eds.), *Crime and Justice: A Review of Research,* vol. 10, pp. 1–37. Chicago: University of Chicago Press.

Snodgrass, J. (1982) *The Jack-Roller at Seventy: A Fifty-Year Follow-Up.* Lexington, MA: Lexington Books.

Sparrow, M. K. (1988) *Implementing Community Policing.* Washington, DC: National Institute of Justice.

Spelman, W. and J. E. Eck (1987) *Problem-Oriented Policing.* Washington, DC: National Institute of Justice.

Steffensmeier, D. J. (1983) "Organization Properties and Sex-Segregation in the Underworld: Building a Sociological Theory of Sex Differences in Crime." *Social Forces* 61:1010–32.

Steffensmeier, D. J. and M. D. Harer (1993) "Bulging Prisons, An Aging U.S. Population, and the Nation's Crime Rate." *Federal Probation* 57 (June):3–10.

Straus, M. A. (1990) "Discipline and Deviance: Physical Punishment of Children and Violence and Other Crimes in Adulthood." *Social Problems* 38:133–54.

Sullivan, M. L. (1989) *"Getting Paid": Youth Crime and Work in the Inner City.* Ithaca: Cornell University Press.

Sutherland, E. H. (1949) *White Collar Crime.* New York: Holt, Rinehart and Winston.

Sutherland, E. H., D. R. Cressey, and D. F. Luckenbill (1992) *Principles of Criminology,* 11th ed. Dix Hills, NY: General Hall.

Sykes, G. M. and F. T. Cullen (1992) *Criminology.* 2nd ed. Fort Worth: Harcourt Brace Jovanovich.

Testa, M., B. A. Miller, W. R. Downs, and D. Panek (1992) "The Moderating Impact of Social Support Following Childhood Sexual Abuse." *Violence and Victims* 7:173–86.

Thrasher, F. M. ([1927] 1963) *The Gang: A Study of 1,313 Gangs in Chicago.* Abridged ed. Chicago: University of Chicago Press.

Thurman, Q. C. (1993) "The Police as a Community-Based Resource." Paper presented to the Oberman Faculty Seminar, University of Iowa.

Van Voorhis, P., F. T. Cullen, R. A. Mathers, and C. C. Garner (1988) "The Impact of Family Structure and Quality on Delinquency: A Comparative Assessment of Structure and Functional Factors." *Criminology* 26:235–61.

Vaux, A. (1988) *Social Support: Theory, Research, and Intervention.* New York: Praeger.

Vaux, A. and M. Ruggiero (1983) "Stressful Life Change and Delinquent Behavior." *American Journal of Community Psychology* 11:169–83.

Visher, C. A. (1987) "Incapacitation and Crime Control: Does a ʾLock 'Em Up' Strategy Reduce Crime?" *Justice Quarterly* 4:513–13.

Vito, G. F. and R. M. Holmes (1994) *Criminology: Theory, Research, and Policy.* Belmont, CA: Wadsworth.

Vold, G. B. and T. J. Bernard (1986) *Theoretical Criminology.* 3rd ed. New York: Oxford University Press.

Walsh, A. and T. A. Petee (1987) "Love Deprivation and Violent Juvenile Delinquency." *Journal of Crime and Justice* 10 (2):45–61.

Ward, J. V. (1988) "Urban Adolescents' Conceptions of Violence." In C. Gilligan, J. V. Ward, and J. M. Taylor (eds.) with B. Bardige, *Mapping the Moral Domain,* pp. 175–200. Cambridge, MA: Harvard University Press.

Wells, L. E. and J. H. Rankin (1991) "Families and Delinquency: A Meta-Analysis of the Impact of Broken Homes." *Social Problems* 38:71–93.

West, D. J. (1982) *Delinquency: Its Roots, Careers and Prospects.* Cambridge, MA: Harvard University Press.

Widom, C. S. (1989) "The Cycle of Violence." *Science* 244 (April 14):160–66.

Wilkinson, K. (1974) "The Broken Family and Juvenile Delinquency: Scientific Explanation or Ideology?" *Social Problems* 21:726–39.

Wilson, J. Q. and R. J. Herrnstein (1985) *Crime and Human Nature.* New York: Simon and Schuster.

Wilson, W. J. (1987) *The Truly Disadvantaged: The Inner City, the Underclass, and Public Policy.* Chicago: University of Chicago Press.

Wright, R N. and K. E. Wright (1992) "Does Getting Married Reduce the Likelihood of Criminality? A Review of the Literature." *Federal Probation* 56 (September):50–56.

Wright, R. A. (1994) *In Defense of Prisons.* Westport, CT: Greenwood.

Wuthnow, R. (1991) *Acts of Compassion: Caring for Others and Helping Ourselves.* Princeton: Princeton University Press.

Wycoff, M. A. (1988) "The Benefits of Community Policing: Evidence and Conjecture." In J. R. Greene and S. D. Mastrofski (eds.), *Community Policing: Rhetoric or Reality,* pp. 103–20. New York: Praeger.

Zimring, F. and G. Hawkins (1991) *The Scale of Imprisonment.* Chicago: University of Chicago Press.

Zuravin, S. J. (1989) "The Ecology of Child Abuse and Neglect: Review of the Literature and Presentation of Data." *Violence and Victims* 4:101–20.

◉ ◉ ◉

Questions

1. Define "social support."

2. In your opinion, which of Cullen's 14 propositions has the most significant ramifications for criminological theory? Why?

3. How would ideas about social support explain racial differences in crime rates and incarceration? Gender differences?

4. How does Cullen integrate ideas from other criminological theories?

Social Learning Theory

RONALD L. AKERS
University of Florida

> *How do people learn how to commit crime? In this selection, Ronald Akers summarizes his work on social learning theory, which itself builds on Edwin Sutherland's differential association theory, which states that people learn to commit crime from others through personal interaction. Akers combines concepts from the two theories to create a general model of how the learning of crime varies with social structures.*

☉ Development of the Theory

Sutherland asserted in the eighth statement of his theory that all the mechanisms of learning are involved in criminal behavior. However, beyond a brief comment that more is involved than direct imitation (Tarde, 1912), he did not explain what the mechanisms of learning are. These learning mechanisms were specified by Burgess and Akers (1966b) in their "differential association-reinforcement" theory of criminal behavior. Burgess and Akers produced a full reformulation that retained the principles of differential association, combining them with, and restating them in terms of, the learning principles of operant and respondent conditioning that had been developed by behavioral psychologists.[1] Akers followed up his early work with Burgess to develop social learning theory, applying it to criminal, delinquent, and deviant behavior in general. He has modified the theory, provided a fully explicated presentation of its concepts, examined it in light of the critiques and research by others, and carried out his own research to test its central propositions (Akers, 1973; 1977; 1985; 1998).

Social learning theory is not competitive with differential association theory. Instead, it is a broader theory that retains all the differential association processes in Sutherland's theory (albeit clarified and somewhat

"Social Learning Theory," reprinted from *Criminological Theories: Introduction, Evaluation, and Application*, Third Edition, by Ronald L. Akers, 2000, pp. 74–82, 98, 257–300. Copyright © 2000 by Roxbury Publishing Company.

modified) and integrates it with differential reinforcement and other principles of behavioral acquisition, continuation, and cessation (Akers, 1985:41). Thus, research findings supportive of differential association also support the integrated theory. But social learning theory explains criminal and delinquent behavior more thoroughly than does the original differential association theory (see, for instance, Akers et al., 1979; Warr and Stafford, 1991).

Burgess and Akers (1966b) explicitly identified the learning mechanisms as those found in modern behavioral theory. They retained the concepts of differential association and definitions from Sutherland's theory, but conceptualized them in more behavioral terms and added concepts from behavioral learning theory. These concepts include differential reinforcement, whereby "operant" behavior (the voluntary actions of the individual) is conditioned or shaped by rewards and punishments. They also contain classical or "respondent" conditioning (the conditioning of involuntary reflex behavior); discriminative stimuli (the environmental and internal stimuli that provides cues or signals for behavior), schedules of reinforcement (the rate and ratio in which rewards and punishments follow behavioral responses), and other principles of behavior modification.

Social learning theory retains a strong element of the symbolic interactionism found in the concepts of differential association and definitions from Sutherland's theory (Akers, 1985:39–70). Symbolic interactionism is the theory that social interaction is mainly the exchange of meaning and symbols; individuals have the cognitive capacity to imagine themselves in the role of others and incorporate this into their conceptions of themselves (Ritzer, 1992). This, and the explicit inclusion of such concepts as imitation, anticipated reinforcement, and self-reinforcement, makes social learning "soft behaviorism" (Akers, 1985:65). As a result, the theory is closer to cognitive learning theories, such as Albert Bandura's (1973; 1977; 1986; Bandura and Walters, 1963), than to the radical or orthodox operant behaviorism of B. F. Skinner (1953; 1959) with which Burgess and Akers began.

◉ The Central Concepts and Propositions of Social Learning Theory

The word *learning* should not be taken to mean that the theory is only about how novel criminal behavior is acquired. "Behavioral principles are not limited to learning but are fundamental principles of performance [that account for] . . . the acquisition, maintenance, and modification of human behavior" (Andrews and Bonta, 1998: 150). Social learning theory offers an explanation of crime and deviance which embraces variables that operate both to motivate and control criminal behavior, both to promote and undermine conformity. . . . The probability of criminal or conforming behavior occurring is a function of the balance of these influences on behavior.

> The basic assumption in social learning theory is that the same learning process in a context of social structure, interaction, and situation, produces both conforming and deviant behavior. The difference lies in the direction . . . [of] the balance of influences on behavior.

> The probability that persons will engage in criminal and deviant behavior is increased and the probability of their conforming to the norm is decreased when they differentially associate with others who commit criminal behavior and espouse definitions favorable to it, are relatively more exposed in-person or symbolically to salient criminal/deviant models, define it as desirable or justified in a situation discriminative for the behavior, and have received in the past and anticipate in the current or future situation relatively greater reward than punishment for the behavior. (Akers, 1998:50)

As these quotations show, while referring to all aspects of the learning process, Akers' development of the theory has relied principally on four major concepts: *differential association, definitions, differential reinforcement,* and *imitation* (Akers et al., 1979; Akers, 1985; Akers, 1998).

Differential Association. Differential association refers to the process whereby one is exposed to normative definitions favorable or unfavorable to illegal or law-abiding behavior. Differential association has both behavioral interactional and normative dimensions. The interactional dimension is the direct association and interaction with others who engage in certain kinds of behavior, as well as the indirect association and identification with more distant reference groups. The normative dimension is the different patterns of norms and values to which an individual is exposed through this association.

The groups with which one is in differential association provide the major social contexts in which all the mechanisms of social learning operate. They not only expose one to definitions, they also present them with models to imitate and with differential reinforcement (source, schedule, value, and amount) for criminal or conforming behavior. The most important of these groups are the primary ones of family and friends, though they may also be secondary and reference groups. Neighbors, churches, school teachers, physicians, the law and authority figures, and other individuals and groups in the community (as well as mass media and other more remote sources of attitudes and models) have varying degrees of effect on the individual's propensity to commit criminal and delinquent behavior. Those associations that occur earlier (priority), last longer and occupy more of one's time (duration), take place most often (frequency), and involve others with whom one has the more important or closer relationship (intensity) will have the greater effect on behavior.

Definitions. Definitions are one's own attitudes or meanings that one attaches to given behavior. That is, they are orientations, rationalizations, definitions of the situation, and other evaluative and moral attitudes that define the commission of an act as right or wrong, good or bad, desirable or undesirable, justified or unjustified.

In social learning theory, these definitions are both general and specific. General beliefs include religious, moral, and other conventional values and norms that are favorable to conforming behavior and unfavorable to committing any deviant or criminal acts. Specific definitions orient the person to particular acts or series of acts. Thus, one may believe that it is morally wrong to steal and that laws against theft should be obeyed, but at the same time one may see little wrong with smoking marijuana and rationalize that it is all right to violate laws against drug possession.

The greater the extent to which one holds attitudes that disapprove of certain acts, the less one is likely to engage in them. Conventional beliefs are negative toward criminal behavior. Conversely, the more one's own attitudes approve of a behavior, the greater the chances are that one will do it. Approving definitions favorable to the commission of criminal or deviant behavior are basically positive or neutralizing. Positive definitions are beliefs or attitudes which make the behavior morally desirable or wholly permissible. Neutralizing definitions favor the commission of crime by justifying or excusing it. They view the act as something that is probably undesirable but, given the situation, is nonetheless all right, justified, excusable, necessary, or not really bad to do. The concept of neutralizing definitions in social learning theory incorporates the notions of verbalizations, rationalizations, techniques of neutralizations, accounts, disclaimers, and moral disengagement (Cressey, 1953; Sykes and Matza, 1957; Lyman and Scott, 1970; Hewitt and Stokes, 1975; Bandura, 1990). . . . Neutralizing attitudes include such beliefs as, "Everybody has a racket," "I can't help myself, I was born this way," "I am not at fault," "I am not responsible," "I was drunk and didn't know what I was doing," "I just blew my top," "They can afford it," "He deserved it," and other excuses and justification for committing deviant acts and victimizing others. These definitions favorable and unfavorable to criminal and delinquent behavior are developed through imitation and differential reinforcement. Cognitively, they provide a mindset that makes one more willing to commit the act when the opportunity occurs. Behaviorally, they affect the commission of deviant or criminal behavior by acting as internal discriminative stimuli. Discriminative stimuli operate as cues or signals to the individual as to what responses are appropriate or expected in a given situation.

Some of the definitions favorable to deviance are so intensely held that they almost "require" one to violate the law. For instance, the radical ideologies of revolutionary groups provide strong motivation for terrorist acts, just as the fervent moral stance of some anti-abortion groups justifies in their minds the need to engage in civil disobedience. For the most part, however, definitions favorable to crime and delinquency do not "require" or strongly motivate action in this sense. Rather, they are conventional beliefs so weakly held that they provide no restraint or are positive or neutralizing attitudes that facilitate law violation in the right set of circumstances.

Differential Reinforcement. Differential reinforcement refers to the balance of anticipated or actual rewards and punishments that follow or are consequences of behavior. Whether individuals will refrain from or commit a crime at any given time (and whether they will continue or desist from doing so in the future) depends on the past, present, and anticipated future rewards and punishments for their actions. The probability that an act will be committed or repeated is increased by rewarding outcomes or reactions to it, e.g., obtaining approval, money, food, or pleasant feelings—positive reinforcement. The likelihood that an action will be taken is also enhanced when it allows the person to avoid or escape aversive or unpleasant events—negative reinforcement. Punishment may also be direct (positive), in which painful or unpleasant consequences are attached to a behavior; or indirect (negative), in which a reward or pleasant consequence is removed. Just as there are modalities of association, there are modalities of reinforcement—amount, frequency, and probability. The greater the value or amount of reinforcement for the person's behavior, the more frequently it is reinforced, and the higher the probability that it will be reinforced (as balanced against alternative behavior), the greater the likelihood that it will occur and be repeated. The reinforcement process does not operate in the social environment in a simple either/or fashion. Rather, it operates according to a "matching function" in which the occurrence of, and changes in, each of several different behaviors correlate with the probability and amount of, and changes in, the balance of reward and punishment attached to each behavior (Herrnstein, 1961; Hamblin, 1979; Conger and Simons, 1995).

Reinforcers and punishers can be nonsocial; for example, the direct physical effects of drugs and alcohol. However, whether or not these effects are experienced positively or negatively is contingent upon previously learned expectations. Through social reinforcement, one learns to interpret the effects as pleasurable and enjoyable or as frightening and unpleasant. Individuals can learn without contact, directly or indirectly, with social reinforcers and punishers. There may be a physiological basis for the tendency of some individuals (such as those prone to sensation-seeking) more than others to find certain forms of deviant behavior intrinsically rewarding (Wood et al., 1995). However, the theory proposes that most of the learning in criminal and deviant behavior is the result of social exchange in which the words, responses, presence, and behavior of other persons directly reinforce behavior, provide the setting for reinforcement (discriminative stimuli), or serve as the conduit through which other social rewards and punishers are delivered or made available.

The concept of social reinforcement (and punishment) goes beyond the direct reactions of others present while an act is committed. It also includes the whole range of actual and anticipated, tangible and intangible rewards valued in society or subgroups. Social rewards can be highly symbolic. Their reinforcing effects can come from their fulfilling ideological, religious, political, or other goals. Even those rewards which we consider to be very tangible, such as money and material possessions, gain their reinforcing value from the prestige and approval value they have in society. Nonsocial reinforcement, therefore, is more narrowly confined to unconditioned phys-iological and physical stimuli. In self-reinforcement the individual exercises self-control, reinforcing or punishing one's own behavior by taking the role of others, even when alone.

Imitation. Imitation refers to the engagement in behavior after the observa-tion of similar behavior in others. Whether or not the behavior modeled by others will be imitated is affected by the characteristics of the models, the behavior observed, and the observed consequences of the behavior (Bandura, 1977). The observation of salient models in primary groups and in the media affects both pro-social and deviant behavior (Donnerstein and Linz, 1995). It is more important in the initial acquisition and performance of novel behavior than in the maintenance or cessation of behavioral patterns once established, but it continues to have some effect in maintain-ing behavior.

● The Social Learning Process: Sequence and Feedback Effects

These social learning variables are all part of an underlying process that is operative in each individual's learning history and in the immediate situa-tion in which an opportunity for a crime occurs. Akers stresses that social learning is a complex process with reciprocal and feedback effects. The reciprocal effects are not seen as equal, however. Akers hypothesizes a typi-cal temporal sequence or process by which persons come to the point of violating the law or engaging in other deviant acts (Akers, 1998).

This process is one in which the balance of learned definitions, imita-tion of criminal or deviant models, and the anticipated balance of reinforcement produces the initial delinquent or deviant act. The facilitative effects of these variables continue in the repetition of acts, although imita-tion becomes less important than it was in the first commission of the act. After initiation, the actual social and non-social reinforcers and punishers affect whether or not the acts will be repeated and at what level of frequency blot only the behavior itself, but also the definitions are affected by the consequences of the initial act. Whether a deviant act will be committed in a situation that presents the opportunity depends on the learning history of the individual and the set of reinforcement contingencies in that situation.

> The actual social sanctions and other effects of engaging in the behavior may be perceived differently, but to the extent that they are more reward-ing than alternative behavior, then the deviant behavior will be repeated under similar circumstances. Progression into more frequent or sustained patterns of deviant behavior is promoted [to the extent] that reinforce-ment, exposure to deviant models, and definitions are not offset by negative formal and informal sanctions and definitions. (Akers, 1985:60)

The theory does not hypothesize that definitions favorable to law viola-tion only precede and are unaffected by the initiation of criminal acts. Acts in violation of the law can occur in the absence of any thought given to right and wrong. Furthermore, definitions may be applied by the individual retroactively to excuse or justify an act already committed. To the extent that such excuses successfully mitigate others' negative sanctions or one's self-punishment, however, they become cues for the repetition of deviant acts. At that point they precede the future commission of the acts.

Differential association with conforming and non-conforming others typically precedes the individual's committing the acts. Families are included in the differential association process, and it is obvious that associ-ation, reinforcement of conforming or deviant behavior, deviant or conforming modeling, and exposure to definitions favorable or unfavorable to deviance occurs within the family prior to the onset of delinquency. On the other hand, it can never be true that the onset of delinquency initiates interaction in the family (except in the unlikely case of the late-stage adop-tion of a child who is already delinquent who is drawn to and chosen by deviant parents). This is also hypothesized as the typical process within peer groups. While one may be attracted to deviant peer groups prior to becom-ing involved in delinquency, associations with peers and others are most often formed initially around attractions, friendships, and circumstances, such as neighborhood proximity, that have little to do directly with co-involvement in some deviant behavior. However, after the associations have been established and the reinforcing or punishing consequences of the deviant behavior are experienced, both the continuation of old and the seek-ing of new associations (over which one has any choice) will themselves be affected. One may choose further interaction with others based, in part, on whether they too are involved in similar deviant or criminal behavior. But the theory proposes that the sequence of events, in which deviant associations precede the onset of delinquent behavior, will occur more frequently than the sequence of events in which the onset of delinquency precedes the beginning of deviant associations.

◉ Social Structure and Social Learning

Akers has proposed a SSSL (social structure and social learning) model in which social structural factors are hypothesized to have an indirect effect on the individual's conduct. They affect the social learning variables of differential association, differential reinforcement, definitions, and imitation which, in turn, have a direct impact on the individual's conduct. The social learning variables are proposed as the main ones in the process by which various aspects of the social structure influence individual behavior (see Figure 1).

> The social structural variables are indicators of the primary distal macro-level and meso-level causes of crime, while the social learning variables

FIGURE 1 *Social Structure and Social Learning*

Social Structure and Social Learning				
Social Structure →			**Social Learning** ⟶ Criminal Behavior ⟶ Conforming Behavior	
I. Society Community IV. Family Peers School Others	II. Age Gender Race Class	III. Social Disorgani- zation Conflict	Differential Association Differential Reinforcement Definitions Imitation Other Learning Variables	Individual Behavior
I. Differential Social Organization II. Differential Location in the Social Structure III. Theoretically Defined Structural Variables IV. Differential Social Location in Groups				

(Adapted from Akers, 1998:331)

120

reflect the primary proximate causes of criminal behavior that mediate the relationship between social structure and crime rates. Some structural variables are not related to crime and do not explain the crime rate because they do not have a crime-relevant effect on the social learning variables. (Akers, 1998:322)

As shown in Figure 1, Akers (1998) identifies four dimensions of social structure that provide the contexts within which social learning variables operate:

(I)   *Differential Social Organization* refers to the structural correlates of crime in the community or society that affect the rates of crime and delinquency including age composition, population density, and other attributes that lean societies, communities, and other social systems "toward relatively high or relatively low crime rates" (Akers, 1998:332).

(II)   *Differential Location* in the Social Structure refers to sociodemographic characteristics of individuals and social groups that indicate their niches within the larger social structure. Class, gender, race and ethnicity, marital status, and age locate the positions and standing of persons and their roles, groups, or social categories in the overall social structure.

(III) *Theoretically Defined Structural Variables* refer to anomie, class oppression, social disorganization, group conflict, patriarchy, and other concepts that have been used in one or more theories to identify criminogenic conditions of societies, communities, or groups.

(IV)   *Differential Social Location* refers to individuals' membership in and relationship to primary, secondary, and reference groups such as the family, friendship/peer groups, leisure groups, colleagues, and work groups.

The differential social organization of society and community, as well as the differential location of persons in the social class, race, gender, religion, and other structures in society, provides the general learning contexts for individuals that increase or decrease the likelihood of their committing crime. The differential location in family, peer, school, church, and other groups provides the more immediate contexts that promote or discourage the criminal behavior of the individual. Differences in the societal or group rates of criminal behavior are a function of the extent to which their cultural traditions, norms, and social control systems provide socialization, learning environments, and immediate situations conducive to conformity or deviance. The structural conditions identified in macro-level theories can affect one's exposure to criminal associations, models, definitions, and reinforcement to induce or retard criminal actions in individuals. It is possible, therefore, to integrate these structural theories with social learning. Although this has not yet been accomplished . . . the SSSL model is a step in that direction.

Endnote

[1]For classic statements of behavioristic "operant conditioning" principles of learning, see Skinner (1953; 1959). See also the full statement of behavioral learning theory in Burgess and Akers (1966a). Prior to the full revision of differential association by Burgess and Akers, C. Ray Jeffery (1965) proposed to replace all of Sutherland's theory with a single statement of operant conditioning, essentially rejecting the theory. Burgess and Akers criticized Jeffery for doing this and retained all the major features of Sutherland's theory in their revision.

References

Akers, Ronald L. 1973. Deviant Behavior: A Social Learning Approach. Belmont, CA: Wadsworth.

_____. 1977. Deviant Behavior: A Social Learning Approach. Second Edition. Belmont, CA: Wadsworth.

_____. 1985. Deviant Behavior: A Social Learning Approach. Third Edition. Belmont, CA: Wadsworth. Reprinted 1992. Fairfax, VA: Techbooks.

_____. 1998. Social Learning and Social Structure: A General Theory of Crime and Deviance. Boston: Northeastern University Press.

Akers, Ronald L., Marvin D. Krohn, Lonn Lanza-Kaduce, and Marcia Radosevich. 1979. "Social learning and deviant behavior: a specific test of a general theory," American Sociological Review 44: 635–655.

Andrews, D. A. and James Bonta. 1998. Psychology of Criminal Conduct. Second Edition. OH: Anderson.

Bandura, Albert. 1973. Aggression: A Social Learning Analysis. Englewood Cliffs, NJ: Prentice Hall.

_____. 1977. Social Learning Theory. Englewood Cliffs, NJ: Prentice Hall.

_____. 1986. Social Foundations of Thought and Action: A Social Cognitive Theory. Englewood Cliffs, NJ: Prentice Hall.

_____. 1990. "Selective activation and disengagement of moral control," Journal of Social Issues 46:27–46.

Bandura, Albert and Richard H. Walters. 1963. Social Learning and Personality Development. New York: Holt, Rinehart, and Winston.

Burgess, Robert L. and Ronald L. Akers. 1966a. "Are operant principles tautological?" Psychological Record 16:305–312.

_____. 1966b. "A differential association-reinforcement theory of criminal behavior," Social Problems 14:128–47.

Conger, Rand D. and Ronald L. Simons. 1995. "Life-course contingencies in the development of adolescent antisocial behavior: a matching law approach," pp. in Terrance P. Thornberry, ed., Developmental Theories of Crime and Delinquency, New Brunswick, NJ: Transaction Publishers.

Donnerstein, Edward and Daniel Linz. 1995. "The media," pp. 237–266 in James Q. Wilson and Joan Petersilia, eds., Crime. San Francisco: ICS Press.

Hamblin, Robert L. 1979. "Behavioral choice and social reinforcement: step function versus matching," Social Forces 57:1141–1156.

Herrnstein, Richard J. 1961. "Relative and absolute strength of response as a function of frequency of reinforcement," Journal of the Experimental Analysis of Behavior 4:267–272.

Hewitt, John P. and Randall Stokes. 1975. "Disclaimers," American Sociological Review 40:1–11.

Jeffery, C. Ray. 1965. "Criminal behavior and learning theory," Journal of Criminal Law, Criminology, and Police Science 56:294–300.

Lyman, Stanford M. and Marvin B. Scott. 1970. A Sociology of the Absurd. New York: Appleton-Century-Crofts.

Ritzer, George. 1992. Sociological Theory. Third Edition. New York: McGraw-Hill.

Skinner, B. F. 1953. Science and Human Behavior: New York: Macmillan.

_____. 1959. Cumulative Record. New York: Appleton-Century-Crofts.

Sutherland, Edwin H. 1947. Principles of Criminology. Fourth Edition. Philadelphia: J. B. Lippincott.

Sykes, Gresham and David Matza. 1957. "Techniques of neutralization: a theory of delinquency," American Journal of Sociology 22:664–670.

Tarde, Gabriel. 1912. Penal Philosophy. Translated by R. Howell. Boston: Little Brown.

Warr, Mark and Mark Stafford. 1991. "The influence of delinquent peers: what they think or what they do?" Criminology 4:851–866.

Wood, Peter B., John K. Cochran, Betty Pfefferbaum and Bruce J. Arneklev. 1995. "Sensation-seeking and delinquent substance use: an extension of learning theory," Journal of Drug Issues 25:173–193.

☻ ☻ ☻

Questions

1. How does Akers' social learning theory differ from Sutherland's differential association theory?

2. How do people learn crime through differential association? Through definitions? Through differential reinforcement? Through imitation?

3. Which elements of social structure are most pertinent to the learning of criminal behavior, and why?

4. How would Akers' theory explain racial differences in arrest rates?

Is "White Collar Crime" Crime?

EDWIN H. SUTHERLAND

In this classic selection, Edwin Sutherland examines "white-collar crime" in the United States. He provides a general definition of crime and assesses the degree to which four types of corporate actions fit this definition. (In particular, he explores laws restricting free trade, misrepresentation in advertising, patent infringement, and unfair labor practices.) Sutherland asks whether these actions are crimes, why criminologists have ignored them in their theoretical work, and why laws make exceptions for corporations.

. . . 980 decisions have been made against the 70 largest industrial and mercantile corporations, with an average of 14.0 decisions per corporation. Although all of these are decisions that the corporations have acted unlawfully, only 158, or 16 percent, of them were made by criminal courts and were ipso facto decisions that the behavior was criminal. Since not all unlawful behavior is criminal behavior, these decisions can be used as a measure of criminal behavior only insofar as the other 822 decisions can be shown to be decisions that the behavior was criminal as well as unlawful.

This is a problem in the definition of crime and involves two types of questions: First, may the word "crime" be applied to the behavior regarding which these decisions were made? Second, if so, why is it not generally applied and why have not criminologists regarded white collar crime as cognate with other crime? The first question involves semantics, the second explanation or interpretation. The following analysis will be limited almost entirely to the laws regarding restraint of trade, misrepresentation in advertising, infringements of patents and analogous rights, and unfair labor practices in violation of the National Labor Relations Law. Little attention is devoted to the other laws, in part because some of the other laws are explicit criminal laws, such as those relating to rebates or adulteration of foods and drugs, and in part because so many different laws are involved in the miscellaneous group of offenses that the analysis would be unduly extended if each of those laws was given specific attention.

The definition of crime, from the point of view of the present analysis, is important only as a means of determining whether the behavior should be included within the scope of a theory of criminal behavior. More specifically, the problem is: From the point of view of a theory of criminal behavior, are the illegal acts of corporations which have been tabulated above cognate with the burglaries, robberies, and other crimes which are customarily included within the scope of theories of criminal behavior? Some writers have argued that an act is criminal only if a criminal court has officially determined that the person accused of that act has committed a crime. This limitation in the definition of crime may be made properly if a writer is interested primarily in administrative questions. The warden of a prison would not be justified in receiving an offender in the penal institution unless that offender had been officially convicted and sentenced to serve a term of imprisonment in that institution. Similarly, public authorities would not be justified in denying civil rights to offenders who had not been convicted of crimes. In contrast, the criminologist who is interested in a theory of criminal behavior needs to know only that a certain class of acts is legally defined as crime and that a particular person has committed an act of this class. The criminologist needs to have certain knowledge on both of these points, but for this purpose a decision of a court is no more essential than it is for certain knowledge in chemistry or biology. However, . . . decisions of courts and commissions have been used as proof that prohibited acts have been committed.

The essential characteristic of crime is that it is behavior which is prohibited by the State as an injury to the State and against which the State may react, at least as a last resort, by punishment. The two abstract criteria generally regarded by legal scholars as necessary elements in a definition of crime are legal description of an act as socially harmful and legal provision of a penalty for the act.[1]

The first of these criteria—legal definition of a social harm—applies to all of the classes of acts which are included in the 980 decisions tabulated above. This can be readily determined by the words in the statutes—"crime" or "misdemeanor" in some, and "unfair," "discrimination," or "infringement" in all the others. The persons injured may be divided into two groups—first, a relatively small number of persons engaged in the same occupation as the offenders or in related occupations, and second, the general public either as consumers or as constituents of the general social institutions which are affected by the violations of the laws.

The antitrust laws are designed to protect competitors and also to protect the institution of free competition as the regulator of the economic system and thereby to protect consumers against arbitrary prices, and to protect the institution of democracy against the dangers of great concentration of wealth in the hands of monopolies. Laws against false advertising are designed to protect competitors against unfair competition and also to protect consumers against fraud. The National Labor Relations Law is designed to protect employees against coercion by employers and also to protect the general public against interferences with commerce due to strikes and lockouts. The laws against infringements are designed to protect the owners of patents, copyrights, and trademarks against deprivation of their property and against unfair competition, and also to protect the institution of patents and copyrights which was established in order to "promote the progress of science and the useful arts." Violations of these laws are legally defined as injuries to the parties specified.

Each of these laws has a logical basis in the common law and is an adaptation of the common law to modern social organization. False advertising is related to common law fraud, and infringement to larceny. The National Labor Relations Law, as an attempt to prevent coercion, is related to the common law prohibition of restrictions on freedom in the form of assault, false imprisonment, and extortion. For at least two centuries prior to the enactment of the modern antitrust laws the common law was moving against restraint of trade, monopoly, and unfair competition.

Each of the four types of laws under consideration, with the possible exception of the laws regarding infringements, grew primarily out of considerations of the welfare of the organized society. In this respect, they are analogous to the laws of the earliest societies, where crimes were largely limited to injuries such as treason, in which the organized society was the victim and particular persons suffered only as they were members of the organized society. Subsequent criminal laws have been concerned principally with person-to-person injuries, as in larceny, and the State has taken jurisdiction over the procedures principally in order to bring private vengeance under public control. The interest of the State in such behavior is secondary or derivative. In this sense, the four laws under consideration may properly be regarded as criminal laws in a more fundamental sense than the laws regarding larceny.

Each of the four laws provides a penal sanction and thus meets the second criterion in the definition of crime, and each of the adverse decisions under these four laws, except certain decisions under the infringement laws to be discussed later, is a decision that a crime was committed. This conclusion will be made more specific by analysis of the penal sanctions provided in the four laws.

The Sherman Antitrust Act states explicitly that a violation of the law is a misdemeanor. Three methods of enforcement of this law are provided, each of them involving procedures regarding misdemeanors. First, it may be enforced by the usual criminal prosecution, resulting in the imposition of fine or imprisonment. Second, the attorney general of the United States and the several district attorneys are given the "duty" of "repressing and preventing" violations of the law by petitions for injunctions, and violations of the injunctions are punishable as contempt of court. This method of enforcing a criminal law was an invention and, as will be described later, is the key to the interpretation of the differential implementation of the criminal law as applied to white collar criminals. Third, parties who are injured by violations of the law are authorized to sue for damages, with a mandatory provision that awarded be three times the injuries suffered. These damages in excess of reparation are penalties for violation of the law. They are payable to the injured party in order to induce him to take the initiative in the enforcement of the criminal law and in this respect are similar to the earlier methods of private prosecutions under the criminal law. All three of these methods of enforcement are based on decisions that a criminal law was violated and therefore that a crime was committed; the decisions of a civil court or a court of equity as to these violations are as good evidence of criminal behavior as is the decision of a criminal court.

Judge Carpenter stated in regard to the injunctions under the antitrust law, "The Supreme Court in upholding them necessarily has determined that the things which were enjoined were crimes, as defined by one at least of the first three sections of the Act."[2]

The Sherman Antitrust Act has been supplemented by the Federal Trade Commission Law, the Clayton Law, and several other laws. Some of these supplementary laws define violations as crimes and provide the conventional penalties, but most of them do not make the criminality explicit. A large proportion of the cases which are dealt with under these supplementary laws could be dealt with, instead, under the original Sherman Act, which is explicitly a criminal law, or under the antitrust laws of the several states, which also are explicit criminal laws. In practice, the supplementary laws are generally under the jurisdiction of the Federal Trade Commission, which has authority to make official decisions as to violations. The commission has two principal sanctions under its control, namely: the stipulation and the cease and desist order. The commission may, after the violation of the law has been proved, accept a stipulation from the corporation that it will not violate the law in the future. Such stipulations are customarily restricted to the minor or technical violations. If a stipulation is violated or if no stipulation is accepted, the commission may issue a cease and desist order; this is equivalent to a court's injunction except that violation is not punishable as contempt. If the commission's desist order is violated, the commission may apply to the court for an injunction, the violation of which is punishable as contempt. By an amendment to the Federal Trade Commission Law in the Wheeler-Lea Act of 1938 an order of the commission becomes "final" if not officially questioned within a specified time and thereafter its violation is punishable by a civil fine. Thus, although certain interim procedures may be used in the enforcement of the laws supplementary to the Sherman Antitrust Act, fines or imprisonment for contempt is available if the interim procedures fail. In this respect the interim procedures are similar to probation in ordinary criminal cases. An unlawful act is not defined as criminal by the fact that it is punished, but by the fact that it is punishable. Larceny is as truly a crime when the thief is placed on probation as when he is committed to prison. The argument may be made that punishment for contempt of court is not punishment for violation of the original law and that, therefore, the original law does not contain a penal sanction. This reasoning is specious since the original law provides the injunction with its penalty as a part of the procedure for enforcement. Consequently all of the decisions made under the amendments to the antitrust law are decisions that the corporations committed crimes.[3]

The laws regarding false advertising, as included in the decisions under consideration, are of two types. First, false advertising in the form of false labels is defined in the Pure Food and Drug Law as a misdemeanor and is punishable by a fine. Second, false advertising generally is defined in the Federal Trade Commission Act as unfair competition. Cases of the second type are under the jurisdiction of the Federal Trade Commission, which uses the same procedures as in antitrust cases. Penal sanctions are available in antitrust cases, as previously described, and are similarly available in these cases of false advertising. Thus, all of the decisions in false advertising cases are decisions that the corporations committed crimes.

The National Labor Relations Law of 1935 defines a violation as "unfair labor practice." The National Labor Relations Board is authorized to make official decisions as to violations of the law and, in case of violation, to issue desist orders and also to make certain remedial orders, such as reimbursement of employees who had been dismissed or demoted because of activities in collective bargaining. If an order is violated, the board may apply to the court for enforcement and a violation of the order of the court is punishable as contempt. Thus, all of the decisions under this law, which is enforceable by penal sanctions, are decisions that crimes were committed.[4]

The laws regarding infringements are more complex than those previously described. Infringements of a copyright or of a patented design are defined in the federal statutes as misdemeanors, punishable by fines. Decisions against the 70 corporations have been made in 7 cases under the copyright laws and in no cases, so far as discovered, on charges of infringement of patented designs. Other infringements are not explicitly defined in the federal statutes on patents and trademarks as crimes, although many states have so defined infringements of trademarks.[5] Nevertheless, these infringements may be criminal acts under federal statutes in either of two respects. First, the statutes provide that damages awarded to injured owners of patents or trademarks may be greater than the injuries actually suffered. These are punitive damages and constitute one form of punishment. Although these punitive damages are not mandatory under the Sherman Antitrust Act, they are not explicitly limited to wanton and malicious infringements. Also, the rule in federal trademark cases is that an account of profits is taken only when the infringement involves wrongful intent to defraud the original owner or deceive the public. These decisions, therefore, are equivalent to convictions in criminal trials. On these principles 3 of the decisions against the 70 corporations in patent cases and 6 in trademark cases are classified as criminal convictions. Second, agents of the Federal Trade Commission may initiate actions against infringers as unfair competition. Infringements proceeded against in this manner may be punished in the same sense as violation of the antitrust law, namely, by stipulations, desist orders, and fines or imprisonment for violation of desist orders. Five decisions in infringement cases against the 70 corporations are classified as criminal actions in this sense. This gives a total of 21 decisions in infringement cases which may be classified as evidence of criminal behavior of the 70 corporations. Of the 222 decisions, 201 are left unaccounted for in terms of criminality. The evidence in some of these cases and in the descriptions of general practices regarding patents and trademarks justifies an estimate that a large proportion of the 201 cases—perhaps half—involved willful appropriation of the property of others and might have resulted in penalties under state or federal laws if the injured parties had approached the behavior from the point of view of crime. In spite of this estimate, the 201 decisions are not included as evidence of criminal behavior.

The law in regard to financial manipulations, such as violations of trust, stock market manipulations, stock watering, misrepresentation in the sale of securities, are generally based on the laws of fraud or violation of trust. A poor man was recently sentenced in Indiana to serve from one to seven years in the state prison on conviction of false pretenses; he had listed with a finance company household goods which he did not own as a means of securing a loan. The same law applies to corporations but it is seldom used when corporations misrepresent their assets. The judicial decisions have tended toward higher standards of protection of stockholders and the public, and the Securities and Exchange Commission has been organized to implement these laws. Most of the regulations imposed by this commission during the last decade and a half were in accordance with some of the earlier decisions of courts.[6]

The penalties presented in the preceding section as definitive of crime were limited to fines, imprisonment, and punitive damages. In addition, the stipulation, the desist order, and the injunction without reference to penalty for contempt have the attributes of punishment. This is evident both in the fact that they result in some suffering on the part of the corporation against which they are issued, and also in the fact that they were designed by legislators and administrators to produce suffering. The suffering takes the form of public shame, which is an important aspect of all penalties. This was illustrated in extreme form in the colonial penalty of sewing the letter "T" on the clothing of a thief. In England the Bread Act of 1836 and the Adulteration of Seeds Act in 1869 provided the penalty of publication in the newspaper of the details regarding the crimes of adulteration of these products; the Public Health Act of 1891 authorized the court to order a person twice convicted of selling meat unfit for human consumption to fix a sign on his place of business of a size to be specified by the court, stating that he had been convicted twice of violating this law. Stipulations, desist orders, and injunctions to some extent resemble these publicity penalties of England. That the publication of the stipulation in Federal Trade Commission cases is a punishment is attested by Lowell B. Mason, a member of the commission.[7]

That this suffering is designed is apparent from the sequence of sanctions used by the Federal Trade Commission. The stipulation involves the least publicity and is used for minor and technical violations. The desist order is used if the stipulation is violated and also if the violation of the law is appraised by the commission as willful and major. The desist order involves more public shame than the stipulation. The shame resulting from the stipulation and the desist order is somewhat mitigated by the argument made by corporations, in exculpation, that such orders are merely the acts of bureaucrats. Still more shameful to the corporation is an injunction issued by a court. The shame resulting from an injunction is sometimes mitigated and the corporation's face is saved by taking a consent decree, or making a plea of nolo contendere. The corporation may insist that the consent decree is not an admission that it violated the law. For instance, the meat packers took a consent decree in an antitrust case in 1921, with the explanation that they had not knowingly violated any law and were consenting to the decree without attempting to defend themselves because they wished to cooperate with the government in every possible way. This patriotic motivation appeared questionable, however, after the packers fought during the next decade and a half for a modification of the decree. The plea of nolo contendere was first used in antitrust cases in 1910 but has been used in hundreds of cases since that date. This plea at the same time saves the face of the corporation and protects the corporation against suits for damages, since the decision in a case in which the plea is nolo contendere may not be used as evidence in other cases.[8] The sequence of stipulation, desist order, and injunction indicates that the variations in public shame are designed; also, the arguments and tactics used by corporations to protect themselves against public shame in connection with these orders indicate that the corporations recognize them as punishments.

The conclusion in this semantic portion of the analysis is that 779 of the 980 decisions against the 70 large corporations are decisions that crimes were committed.

This conclusion may be questioned on the ground that the rules of proof and evidence used in reaching many of these decisions were not the same as the rules used in criminal courts. This involves, especially, the proof of criminal intent and the presumption of innocence. These rules of criminal intent and presumption of innocence, however, are not required in all prosecution in criminal courts and the number of exceptions authorized by statutes is increasing. In many states a person may be committed to prison without protection of one or both of these rules on charges of statutory rape, bigamy, adultery, passing bad checks, selling mortgaged property, defrauding a hotel keeper, and other offenses.[9] Jerome Hall and others who include *mens rea* or criminal intent as one of the essential and universal criteria of crime, justify this inclusion by the argument that exceptions such as those just listed are "bad law."[10] The important consideration here is that the criteria which have been used in defining white collar crimes are not categorically different from the criteria used in defining some other crimes. The proportion of decisions rendered against corporations without the protection of the rules of criminal intent and presumption of innocence is probably greater than the proportion rendered against other criminals, but a difference in proportions does not make the violations of law by corporations categorically different from the violations of laws by other criminals. Moreover, the difference in proportion, as the procedures actually operate, is not great. On the one hand, many of the defendants in usual criminal cases, being in relative poverty, do not get good defense and consequently secure little benefit from these rules; on the other hand, the commissions come close to observing these rules of proof and evidence although they are not required to do so. This is illustrated by the procedure of the Federal Trade Commission in regard to advertisements. Each year it examines several hundred thousand advertisements and appraises about 50,000 of them as probably false. From the 50,000 it selects about 1,500 as patently false. For instance, an advertisement of gumwood furniture as "mahogany" would seldom be an accidental error and would generally result from a state of mind which deviated from honesty by more than the natural tendency of human beings to feel proud of their handiwork.

The preceding discussion has shown that these 70 corporations committed crimes according to 779 adverse decisions, and also has shown that the criminality of their behavior was not made obvious by the conventional procedures of the criminal law but was blurred and concealed by special procedures. This differential implementation of the law as applied to the crimes of corporations eliminates or at least minimizes the stigma of crime. This differential implementation of the law began with the Sherman Antitrust Act of 1890. As previously described, this law is explicitly a criminal law and a violation of the law is a misdemeanor no matter what procedure is used. The customary policy would have been to rely entirely on criminal prosecution as the method of enforcement. But a clever invention was made in the provision of an injunction to enforce a criminal law; this was an invention in that it was a direct reversal of previous case law. Also, private parties were encouraged by treble damages to enforce a criminal law by suits in civil courts. In either case, the defendant did not appear in the criminal court and the fact that he had committed a crime did not appear on the face of the proceedings.

The Sherman Antitrust Act, in this respect, became the model in practically all the subsequent procedures authorized to deal with the crimes of corporations. When the Federal Trade Commission bill and the Clayton bill were introduced in Congress, they contained the conventional criminal procedures; these were eliminated in committee discussions, and other procedures which did not carry the external symbols of criminal process were substituted. The violations of these laws are crimes, as has been shown above, but they are treated as though they were not crimes, with the effect and probably the intention of eliminating the stigma of crime.

This policy of eliminating the stigma of crime is illustrated in the following statement by Wendell Berge, at the time assistant to the head of the antitrust division of the Department of Justice, in a plea for abandonment of the criminal prosecution under the Sherman Antitrust Act and the authorization of civil procedures with civil fines as a substitute.

> While civil penalties may be as severe in their financial effects as criminal penalties, yet they do not involve the stigma that attends indictment and conviction. Most of the defendants in antitrust cases are not criminals in the usual sense. There is no inherent reason why antitrust enforcement requires branding them as such.[11]

If a civil fine were substituted for a criminal fine, a violation of the antitrust law would be as truly a crime as it is now. The thing which would be eliminated is the stigma of crime. Consequently, the stigma of crime has become a penalty in itself, which may be imposed in connection with other penalties or withheld, just as it is possible to combine imprisonment with a fine or have a fine without imprisonment. A civil fine is a financial penalty without the additional penalty of stigma, while a criminal fine is a financial penalty with the additional penalty of stigma.

When the stigma of crime is imposed as a penalty, it places the defendant within the popular stereotype of "the criminal." In primitive society "the criminal" was substantially the same as "the stranger,"[12] while in modern society the stereotype is limited largely to the lower socioeconomic class. Seventy-five percent of the persons committed to state prisons are probably not, aside from their unesteemed cultural attainments, "criminals in the usual sense of the word." It may be excellent policy to eliminate the stigma of crime from violations of law by both the upper and the lower classes, but we are not here concerned with policy.

White collar crime is similar to juvenile delinquency in respect to the stigma. In both cases the procedures of the criminal law are modified so that the stigma of crime will not attach to the offenders. The stigma of crime has been less completely eliminated from juvenile delinquency than from white collar crimes because the procedures for the former are a less complete departure from conventional criminal procedures, because most juvenile delinquents come from the lower class, and because the juveniles are not organized to protect their good names. Because these juvenile delinquents have not been successfully freed from the stigma of crime, they have been generally held to be within the scope of the theories of criminal behavior and in fact provide a large part of the data for criminology. Because the external symbols have been more completely eliminated from white collar crimes, white collar crimes have not generally been included within the scope of criminology. These procedural symbols, however, are not the essential elements in criminality and white collar crimes belong logically within the scope of criminology, just as do juvenile delinquencies.

Those who insist that moral culpability is a necessary element in crime may argue that criminality is lacking in the violations of laws which have eliminated the stigma from crime. This involves the general question of the relation of criminal law to the mores. The laws with which we are here concerned are not arbitrary, as is the regulation that one must drive on the right side of the street. The Sherman Antitrust Act, for instance, represents a settled tradition in favor of free competition and free enterprise. This ideology is obvious in the resentment against communism. A violation of the antitrust laws is a violation of strongly entrenched moral sentiments. The value of these laws is questioned principally by persons who believe in a more collectivistic economic system, and these persons are limited to two principal groups, namely, socialists and the leaders of Big Business. When the leaders of business, through corporate activities, violate the antitrust law, they are violating the moral sentiments of practically all parts of the American public except the socialists.

The other laws for the regulation of business are similarly rooted in moral sentiments. Violations of these laws, to be sure, do not call forth as much resentment as do murder and rape, but not all laws in the penal code involve equal resentments by the public. We divide crimes into felonies, which elicit more resentment, and misdemeanors, which elicit less resentment. Within each of these classes, again, the several statutes may be arranged in order of the degree of atrocity. White collar crimes, presumably, would be in the lower part of the range, in this respect, but not entirely out of the range. Moreover, very few of the ordinary crimes arouse much resentment in the ordinary citizen, unless the crimes are very spectacular or unless he or his immediate friends are affected. The average citizen, reading in the morning newspaper that the home of an unknown person has been burglarized by another unknown person, has no appreciable increase in blood pressure. Fear and resentment develop in the modern city principally as the result of an accumulation of crimes, as depicted in crime rates or in general descriptions. Such resentment develops under those circumstances both as to white collar crimes and other crimes. Finally, not all parts of the society react in the same manner against the violation of a particular law. It is true that one's business associates do not regard a violation of a business regulation as atrocious. It is true, also, that people in certain city slum areas do not regard larceny by their neighbors as atrocious, for they will ordinarily give assistance to these neighbors who are being pursued by the agents of criminal justice.

The differential implementation of the law as it applies to large corporations may be explained by three factors, namely, the status of the businessman, the trend away from punishment, and the relatively unorganized resentment of the public against white collar crimes. Each of these will be described.

First, the methods used in the enforcement of any law are an adaptation to the characteristics of the prospective violators of the law, as appraised by the legislators and the judicial and administrative personnel. The appraisals regarding businessmen, who are the prospective violators of the laws which are now under consideration, include a combination of fear and admiration. Those who are responsible for the system of criminal justice are afraid to antagonize businessmen; among other consequences, such antagonism may result in a reduction in contributions to the campaign funds needed to win the next election. The amendment to the Pure Food and Drug Law of 1938 explicitly excludes from the penal provisions of that law the advertising agencies and media (that is, principally, newspapers and journals) which participate in the misrepresentation. Accessories to crimes are customarily included within the scope of the criminal law, but these accessories are very powerful and influential in the determination of public opinion and they are made immune. Probably much more important than fear, however, is the cultural homogeneity of legislators, judges, and administrators with businessmen. Legislators admire and respect businessmen and cannot conceive of them as criminals; businessmen do not conform to the popular stereotype of "the criminal." The legislators are confident that these respectable gentlemen will conform to the law as the result of very mild pressures. The most powerful group in medieval society secured relative immunity by "benefit of clergy," and now our most powerful group secures relative immunity by "benefit of business," or more generally "high social status." The statement of Daniel Drew, a pious old fraud, describes the working of the criminal law with accuracy, "Law is like a cobweb: it's made for flies and the smaller kind of insects, so to speak, but lets the big bumblebee break through. When technicalities of the law stood in my way, I have always been able to brush them aside easy as anything."

This interpretation meets with considerable opposition from persons who insist that this is an egalitarian society in which all men are equal in the eyes of the law. It is not possible to give a complete demonstration of the validity of this interpretation but four types of evidence are presented in the following paragraphs as partial demonstration.

The Department of Justice is authorized to use both criminal prosecutions and petitions in equity to enforce the Sherman Antitrust Act. The department has selected the method of criminal prosecution in a larger proportion of cases against trade unions than of cases against corporations, although the law was enacted primarily because of fear of the corporations. From 1890 to 1929 the Department of Justice initiated 438 actions under this law with decisions favorable to the United States. Of the actions against business firms, 27 percent were criminal prosecutions, while of the actions against trade unions 71 percent were criminal prosecutions.[13] This shows that the Department of Justice has been comparatively reluctant to use a method against business firms which carries with it the stigma of crime.

The method of criminal prosecution in enforcement of the Sherman Antitrust Act has varied from one presidential administration to another. It was seldom used in the administrations of the presidents who were popularly appraised as friendly toward business, namely, McKinley, Harding, Coolidge, and Hoover.

Businessmen suffered their greatest loss of prestige in the depression which began in 1929. It was precisely in this period of low status of businessmen that the most strenuous efforts were made to enforce the old laws and enact new laws for the regulation of businessmen. The appropriations for this purpose were multiplied several times and persons were selected for their vigor in administration of the law, with the result that the number of decisions against the 70 corporations was quadrupled in the next decade.

The Federal Trade Commission Law states that a violation of the law by a corporation shall be deemed to be also a violation by the officers and directors of the corporation. Businessmen, however, are seldom convicted in criminal courts, and several cases have been reported, like the 6 percent case of the automobile industry, in which corporations were convicted and the persons who directed the corporation were all acquitted. Executives of corporations are convicted in criminal courts principally when they use methods of crime similar to the methods of the lower socioeconomic class.

A second factor in the explanation of the differential implementation of the law as applied to white collar criminals is the trend away from penal methods. This trend advanced more rapidly in the area of white collar crimes than of other crimes. The trend is seen in general in the almost complete abandonment of the extreme penalties of death and physical torture; in the supplanting of conventional penal methods by nonpenal methods such as probation and the case work methods which accompany probation; and in the supplementing of penal methods by nonpenal methods, as in the development of case work and educational policies in prisons. These decreases in penal methods are explained by a series of social changes: the increased power of the lower socioeconomic class upon which previously most of the penalties were inflicted; the inclusion within the scope of the penal laws of a large part of the upper socioeconomic class as illustrated by traffic regulations; the increased social interaction among the classes, which has resulted in increased understanding and sympathy; the failure of penal methods to make substantial reductions in crime rates; and the weakening hold on the legal profession and others of the individualistic and hedonistic psychology which had placed great emphasis on pain in the control of behavior. To some extent overlapping those just mentioned is the fact that punishment, which was previously the chief reliance for control in the home, the school, and the church, has tended to disappear from those institutions, leaving the State without cultural support for its own penal methods.[14]

The third factor in the differential implementation of the law in the area of white collar crime is the relatively unorganized resentment of the public toward white collar crimes. Three reasons for the different relation between law and mores in this area may be given. (a) The violations of law by businessmen are complex and their effects diffused. They are not simple and direct attack by one person on another person, as is assault and battery. Many of the white collar crimes can be appreciated only by persons who are experts in the occupations in which they occur. A corporation often violates a law for a decade or longer before the administrative agencies or the public becomes aware of the violation. The effects of these crimes may be diffused over a long period of time and perhaps millions of people, with no particular person suffering much at a particular time. (b) The public agencies of communication do not express the organized moral sentiments of the community as to white collar crimes, in part because the crimes are complicated and not easily presented as news, but probably in greater part because these agencies of communication are owned or controlled by businessmen and because these agencies are themselves involved in the violations of many of these laws. Public opinion in regard to picking pockets would not be well organized if most of the information regarding this crime came to the public directly from the pickpockets themselves. This failure of the public agencies of communication may be illustrated by the almost complete lack of attention by newspapers to the evidence presented in the trial of A. B. Dick and other mimeographing companies that these companies maintained a sabotage school in Chicago in which their employees were trained to sabotage the machines of rival companies, and even their own machines if the supplies of rival companies are being used.[15]

Analogous behavior of trade unions, with features as spectacular as in this case, would have been described in hundreds of newspapers with large headlines on the front page, while many newspapers did not even mention this decision, and those which did mention it placed a brief paragraph on an inner page. (c) These laws for the regulation of business belong to a relatively new and specialized part of the statutes. The old common law crimes, as continued in the regular penal codes, were generally limited to person-to-person attacks, which might be committed by an person in any society. In the more complex society of the present day, legislatures have felt compelled to regulate many special occupations and other special groups. The penal code of California, for instance, contains an index of penal provisions in the statutes outside of the penal code, which are designed to regulate barbers, plumbers, farmers, corporations, and many other special groups. This index occupies 46 pages, and the complete statutes to which reference is made in the index would occupy many hundreds of pages. This illustrates the great expansion of penal provisions beyond the simple requirements of the earlier societies. The teachers of criminal law, who generally confine their attention to the old penal code, are missing the larger part of the penal law of the modern state. Similarly, the general public is not generally aware of many of these specialized provisions and the resentment of the public is not organized.

For the three reasons which have been presented, the public does not have the same organized resentment toward white collar crimes as toward certain of the serious felonies. The relation between the law and mores, finally, tends to be circular. The laws, to a considerable extent, are crystallizations of the mores, and each act of enforcement of the laws tends to reenforce the mores. The laws regarding white collar crimes, which conceal the criminality of the behavior, have been less effective than other criminal laws in reenforcing the mores.

The answers to the questions posed at the beginning of this chapter may be given in the following propositions: First, the white collar crimes which are discussed . . . have the general criteria of criminal behavior, namely, legal definition of social injuries and penal sanctions, and are therefore cognate with other crimes. Second, these white collar crimes have generally not been regarded by criminologists as cognate with other crimes and as within the scope of theories of criminal behavior because the administrative and judicial procedures have been different for these violations of criminal law than for other violations of criminal law. Third, this differential implementation of the criminal law as applied to businessmen is explained by the status of the businessman, the trend away from reliance on punitive methods, and the relatively unorganized resentment of the public toward white collar crimes.

Since this analysis is concerned with violations of laws by corporations, a brief description of the relation of the corporation to the criminal law is necessary. Three or four generations ago the courts with unanimity decided that corporations could not commit crimes. These decisions were based on one or more of the following principles. First, since the corporation is a legislative artifact and does not have a mind or soul, it cannot have criminal intent and therefore cannot commit a crime. Second, since a corporation is not authorized to do unlawful acts, the agents of a corporation are not authorized to do unlawful acts. If those agents commit unlawful acts, they do so in their personal capacity and not in their capacity as agents. They may be punished, therefore, as persons but not as agents. Third, with a few exceptions the only penalties that can be imposed on corporations, if found guilty of crimes, are fines. These fines are injurious to stockholders, and consequently, as a matter of policy, should not be imposed.

These principles have now been reversed by the courts and corporations are now frequently convicted of crimes. Corporations have been convicted of larceny, manslaughter, keeping disorderly houses, breaking the Sabbath, destruction of property and a great variety of other crimes.[16] Such decisions involved reversal of the three principles on which the earlier decisions were based. First, the corporation is not merely a legislative artifact. Associations of persons existed prior to the law and some of these associations have been recognized as entities by legislatures. These corporations and other associations are instrumental in influencing legislation. Consequently legislation is in part an artifact of corporations, just as corporations are in part an artifact of legislatures.[17] Second, the requirement that criminal intent be demonstrated has been eliminated from an increasing number of criminal laws, as was described above. Third, the location of responsibility has been extremely difficult in many parts of modern society, and responsibility is certainly a much more complicated concept than is ordinarily believed. The old employers' liability laws, which were based on the principle of individual responsibility, broke down because responsibility for industrial accidents could not be located. Workmen's compensation laws were substituted, with their principle that the industrial establishment should bear the cost of industrial accidents. Some attention has been given to the location of responsibility for decisions in the large corporations.[18] Although responsibility for actions of particular types may be located, power to modify such actions lies also at various other points. Due largely to the complexity of this concept, the question of individual responsibility is frequently waived and penalties are imposed on corporations. This does, to be sure, affect the stockholder who may have almost no power in making decisions as to policy, but the same thing is true of other penalties which have been suggested as substitutes for fines on corporations, namely, dissolution of the corporation, suspension of business for a specified period, restriction of sphere of action of the corporation, confiscation of goods, publicity, surety for good behavior, and supervision by the court.

Two questions may be raised regarding the responsibility of corporations from the point of view of the statistical tabulation of violations of law. The first is whether a corporation should be held responsible for the action of a special department of the corporation. The advertising department, for instance, may prepare and distribute advertising copy which violates the law. The customary plea of the executives of the corporation is that they were ignorant of and not responsible for the action of the special department. This plea is akin to the alibi of the ordinary criminal and need not to be taken seriously. The departments of a corporation know that their recognition by the executives of the corporation depends on results and that few questions will be asked if results are achieved. In the rare case in which the executives are not only unaware of but sincerely opposed to the policy of a particular department, the corporation is customarily held responsible by the court. That is the only question of interest in the present connection. Consequently, an illegal act is reported as the act of the corporation, without consideration of the location of responsibility within the corporation.

The second question is concerned with the relation between the parent corporation and the subsidiaries. This relationship varies widely from one corporation to another and even within one corporate system. When subsidiaries are prosecuted for violations of law, the parent company generally pleads ignorance of the methods which have been used. This, again, is customarily an alibi, although it may be true in some cases. For instance, the automobile corporations generally insist that the labor policy of each subsidiary is determined by that subsidiary and is not within the control of the parent company. However, when a labor controversy arose in a plant in Texas and a settlement was proposed by the labor leaders, the personnel department of that plant replied, "We must consult Detroit." They reported the following morning, "Detroit says 'No.'" For the present purpose, the corporation and its subsidiaries are treated as a unit, without regard to the location of responsibility within that unit.

*Σ*ndnotes

[1]The most thorough analysis of crime from the point of view of the legal definition is Jerome Hall, *Principles of Criminal Law* (Indianapolis, 1947). He lists seven criteria of crime: "(1) certain external consequences ('harms'), (2) which are legally forbidden (principle of legality); (3) conduct; (4) *mens rea*; (5) the fusion, 'concurrence,' of *mens rea* and conduct; (6) a 'causal' relationship between the legally forbidden harms and the voluntary misconduct; and (7) (legally

prescribed) punishment" (p. 11). The position taken . . . is in most respects consistent with Hall's definition; certain differences will be considered later.

[2]U.S. vs. Swift, 188 F 92 (1911).

[3]Some of the antitrust decisions were made against meat packers under the Packers and Stockyards Act. The penal sanctions in this act are essentially the same as in the Federal Trade Commission Act.

[4]Violations of the federal Fair Labor Standards Act and of most of the state labor laws are defined as misdemeanors.

[5]For a list of such states, see Walter J. Derenburg, *Trade Mark Protection and Unfair Trading* (New York, 1936), pp. 861–1012.

[6]Orville C. Snyder, "Criminal Breach of Trust and Corporate Mismanagement," *Miss. Law Jour.*, 11:123–51, 262–89, 368–89, December 1938 and April 1939; A. A. Berle, "Liability for Stock Market Manipulation," *Columbia Law Rev.*, 31:264–79, February 1931; David L. Dodd, *The Judicial Valuation of Property for Stock-Issue Purposes* (New York, 1930).

[7]Lowell B. Mason, "FTC Stipulation—Friend of Advertiser?" *Chicago Bar Record*, vol. 26, pp. 310 f., May 1945.

[8]Paul E. Hadlick, *Criminal Prosecutions under the Sherman Antitrust Act* (Washington, 1939), pp. 131–32.

[9]Livingston Hall, "Statutory Law of Crimes, 1887–1936," *Harvard Law Rev.*, 50:616–53, February 1937.

[10]Hall, *Principles of Criminal Law*, ch. x.

[11]Wendell Berge, "Remedies Available to the Government under the Sherman Act," *Law and Contemporary Problems*, 7:111, January 1940.

[12]On the role of the stranger in punitive justice, see Ellsworth Faris, "The Origin of Punishment," *Intern. Journ. of Ethics*, 25:54–67, October 1914; George H. Mead, "The Psychology of Punitive Justice," *Amer. Journ. Sociol.*, 23:577–602, March 1918; Florian Znaniecki, *Social Actions* (New York, 1936), pp. 345–408.

[13]Percentages compiled from cases listed in the report of the Department of Justice "Federal Antitrust Laws, 1938."

[14]The trend away from penal methods suggests that the penal sanction may not be a completely adequate criterion in the definition of crime.

[15]*New York Times*, March 26, 1948, pp. 31, 37.

[16]George F. Canfield, "Corporate Responsibility for Crime," *Columbia Law Rev.*, 14:469–81, June 1941; Frederic P. Lee, "Corporate Criminal Liability," ibid., 28:1–28, February 1928; Max Radin, "Endless Problem of Corporate Personality," ibid., 32:643–67, April 1932.

[17]For a summary of classical theories of corporate personality, see Frederick Hallis, *Corporate Personality* (London, 1930). See also Henri Levy-Bruhl, "Collective Personality in the Law," *Annales Sociologique*, ser. C, fasc. 3, 1938.

[18]Robert A. Gordon, *Business Leadership in the Large Corporation* (Washington, D.C., 1945).

◉ ◉ ◉

Questions

1. How does Sutherland define "crime." Do you agree with this definition? If not, how would you change it?

2. According to Sutherland, does "white-collar crime" fit the definition that he lays out?

3. How do government rules and regulations help remove the stigma of "crime" from various corporate infractions?

4. According to Sutherland, why do laws make exceptions for large corporations? Which of these reasons do you think is most important? Why?

5. Why is it important to determine whether white-collar crime is actually crime? What do we gain, theoretically and practically?

The Culture of the Corporation and Illegal Behavior

MARSHALL B. CLINARD AND PETER C. YEAGER

Why do some corporations commit deviant and illegal acts? Does the responsibility for such behavior rest solely on senior executives, or do cultural norms and expectations for employees also play a role? In this selection, Marshall Clinard and Peter Yeager examine how corporations and entire industries establish cultural norms and expectations for their employees. According to the authors, these norms and expectations make executives feel pressured into committing deviant, unethical, and illegal behavior.

• • •

Although the ethical behavior of a firm is influenced by the economic and political climate, it is also a product of cultural norms operating within a given corporation or even an industry that may be conducive to law violation. In a sense, one may speak of internal cultural factors and external economic factors, which may not be independent but tend to interact to produce violations. For example, Sutherland (1949), although he stressed unethical and illegal cultural factors (differential association), found that "position in the economic structure has great significance in the variations among the corporations as to the number of violations" (p. 259). He argued that differential association with corporate criminal and unethical norms is crucial, yet he also stressed that violations may result when firms face similar economic conditions in an industry. The living code of a corporation "is an ever-shifting pattern of guidelines set by the necessities of the market, the conditions and traditions of the industry, the goals of the corporation, the aspirations of management, and the nature of the executives themselves" (Goodman, 1963, p. 82).

The cultural environment within which the modern American corporation operates may actually encourage or discourage criminal or deviant behavior. Some corporations appear to be more legally ethical in their business operations. In research conducted . . . it was found that approximately 40 percent of the largest U.S. manufacturing corporations were not charged with a law violation by any of the 25 federal agencies during 1975 and 1976 (p. 113). Some of the *Fortune* 500, such as the Digital Equipment Corporation, have a reputation for high ethical standards. (*Wall Street Journal,* October 24, 1977). Many corporations, for example, appear not to have made illegal political contributions to the Nixon campaign or to have been charged with violations connected with foreign payments (p. 171). On the other hand, some corporations have been charged with numerous violations of various types (p. 116).

Corporate norms of doing business may conflict with one or several ethical and legal norms. The interplay among corporate norms of unethical behavior, societal norms, and law violations may run throughout a given corporation and be present in much of the decisionmaking (Clark and Hollinger, 1977). Businessmen are subject to contradictory expectations—a universalistic one (as citizen) and a particularistic one (as businessman)—with the obligation to the firm generally guiding behavior. A corporation that emphasizes profits above business ethics and ignores corporate responsibility to the community, the consumer, or society is likely to have difficulty complying with legal norms. The policies of some corporations can encourage the "criminal tendencies" of particular executives. For example, the persons involved in the electrical price-fixing case of the 1960s found illegal activity "an established way of life" when they began their jobs (Geis, 1973, p. 109).

In this connection, it has been suggested that we should begin our studies of why corporations break the law by learning more about why different corporations, like different political administrations, appear to become permeated with their own particular attitudes and stands in relation to law obedience and good citizenship generally (Stone, 1975, p. 237). Stone has referred to the "culture of a corporation," which is an entire constellation of attitudes and forces, some of which contribute to illegal behavior. Those factors contributing to illegal behavior include

> a desire for profits, expansion, power; desire for security (at corporate as well as individual levels); the fear of failure (particularly in connection with shortcomings in corporate innovativeness); group loyalty identification

(particularly in connection with citizenship violations and the various failures to "come forward" with internal information); feelings of omniscience
(in connection with adequate testing); organizational diffusion of responsibility (in connection with the buffering of public criticism); corporate
ethnocentrism (in connection with limits in concern for the public's wants
and desires). (Stone 1975, p. 236)

In a follow-up of Baumhart's mid-1950s survey of corporate ethics,
Brenner and Molander (1977) found that superiors continued to be ranked
as the primary influence in unethical decisionmaking. About half of those
surveyed in the 1977 study thought that their superiors frequently did not
wish to know how results were obtained as long as they achieved the desired
outcome: "Respondents frequently complained of superiors' pressure to
support incorrect viewpoints, sign false documents, overlook superiors'
wrongdoing, and do business with superiors' friends" (p. 60).

Under conditions such as these the use of sanctions to accomplish
compliance with law is but one of the various forces operating within a
corporation encouraging or opposing violations of law. The success of law
enforcement

> ultimately depends upon its consistency with and reinforcement from
> other vectors—the organization's rules for advancement and reward, its
> customs, conventions, and morals. If the law is too much at odds with
> these other forces, its threats will make the employees more careful to
> cover their tracks before it makes them alter their institutionally support-
> ive behavior. (Stone, 1975, p. 67)

Woodmansee, writing in 1975, illustrated what happens when corporate
codes of conduct clash with legal norms.

> General Electric has been charged with price fixing and other monopoly
> practices not only for its light bulbs, but for turbines, generators, trans-
> formers, motors, relays, radio tubes, heavy metals, and lightning arresters.
> At least 67 suits have been brought against General Electric by the
> Antitrust Division of the Justice Department since 1911, and 180 antitrust
> suits were brought against General Electric by private companies in the
> early 1960s alone. General Electric's many trips to court hardly seem to
> have "reformed" the company; in 1962, after 50 years experience with
> General Electric, even the Justice Department was moved to comment on
> "General Electric's proclivity for frequent and persistent involvement in
> antitrust violations." And there have been new suits in the years since
> 1962. (p. 52)

Lawbreaking can become a normative pattern within a corporation, with or without pressure for profits or from the economic environment. In confidential interviews with a number of board chairmen and chief executive officers of very large corporations, a consensus emerged that the top management, particularly the chief executive officer, sets ethical tone. The president and chief executive officer of a large manufacturing corporation noted that "by example and holding a tight rein a chief executive . . . can set the level of ethical or unethical practices in his organization. This influence can spread throughout the organization." As another high executive pointed out, price fixing or kickbacks must be "congenial to the climate of the corporation." Still another board chairman said, "Some corporations, like those in politics, tolerate corruption."

● Diffusion of Illegal Behavior Within Industries

Corporate wrongdoing sometimes reflects the normative structure of a particular industry. That is, criminal behavior by the corporation and its executives often is the result of the diffusion of illegal practices and policies within the industry (Sutherland, 1949, p. 263). Frequently it is not the corporate organization itself that must be examined but the corporation's place in the industry (Riedel, 1968, p. 94).

In a recent reanalysis of some old data on restraint of trade collected by Sutherland during the 1930s and 1940s for his study of corporate crime, Cressey (1976) found that generally corporations in the same industry have similar rates of recidivism. "For example, neither of the two mail-order houses included in Sutherland's study were repeaters of the restraint of trade offense—Sears Roebuck had no adverse decisions against it, and Montgomery Ward had only one. But all three motion-picture companies had high recidivism rates—Paramount and Warner Brothers each had 21, and Loew's had 22. Two dairy companies, Borden and National Dairy Products, had middle-range rates of 7 and 8" (pp. 216–217). A study of price fixing reported that this offense is more likely to occur when the companies deal with a homogeneous product line (Hay and Kelley, 1974). Relying on his studies of corporate crime in the Federal German Republic, Tiedemann (1974, 1976) concluded that much of this activity is a response to competition in certain industries. For example, 50 percent of all scrap imports in the European Coal and Steel Community were found to be faked: one-third of the subsidized scrap metal was nonexistent. In 1978 almost all Mercedes establishments in Germany, as well as their clients, were charged with having changed the contract dates on motor cars and trucks so that they could get the high subsidies paid by the German government in 1976 in an effort to stimulate the national economy (*Frankfurter Allgemeine Zeitung,* November 17, 1978).

The atmosphere thus becomes one in which participants, as in the Equity Funding case, learn the necessary values, motives, rationalizations, and techniques favorable to particular kinds of crimes. A corporation may socialize its members to normative systems conducive to criminality. The head of the Enforcement Division of the SEC has said: "Our largest corporations have trained some of our brightest young people to be dishonest" (*New York Times Magazine,* September 25, 1976, p. 58). Diffusion of industry practices was evident in the electrical price fixing conspiracy of the 1960s in the manner in which the corporation representatives arranged meetings far from the home offices of the corporation, used code names in meetings of representatives of the corporations, sent mail in plain envelopes rather than business envelopes, used public telephones to avoid wiretaps, and falsified accounts to conceal their meeting places. (Herling, 1962). Although large aircraft manufacturers commonly made foreign payoffs, particularly in Japan, Lockheed is generally believed to have set the pace. As the chairman of the board testified before a Senate subcommittee, "If you are going to win it is necessary." Still, officials of the Northrop Corporation, "which, like Lockheed, made similar payments through a special subsidiary company established in Switzerland to handle the financing," told the subcommittee, Senator Church said, that *"they learned how to do that from Lockheed"* (Shaplen, 1978, p. 54).

The role of industry ethics in law violations is shown in a widespread price conspiracy that resulted in the indictment of 23 carton manufacturing corporations and 50 of their executives in 1976 (United States of America, Plaintiff, v. Alton Box Board Company, et. al., Defendants, Criminal Action No. 76, CR 199, U.S. District Court, Northern District of Illinois, Eastern Division. All references and quotes are from court documents). Included were International Paper Company, Container Corporation of America, Packaging Corporation of America, Weyerhauser, Diamond International Corporation, and Alton Box. American industry and consumers depend enormously on goods packaged in folding cartons, and in terms of corporate annual sales (over $1 billion), number of defendants, duration of the conspiracy (1960 to 1974), and number of transactions involved, this case represents one of the most flagrant violations of the Sherman Antitrust Act in the law's 86-year history. In the indictment the conspirators were charged with the following crimes:

1. Disclosing to other members of the conspiracy the price being charged or to be charged for a particular folding carton to the buyer of that folding carton, with the understanding that the other members of the conspiracy would submit a noncompetitive bid, or no bid, on that folding carton to that buyer.

2. Agreeing with other members of the conspiracy who were supplying the same folding carton to a buyer on the price to be charged to that buyer.

3. Agreeing with other members of the conspiracy on increases in list prices of certain folding cartons.

Shortly after being indicted, all but one of the corporate executives pleaded guilty; later some tried to change their pleas to *nolo contendere*, an effort that was vigorously opposed by the government. According to the government statement,

> These defendants were not engaged in a short-term violation based on sudden market pressures; price-fixing was their way of doing business. The participants demonstrated a knowing, blatant disregard for antitrust laws. One grand jury witness testified that during a six-year period he personally engaged in thousands of price-fixing transactions with competitors which were illegal.[1] This illegal conduct was carried on in all parts of the country by all management levels in the billion-dollar folding-carton industry. The thousands upon thousands of exchanges of prices with competitors, the dozens upon dozens of meetings with competitors were done with a single purpose and design—to eliminate price competition in this industry. (Government's Statement of Reasons and Authorities in Opposition to Defendants' Motions to Plead *Nolo Contendere, United States v. Alton Box Board Company*, Criminal Action No. 76 CR 199 [May 7, 1976] at 10–11)

One executive of a large corporation stated: "The meetings and exchange of price information were well known to the senior management and in the industry as a whole." Another stated: "Meetings of competitors were a way of life in the folding carton industry."

Community standards can also encourage wrongdoing in an industry. Some businessmen may be able to justify illicit behavior if they see it as conforming to community norms (Chibnall and Saunders, 1977). Discussing the variations in obedience to laws by a group of manufacturing companies within the shoe industry, Lane (1953) concluded that "the [community's] attitude toward the law, government, and the morality of illegality" (p. 160) is highly influential. Even though the companies he studied were in the same industry and were subject to the same laws, variation in law disobedience was great. In Haverhill, Massachusetts, 7 percent of the companies were in violation, while in Auburn, Maine, 44 percent were. Lane concluded that such differences might be explained by the home community's attitudes about the importance of law and government and its tolerance of illegal behavior.

◉ The Executive in the Corporation: The Making of a Corporate Criminal

In their well-known analysis of large-scale organization, March and Simon (1958) developed a theory to explain how employees can be induced to make decisions that are correct from the standpoint of an organization such as a corporation. Basically, they claimed that the organization's elite controls the premises of decisionmaking for subordinates by setting priorities and regulating the flow of communication; thus, top officials manipulate subordinates' assessments of situations in a system of unobtrusive control (cf. Perrow, 1972, pp. 152–157).

In his discussion of the nature of corporations, Drucker (1972, p. 40) affirmed that a natural tendency exists in every large-scale organization to discourage initiative and encourage conformity. A primary means of fostering conformity in corporations is through the training of persons who are likely to hold positions of responsibility. Studies have been made in detail of how corporations lead new managers through an initiation period designed to weaken their ties with external groups, including their own families, and encourage a feeling of dependence on and attachment to the corporation (Madden, 1977; Margolis, 1979). Outside connections are reduced, and a club mentality is bred through overwork, frequent transfers, which inhibit attachment to local communities, and provisions for recreational and educational needs during leisure time. Co-workers and higher-ups become "significant others" in the individual's work and social life. "Briefly, this all suggests that organization members can be socialized to accept the goal structure of the organization" (Meier, 1975, p. 10). After interviews with corporate executives, Margolis (1979) concluded that executive transfers to other communities play a key role in the psychological initiation of managers. By last-minute assignments and out-of-town work the priority of the corporation is established. Not surprisingly, recruiters of top executives claim that corporations tend to hire "our kind of person" in terms of managerial style and family commitments, which might interfere with corporate responsibilities, "physical appearance, and personal habits" (*Wall Street Journal,* September 19, 1979). In an advertisement in the *Wall Street Journal* (September 20, 1979), the president of Solfan Corporation bluntly noted: "The job of personnel director at our company is not for everyone. I know because this year I have already had two men in this position. It wasn't for them. If your family or your 'lifestyle' or your kid's boy scout experience is more important to you than your job, then this isn't for you."

Ability to socialize employees so thoroughly into the corporate world insures one of the main characteristics of bureaucratic organizations described by Max Weber: "The very nature of a bureaucracy, as Weber so well demonstrated, is to make the *individual dispensable*" (Stone, 1975, p. 65). In this sense, the corporation is constructed not of persons but of roles and positions that it has created and defined and therefore over which it has control. This permits individual movement into and out of the corporation without a disruption of activity; the only function of persons is to carry out the activities that belong to those positions they hold (Coleman, 1978, p. 26).

The end product in many cases is what has been called a "functionary" in other contexts, "a new kind of man who in his role of serving the organization is morally unbounded. . . . His ethic is the ethic of the good soldier: take the order, do the job" (Howton, 1969, pp. 5–6). Given the outcomes desired at the higher levels, generally the employee neither questions these ends nor his use of the most efficient or quickest means of achieving them. In his examination of the electrical price-fixing conspiracy, Cook (1966) discussed at length the mentality of the organizational man that encouraged illegal behavior throughout the entire industry: "They were men who surrendered their own individualities to the corporate gods they served. Though they knew that their acts were illegal, not to say unethical, though the shady maneuvering at times affronted their sense of decency, not one found it possible to pronounce an unequivocal 'no'" (p. 38). Similarly, in a case involving the side effects of an anticholesterol drug HE/14 several pharmaceutical corporation executives were convicted of lying about animal studies testing the drug's effects: "No one involved expressed any strong repugnance or even opposition to selling the unsafe drug. Rather they all seemed to drift into the activity without thinking a great deal about it" (Carey, 1978, p. 384).

In his study of the electrical industry price-fixing conspiracy, Geis (1967) discussed a theme common to many studies of individuals involved in corporate crime. That is, the individual has been trained in the illegal behavior as a part of his occupational role. Schrager and Short (1978) believe that individual personality becomes unimportant; criminal behavior stemmed more from the roles they were expected to fulfill than from individual pathology (p. 410).

Some of the testimony in the folding carton price conspiracy specifically indicated how an individual executive learns to use price fixing as an accepted business practice in the industry. One corporate executive said: "Each was introduced to price-fixing practices by his superiors as he came to that point in his career when he had price-fixing responsibility." Another testified as follows:

Q.: Mr. DeFazia, how were you informed that discussing prices was part of your job?

A.: I don't think I was ever really told it was part of my job. I think it was just something I sort of worked right into. That was Mr. Cox's responsibility back in those years. I was young, I was still a green kid, I just picked it right up from working along with him.

Q.: Mr. Cox provided guidance to you? Kind of discussed?

A.: No. We worked in the same office. I guess you just pick it up. I don't know how you would want to say it, just like learning your ABC's, you hear it repeated so often that it's just part of your daily activity.

Lockheed's special review committee established to investigate foreign and domestic illegal payments and practices reported to the SEC in 1976 that senior corporate management was responsible for this strategy. Accountants as well as other employees, however, were aware of the devious methods used in securing, recording, and transferring money to foreign sources for bribes: "Employees learned not to question deviations from standard operating procedures and practices. Moreover, the Committee was told by several witnesses that employees who questioned foreign marketing practices damaged their claims for career advancement." A similar committee for the 3M Company reported to the SEC in 1976: "We felt that employees should have asked more questions and should have challenged their supervisors more, but realistically, the internal control systems did not provide a means or an atmosphere for challenges to executives at the level of president, chairman of the board, and chief executive officer" (p. 31). And yet another review committee, this time of J. Ray McDermott and Co., in a 1977 report to the SEC, stated that the corporation (extracts)

> has retained the atmosphere of a privately held company. Employees from senior management on down have taken the position that "the boss's word is law." The critical issue, even in questionable payments, was whether the boss was aware and approved the transaction. . . . Employees who balked at orders from the boss were likely to be fired (p. 6).

Pressures often exist at all levels of the corporation to promote attitudes and behaviors conducive to corporate goals regardless of means. At the lower and middle levels, the corporate actors are encouraged to develop a short-term perspective that "leads them to believe the future is now," thereby producing an overemphasis on corporate objectives and short-run advantages (Madden, 1977, p. 60). Some characterize this process in terms of a great moral struggle between the individual and the "massed corporate hierarchy"—"a man can be crushed and beaten and forced into actions against which his ethical sense rebels" by a hierarchy "supreme in its power and a law unto itself" (Cook, 1966, p. 72). It is far more likely, however, that this process is subtle, and the individual, in the course of his work, gradually comes to identify with the main goals and ideology of the corporation: "If operative goals take on qualities of normative requirements for organizational behavior, and if these norms conflict with those of the legal order, then corporate crime may be indigenous to organizational processes" (Meier, 1975, p. 10).

It would be a mistake to imagine a scenario in which the corporation's directors or highest officers generate these pressures for the lower levels without being affected themselves. Like other social organizations, corporations have inherent socialization pressures that are passed on through the generations. Corporate executives assume roles into which they are duly socialized by the structure and nature of work and the status system, as are lower level employees. Socialization is therefore structural and cultural.

Executives are subject, in fact, to the same kinds of indoctrination into the corporate mind as are employees at lower levels—through their associations with others who play similar roles, through their training and education, and through their isolation from potentially countervailing influences (Henning, 1973, p. 158). Drucker (1972) noted that executives' contacts outside business tend to be restricted to persons of similar background if not those who work for the same organization. And the very insistence upon loyalty and the restriction of competing interests characteristic of the army is typical of corporations: "Hence executive life not only breeds a parochialism of the imagination comparable to the 'military mind' but places a considerable premium on it" (p. 81).

One does not have to picture a corporation composed of automatons marching to the same beat in order to understand how individuals as corporate actors could participate in activities that they might never consider outside the corporate environment.[2] Motivations besides the ones discussed here range from altruistic loyalty to the corporate good to outright self-interest. Many involved in illegal corporate activities regard their acquiescence and active participation as necessary in order to keep their jobs, although they may have no illusions about the illegal and immoral nature of their behavior. A former high-ranking General Motors executive, John Z. DeLorean, contended, for example, that the company knew about the safety problems of the Corvair before production began but failed to take remedial action: "Claims DeLorean: 'Charlie Chayne, vice president of engineering, along with his staff, took a very strong stand against the Corvair as an unsafe car long before it went on sale in 1959. He was not listened to but instead told in effect: "You're not a member of the team. Shut up, or go looking for another job"'" (*Time*, November 19, 1979, p. 85). The decisionmakers were "not immoral men," said DeLorean, but he claimed that they were operating in a business atmosphere in which all was reduced to costs, atmosphere in which approval was given to a product that the individuals acting alone would not have considered approving (Wright, 1979).

£xecutives' Rationalizations

A variety of justifications are available to those executives who are confronted with doubt or guilt about illegal or unethical behavior; these justifications allow them to neutralize the negative connotations of their behavior. In an examination of a famous case of business corruption and bribery in England, Chibnall and Saunders (1977) pointed out that an individual can fully understand the illegal nature of his actions but can justify them by citing the pervasiveness of such practices in the business world. There is considerable evidence that business executives believe that unethical practices are common. A *Harvard Business Review* survey found that four out of five executives maintained that at least some generally accepted practices in their industries were unethical, and when asked whether they thought that other executives would violate a code of ethics if they knew they would not be caught, four out of seven replied affirmatively (Baumhart, 1961). Studies made in 1976 by Uniroyal and a University of Georgia professor found that 70 percent of Uniroyal managers and 64 percent of a random sample of corporate managers perceived company pressure on personal ethics. "Most managers believed that their peers would not refuse orders to market off-standard and possibly dangerous products (although an even larger majority insisted they would personally reject such orders), and a majority thought young managers automatically go along with superiors to show loyalty" (Madden, 1977, p. 66). Confidential interviews with top officials, usually chief executive officers, of 57 of the largest U.S. corporations in 1975 indicated that they felt unethical behavior was widespread in industry and, for the most part, had to be accepted as part of daily business (Silk and Vogel, 1976). Business results and the survival of the corporation inevitably came before personal ethics: "If we wait until all businessmen are ethical before we start our sales job, we will never get started" (p. 228). Moreover, there was great reluctance to criticize other businessmen for illegal actions. Finally, the behavior was legitimized through the good intentions of the actors and through its consequences; that is, no one was actually harmed, the firm benefited, and customer needs were served.

The issue of morals and corporate conduct became a topic of discussion in 1979 when it was reported that a Harvard Business School professor, in his business decisionmaking course, trained students to misrepresent their positions in negotiations and other business dealings (*Wall Street Journal,* January 15, 1979). Students found that hiding certain facts, bluffing, and even outright lying got them a better deal and, in part, a better grade. The course was designed to teach budding businessmen to negotiate in the "real world," in which "lying"—or "strategic misrepresentation"—is resorted to in some cases. As the article in the *Wall Street Journal* commented, "It's a safe bet that in the course students will eventually get to practice what they learn." (According to surveys by the school, 14 percent of its alumni are presidents or chief executive officers of their firms, and 19 percent of the top three officers of all *Fortune* 500 companies are Harvard Business School graduates.)

● *C*orporate *D*efenses for *L*aw *V*iolations

The diverse defenses continually offered by corporations, their executives and counsel, business organizations, and trade and other journals, particularly the editorials in the prestigious *Wall Street Journal,* to explain corporate violations of law serve to justify illegal activity in a society that professes law obedience to be one of its highest ideals. In so rationalizing their behavior, however, corporations follow a general tendency in our society to obey laws selectively, that is, according to one's situational needs as determined by such factors as social class and occupation. Many businessmen, for example, firmly believe, and act accordingly, that the laws regulating securities and banking procedures, trade, labor arrangements, and environmental pollution are not as formally binding on individual decisionmakers as are burglary and robbery laws.

To a certain degree corporate executives are insulated from persons who might disagree with their beliefs (Sutherland, 1949, p. 247). As we have seen, they tend to associate almost exclusively with persons who are pro-business, politically conservative, and generally opposed to government regulation. Many of the beliefs held within the corporate world about laws and government are nourished in a climate in which there is a lack of consensus about the values society is trying to advance. On the one hand, people do not want to deplete natural resources too rapidly or to pollute the air, land, and water, but on the other, they want abundant consumer goods at the lowest possible prices. The question also arises as to how much future generations must be considered in planning the use of our natural resources: "Problems of this sort exist everywhere we look. Consider a drug that can benefit 99 percent of people who suffer from a disease but seriously injures 1 percent. Should it be banned from the market?" (Stone, 1975, p. 97).

Some maintain that laws affecting corporations often fail because the public does not regard the behavior to be regulated as "morally reprehensible" (Kadish, 1963, p. 436). Moreover, numerous beliefs of the corporate world help to neutralize government efforts to deter or to prevent violations and thus reduce the effectiveness of legal sanctions applied to corporations and their executives. It would of course be unfair to presume that everyone in top corporate management accepts these beliefs without question, but some were widely expressed by top executives of the largest corporations in confidential interviews done by Silk and Vogel (1976). From various sources the following beliefs have been identified as most significant;[3] in general, however, they lack validity or they are greatly exaggerated.

1. *All legal measures proposed constitute government interference with the free enterprise system.* Since we have had 200 years of prosperity under a capitalist system, the argument goes, we should not interfere with the system. This argument obviously disregards consumer protection, the protection of the environment, and the protection of free competition afforded by antitrust laws. In this connection one might mention Ralph Nader's often-quoted reply as a witness during a congressional hearing. When a senator insisted that Nader's criticism of the auto industry failed to recognize the industry's contribution to American society, he responded, "Do you give credit to a burglar because he doesn't burglarize 99 percent of the time?" (Geis, 1973, p. 183).

2. *Government regulations are unjustified because the additional costs of regulations and bureaucratic procedures cut heavily into profits.* This represents an effort to condemn the condemners by expressing contempt for government interference and law enforcement staffs. Compliance with federal regulations such as those of the Environmental Protection Agency (EPA), the Consumer Product Safety Commission (CPSC), and the Occupational Safety and Health Administration (OSHA) has been estimated to cost nearly $103 billion. (*Wall Street Journal,* December 1, 1978). As a result, it has been estimated, business must invest $10 billion in new capital spending each year merely to meet these regulations. According to Dow Chemical, compliance with federal regulations cost the company $147 million in 1975 and, a year later, $186 million, an increase of 27 percent. Dow reported that costs of federal regulations for 1976 constituted 50 percent of after-tax profits and 6 percent of sales. Many corporate cost estimates for compliance have been challenged as highly exaggerated. The National Association of Automobile Dealers publicly stated in 1979 that adoption of the proposed FTC rule requiring inspection and stricter disclosure of the condition of used cars would raise prices by hundreds of dollars. Yet research conducted under the

auspices of the Center for Public Representation for the congressional hearings indicated that a similar Wisconsin law increased the prices of automobiles by no more than $15, even adjusting for inflation (private conversations with Professor Gerald Thain, University of Wisconsin Law School). In fact, the differences between what corporations report as excessive regulatory costs to government agencies such as the EPA and the less glowing story, or none at all, that they report to their shareholders and the SEC became a subject of congressional interest and of Ralph Nader's Public Citizen group in 1980 (*Wall Street Journal,* May 6, 1980). According to the *Wall Street Journal* article, officials of the EPA and OSHA planned "to take a closer look at SEC filings so that they can assess more critically the cost estimates filed with their agency."

3. *Regulation is faulty because most government regulations are incomprehensible and too complex.* In addition, according to this argument, regulations are so numerous that no corporation could be well informed on all of them; for example, the steel industry is controlled by some 5,600 regulations involving 27 different federal agencies (Madden, 1977, p. 52). Even though they have existed for nearly a century,

> antitrust laws are seen as inconsistent, hypocritical, poorly defined, and rarely enforced. Although the interpretation of these laws is constantly evolving, many businessmen who violate the law are aware that they are taking a risk when they engage in certain actions. They test the limits of the law and try to keep "just inside an imaginary boundary thought to separate the condoned from the condemned." Price-fixing is a clear violation of the law which is regularly prosecuted by the Department of Justice's Antitrust Division, but even businessmen who are charged with this crime often claim that the law is excessively vague. (Conklin, 1977, p. 92)

Most regulations must be written in detail, however, in order to cover as many contingencies as possible; otherwise, they could not be enforced and they would not hold up in the courts. In any event, large corporations generally employ adequate legal counsel to interpret government regulations.

4. *Regulation is unnecessary because the matters being regulated are unimportant.* OSHA regulations have been a favorite subject for such attacks in recent years. The chairman of United States Steel, in an address on February 7, 1977, spoke about OSHA regulations that had just gone into effect.

These new requirements run from the ridiculous to the extreme. For example, the performance standard says that no employee can be exposed to more than 0.15 milligrams of particulates per cubic meter of air during an eight-hour period. And that 0.15 milligrams is roughly equivalent to an ounce of material dispersed in an air space twenty feet high and three football fields long. Other requirements call for collecting air samples at every coke battery—perhaps a minimum of 600 samples a month at our Clairton Works and 14,000 a year across our entire company . . . providing annual and semi-annual physical examinations for coke oven employees . . . supplying work clothes and laundering them every week . . . making employees take a shower before they go home . . . forbidding them from eating or using tobacco on the job . . . and like mothers of old, requiring them to wash their hands and faces before they eat their lunch. (Madden, 1977, pp. 52–53)

Although it is true that some rules may be overzealous, as also happens within a corporation itself, it is unreasonable to include in this category the vast majority of laws that regulate trusts, advertising, environmental pollution, taxes, and other important areas of corporate behavior. Syndicated economic columnist Sylvia Porter wrote in 1979, for example, that corporations in virtually all sectors of the economy are "fiercely defending" arrangements that keep prices high and restrain trade. She cited the following activities.

Prescription drug companies are in a last-ditch fight to preserve state laws that prevent pharmacists from selling lower-priced generic drugs instead of more expensive brand-name equivalents. The Federal Trade Commission along with the Department of Health, Education and Welfare are drawing up a model state law to encourage feasible drug substitution. Potential consumer savings: an estimated $70 million a year.

Industries ranging from blue jeans manufacturers to makers of footwear and audio components have been charged with fixing retail prices through a variety of means. The FTC, for instance, recently sued and obtained a consent order against Levi Strauss. The day the agency sued, Levi's were selling for $15–$17. Today, in many areas of the U.S., they sell for $10–$14. (*Wisconsin State Journal,* February 4, 1979)

5. There is little deliberate intent in corporate violations: many of them are errors of omission rather than commission, and many are mistakes. There is some truth to this claim but ample evidence has also been cited of highly concealed conspiracies in many antitrust cases and clear intent to violate in domestic and foreign illegal payments, as is the case with many other corporate violations.

6. *Other concerns in the same line of business are violating the law, and if the government cannot prevent this situation there is no reason why competing corporations should not also benefit from illegal behavior.* Obviously, the government lacks the resources to prosecute all violators; it must be selective. The general belief among businessmen that the "other fellow" is regularly violating the law with relative impunity does constitute a major support to those who do violate. A 1961 Harvard Business Review survey found that this belief was extraordinarily widespread (Baumhart, 1961).

7. *Although it is true, as in price-fixing cases, for example, that some corporate violations involve millions of dollars, the damage is so diffused among a large number of consumers that individually there is little loss.* In this sense corporate violations are not like ordinary crimes, but price fixing is theft regardless of what it is called. C. Wright Mills (1956) once wrote that "it is better, so the image runs, to take one dime from each of ten million people at the point of a corporation than $100,000 from each of ten banks at the point of a gun" (p. 95); Mills added that it is also safer. Geis (1973, p. 183) explained that although corporate crime is serious, it is less infuriating as well as less frightening to be victimized a little bit at a time over a long period than to be victimized all at once.

8. *If there is no increase in corporate profits a violation is not wrong.* According to this view, some corporate violations do not necessarily result in an increase in profit; in fact, some simply are efforts to prevent profit loss. The plumbing industry price-fixing conspirators used this argument as a defense. This defense views violations in terms of a corporation's right to exercise selective obedience to law. Actually, many violations do result in increased profits, and violations are often for this purpose.

9. *Corporations are actually owned by the average citizen so that the claims that big business can dominate American society and violate the law with impunity are false.* It is a fact that stock ownership of most corporations is widely dispersed. In 1970, for example, some 31 million persons owned some stock: the ownership of stocks, however, and therefore of corporations, is

heavily concentrated in a small group of institutions such as banks, insurance companies, and universities, and individuals. A few large corporations are principally owned by families like the DuPonts, Mellons, Rockefellers, Fords, Dukes, and Firestones. Moreover, as has been previously indicated, control of corporate activities remains largely in the hands of management, not stockholders.

10. *Violations are caused by economic necessity: they aim to protect the value of stock, to insure an adequate return for stockholders, and to protect the job security of employees by insuring the financial stability of the corporation.* This argument again represents the belief that laws can be selectively obeyed with impunity.

Sometimes indicted corporations will submit multiple defenses for their actions. In the folding carton price conspiracy, numerous arguments were presented to the court by various corporations for the reduction of their penalties. Among them were: (1) abysmal losses were jeopardizing the folding carton industry generally, and some corporations particularly; (2) a given corporation does not play a serious economic part in total industry sales; (3) some corporations had no record of antitrust cases brought against them; (4) corporate management had changed since the violations had occurred; and (5) a new antitrust compliance program was in effect and determined efforts were being made to follow it. But, as the government contended, "Neither ruinous competition, competitive evils, nor good intentions or motives of the parties constitute any legal excuse for such agreement. . . . Profitability is irrelevant to the determination of guilt or innocence in a price-fixing case."

We have seen how both the internal and external environments of the corporation often facilitate the use of illegal behavior. The culture of the corporation is also likely to furnish a set of facilitating beliefs or rationale— either in defense of deviant acts or as charges against the propriety of government regulation. Clearly, however, the corporate record does not warrant placing the onus for illegal and unethical behavior on the laws. In view of the tremendous potential for harm carried by these massive, complex organizations, special measures of social control are necessary. . . .

Endnotes

[1] Illegal telephone calls between corporate executives were frequent. As one conspirator put it concerning price increases of cartons sold to the frozen food industry, "If there was a need for an increase he would call the others, see if [the] . . .

percentage increase that he proposed was acceptable to them and if it was, then all the companies would move in the general area of the same percentage."

[2]"Some may even find covert activity exciting, as noted in the case of Equity Funding. In this environment of fun, excitement, and do-as-you're-told corporate loyalty, the law's threats are simply no guarantee that people are going to comply. Indeed, what is worse, I have a strong suspicion—shared by others who have represented corporate clients in their tangled affairs—that being on the edge of the law can even lend a tingle of 007 intrigue to the life of middle-level corporate operatives" (Stone, 1975, p. 69).

[3]Some of these beliefs are from Silk and Vogel and some are from business journal editorials and statements of business executives; others were expressed in interviews with government enforcement officials questioned about the explanations given by corporate counsels and others for a corporation's law violations. Irving Kristol (1978), an influential contributor to the *Wall Street Journal*, offered several of these defenses of corporate behavior, although, in fairness, he at times somewhat tempered them.

References

Baumhart, Raymond C. (1961). "How Ethical Are Businessmen?" *Harvard Business Review* 39 (July–August):5–176.

Brenner, S. N., and E. A. Molander (1977). "Is the Ethics of Business Changing?" *Harvard Business Review* 55(January–February):59–70.

Carey, James T. (1978). *Introduction to Criminology*. Englewood Cliffs: Prentice-Hall.

Chibnall, S., and P. Saunders (1977). "Worlds Apart: Notes on the Social Reality of Corruption." *British Journal of Sociology* 28(June):138–153.

Clark, John P., and Richard Hollinger (1977). "On the Feasibility of Empirical Studies of White-Collar Crime," in Robert F. Meier (ed.), *Theory in Criminology: Contemporary Views*. Beverly Hills: Sage.

Conklin, John E. (1977). *Illegal but Not Criminal: Business Crime in America*. Englewood Cliffs: Prentice-Hall.

Cook, Fred J. (1966). *The Corrupted Land: The Social Morality of Modern America*. New York: Macmillan.

Cressey, Donald R. (1976). "Restraint of Trade, Recidivism, and Delinquent Neighborhoods." In James F. Short, Jr. (ed.), *Delinquency, Crime, and Society*. Chicago: University of Chicago Press.

Drucker, Peter F. (1972). *Concept of the Corporation*. Revised edition. New York: Mentor.

Geis, Gilbert (1967). "White Collar Crime: The Heavy Electrical Equipment Antitrust Cases of 1961." In Marshall B. Clinard and Richard Quinney (eds.), *Criminal Behavior Systems: A Typology*. New York: Holt, Rinehart & Winston.

———. (1973). " Deterring Corporate Crime." In Ralph Nader and Mark J. Green (eds.), *Corporate Power in America*. New York: Grossman.

Goodman, Walter (1963). *All Honorable Men: Corruption and Compromise in American Life*. Boston: Little, Brown.

Hay, George, and Daniel Kelley (1974). "An Empirical Survey of Price-fixing Conspiracies." *Journal of Law and Economics* 17(April):13–39.

Henning, Joel F. (1973). "Corporate Social Responsibility: Shell Game for the Seventies?" In Ralph Nader and Mark J. Green (eds.), *Corporate Power in America*. New York: Grossman.

Herling, John (1962). *The Great Price Conspiracy: The Story of the Antitrust Violations in the Electrical Industry*. Washington, D.C.: Luce.

Howton, F. W. (1%9). *Functionaries*. Chicago: Quadrangle.

Kadish, Sanford H. (1963). "Some Observations on the Use of Criminal Sanctions in Enforcing Economic Regulations." *University of Chicago Law Review* 30(Spring):423–449.

Lane, Robert E. (1953). "Why Businessmen Violate the Law." *Journal of Criminal Law, Criminology, and Police Science* 44(July):151–165. Reprinted in Gilbert Geis and Robert F. Meier (eds.), *White-collar Crime: Offenses in Business, Politics, and the Professions*. Revised edition. New York: Free Press.

Madden, Carl (1977). "Forces which Influence Ethical Behavior." In Clarence Walton (ed.), *The Ethics of Corporate Conduct*. Englewood Cliffs: Prentice-Hall.

March, J., and H. Simon (1958). *Organizations*. New York: Wiley.

Margolis, D. R. (1979). *The Managers: Corporate Life in America*. New York: Morrow.

Meier, Robert F. (1975). "Corporate Crime as Organizational Behavior." Address presented at the American Society of Criminology meeting, November.

Mills, C. Wright (1956). *The Power Elite*. New York: Oxford University Press.

Perrow, Charles (1972). *Complex Organizations: A Critical Essay*. Chicago: Scott, Foresman.

Riedel, Marc (1968). "Corporate Crime and Interfirm Organization: A Study of Penalized Sherman Act Violations." *Graduate Sociology Club Journal* 8:74–97.

Schrager, Laura S., and James R. Short, Jr. (1978). "Toward a Sociology of Organizational Crime." *Social Problems* 25(No. 4):407–419.

Shaplen, Robert (1978). "Annals of Crime: The Lockheed Incident." *New Yorker* (January 23):48–74, (January 30):78–91.

Silk, L. Howard, and David Vogel (1976). *Ethics and Profits: The Crisis of Confidence in American Business.* New York: Simon and Schuster.

Stone, Christopher (1975). *Where the Law Ends: The Social Control of Corporate Behavior.* New York: Harper & Row.

Sutherland, Edwin H. (1949). *White Collar Crime.* New York: Holt.

Tiedemann, Klaus (1974). *Subventions: Kriminalität in der Bundesrepublik.* Reinbek bei Hamburg: Rowohlt.

Woodmansee, John (1975). *The World of a Giant Corporation: A Report from the GE Project.* Seattle: North Country.

Wright, J. Patrick (1979). *On a Clear Day You Can See G.M.* Detroit: Wright Enterprises.

◉ ◉ ◉

Questions

1. What are some examples of internal cultural factors? What are some examples of external economic factors? How are these factors related?

2. Explain the relationship between cultural norms of corporations and various ethical and legal actions that corporations and executives take.

3. How does a corporation ensure that its members learn the necessary values, norms, rationalizations, and techniques to ensure that employees make the corporation's well-being a priority?

4. How do executives justify their actions, especially unethical or illegal ones?

5. Of the various beliefs regarding the defensibility of corporate crime, which seems most valid to you? Which of these beliefs strike you as primarily myth?

6. Corporate criminal rationalizations would also apply to what other forms of deviant or criminal behavior?

7. After reading this article, what changes do you think would have to occur to reduce the incidence of corporate crime?

Fighting a War Against Terrorism, at Home and Abroad

DAVID COLE AND JAMES X. DEMPSEY

The terrorist attacks of September 11, 2001 altered life in the United States in many ways. In an effort to enhance domestic security against terrorism, the government immediately passed the USA PATRIOT Act (USAPA). In this provocative chapter, however, David Cole and James Dempsey argue that provisions in the USAPA fundamentally violate individual liberties that are guaranteed in the U.S. Constitution. Among the violations Cole and Dempsey cite are insufficient due process, inappropriate searches and access to information, and ethnic profiling.

*W*hen terrorists hijacked four airplanes on a crisp Tuesday morning in September 2001, turning them into devastating explosives directed at the World Trade Center, the Pentagon, and a third location still unknown, they not only killed thousands of innocent civilians in the most brutal act of terrorism mankind has yet perpetrated, but they also threatened to change the fabric of American life. Before September 11, we had been relatively free of foreign attacks on our soil, at least since Pearl Harbor. After September 11, we all confront a new vulnerability. Before September 11, terrorists had done many unspeakable things, but never had they committed an act so heinous and so devastating. The attacks of September 11 made the unthinkable gruesomely real. The anthrax scare that followed in the ensuing weeks only exacerbated the threat.

In the wake of these attacks, calls for new security measures are undoubtedly warranted, particularly in light of the ongoing threats that the country faces as it fights a war against terrorism, and specifically against

Osama bin Laden and his al Qaeda network. Airport security has been a particular focus, but to stop there would fail to address the threat that the next attack will likely take a very different form. We must improve all of our defenses against terrorism, by improving intelligence and law enforcement capabilities. The fact that the U.S. intelligence agencies apparently had no foreknowledge of the September 11 attacks points to a failure of intelligence with massive consequences.

But in responding to the threat of terrorism, we must not trample upon the very freedoms that we are fighting for. Nothing tests our commitments to principle like fear and terror. Precisely because the terrorists violated every principle of civilized society and human dignity, we must maintain our commitment to principle as we fashion a response.

Three principles in particular should guide our response. First, we should not overreact in a time of fear, a mistake we have made all too often in the past. Second, we should not sacrifice the bedrock foundations of our constitutional democracy—political freedom, due process, and equal treatment—absent compelling showings of necessity. And third, in balancing liberty and security, we should not trade a vulnerable minority's liberties, namely the liberties of immigrants in general or Arab and Muslim immigrants in particular, in a misguided effort to obtain security for the rest of us.

Unfortunately, the immediate response to the events of September 11 has violated all three principles. Some measures in the anti-terrorism legislation enacted hastily in October 2001 were undoubtedly justified—in particular those that seek to reduce barriers to coordination between law enforcement and intelligence in terrorism investigations, to shore up airport security, border control and visa review procedures, and to improve controls over biochemical toxins. But in several critical areas, Congress has given the Executive Branch (and the Executive Branch has claimed for itself) broad new powers that go far beyond the fight against terrorism, and that infringe on fundamental liberties.

The government has detained over 1,200 persons in connection with its investigation of the attacks of September 11, yet as of late December only one had been charged with any involvement in the crimes under investigation, and the government claims that only ten or twelve of the detained are members of al Qaeda, the organization said to be responsible for the attacks. The vast majority are being held on routine immigration charges under unprecedented secrecy. The government will not disclose most of their names, their trials are held in secret, and their cases are not listed on any public docket.

At the same time, ethnic profiling is being broadly engaged in, and widely defended as reasonable. The Justice Department has assumed the authority to listen in on attorney-client communications without a judge's approval and is considering relaxing the limits on FBI spying that were created in the wake of COINTELPRO. And President Bush has authorized the use of military tribunals, not only against al Qaeda members captured abroad, but against any of the 20 million noncitizens residing among us whom the President accuses of engaging in "international terrorism" or of harboring someone who has so engaged. In such tribunals, the military would be prosecutor, judge, jury and executioner, the trials could be held in secret, classified evidence could be used against the defendant without affording him an opportunity to confront it, and there would be no judicial review. And these responses mark only the first three months of the new "war on terrorism." Already, we fear, the government has overreacted in a time of fear, assuming powers in the name of fighting terrorism that are in no way limited to counterterrorist investigations. It has not shown that the new powers it has asserted are necessary to fight terrorism. And it has targeted the lion's share of its infringements on liberty at immigrants, and particularly Arab and Muslim immigrants.

❧ Repeating History

Before turning to the specifics of the post-September 11 response, it is worth reviewing a little history, and assessing what powers government already has in the fight against terrorism. Both assessments are critical to asking whether the government's response to September 11 is measured and likely to be effective.

This is not the first time our nation has responded to fear by targeting immigrants and treating them as suspect because of their group identities rather than their individual conduct. In World War I, we imprisoned dissidents for merely speaking out against the war, most of them immigrants. In 1919, the federal government responded to a politically motivated bombing of Attorney General A. Mitchell Palmer's home in Washington, DC by rounding up more than 6,000 suspected immigrants in 33 cities across the country—not for their part in the bombings, but for their political affiliations. They were detained in overcrowded "bull pens" and beaten into signing confessions. Many of those arrested turned out to be citizens. In the end, 556 immigrants were deported, but for their political affiliations, not for their part in the bombings.

In World War II, we interned 110,000 persons, over two-thirds of whom were citizens of the United States, not because of individualized determinations that they posed a threat to national security or the war effort, but solely for their Japanese ancestry. And in the fight against Communism, which reached its height in the McCarthy era, we made it a crime even to be a member of the Communist Party, and passed the McCarran-Walter Act, which authorized the government to keep out and expel noncitizens who advocated Communism or other proscribed ideas, or who belonged to the Communist Party or other groups that advocated proscribed ideas. As noted above, under the McCarran-Walter Act, the United States denied visas to famous writers and artists, as well as to Nino Pasti, former Deputy Commander of NATO, simply because he was coming to speak against the deployment of nuclear cruise missiles. And as the preceding chapters of this book have illustrated, misguided enforcement directed at political dissidents rather than criminals has continued into the present day.

All of these past responses are now seen as mistakes. Yet while the post-September 11 response does not yet match these historical overreactions, it nonetheless features some of the same mistakes of principle—in particular, targeting vulnerable groups not for illegal conduct, but for political speech, political activity, or group identity, and relying on broad investigatory sweeps rather than focusing on objective individualized suspicion. The present story begins with the awkwardly titled "United and Strengthening America by Providing Appropriate Tools Required to Intercept and Obstruct Terrorism Act of 2001"[1]—the PATRIOT Act for short—enacted within six weeks of the fateful attacks.

❧ The Patriot Act

In legislative time, Congress enacted the PATRIOT Act virtually overnight. Attorney General John Ashcroft, its principal proponent, exerted extraordinary pressure, essentially threatening Congress that the blood of the victims of future terrorist attacks would be on its hands if it did not swiftly enact the Administration's proposals. The bill was never the subject of a Committee debate or mark-up in the Senate. There was a truncated process in the House, which heard no official testimony from opponents of the bill but at least held a full Committee mark-up. But the result of that process was put aside by the Administration and the House leadership and never brought to a vote in the full House. Instead, after three weeks of behind-the-scenes discussions between a few Senators and the Administration, a bill was introduced in the Senate on October 5 that included essentially all of the Administration's proposals. That bill passed the Senate on October 11, following a brief debate that made it clear that even supporters of the legislation had not read it and did not understand its provisions. The next day, a slightly different bill was introduced in the House, and was taken up and passed the same day under a procedure barring the offering of any amendments. It is virtually certain that not a single member of the House read the bill for which he or she voted. Differences between the two bills were reconciled without the normal convening of a conference committee. The President signed the bill into law on October 26.

Some measures in the omnibus act make sense. These include provisions ensuring adequate personnel on the northern border, some provisions strengthening the laws on money laundering, some provisions intended to break down institutional barriers that had limited the sharing of information between law enforcement agencies and intelligence agencies, and provisions intended to improve the processing of visas. (Making these things actually work, however, is largely beyond Congress's control.) Some of the expanded electronic surveillance provisions would also have made sense had they included appropriate limitations and judicial controls.

But in many respects, the PATRIOT Act reflects an overreaction all too typical in American history. It casts a cloak of secrecy over the exercise of government power by removing limitations and judicial controls on investigative authorities, and short-circuits procedures designed to protect the innocent and punish the guilty. It violates core constitutional principles, rendering immigrants deportable for their political association and excludable for pure speech. It fundamentally alters the power of the FBI and the role of the CIA within the United States, without adequate checks to protect against abuses. And by reserving its harshest measures for immigrants, measures that in the immediately foreseeable future will be directed predominantly at Arab and Muslim immigrants, it sacrifices commitments to equality by trading a minority group's liberty for the majority's purported security—a trade that will in all likelihood be ineffective. Painting with a broad brush is simply not a good law enforcement tool; it wastes resources on innocents and alienates communities, making it all the more difficult for law enforcement to distinguish the true threats from the innocent bystanders.

The PATRIOT Act: (1) imposes guilt by association on immigrants, extending the reach of that philosophy beyond the 1996 Act; (2) authorizes executive detention on mere suspicion that an immigrant has at some point engaged in a violent crime or provided humanitarian aid to a proscribed organization; (3) authorized the government to deny entry to aliens for pure speech, resurrecting yet another long-interred relic of the McCarthy era; (4) expands the government's authority to conduct criminal searches and wiretaps without first showing probable cause that the subject is engaged in criminal activity; (5) authorizes secret searches in cases having nothing to do with terrorism; (6) gives the Central Intelligence Agency access to the awesome power of criminal grand juries; and (7) reduces judicial oversight of intrusive information-gathering powers and expands the scope of FBI access to a wide range of records, essentially sanctioning fishing expeditions.

❧ *Guilt* by *Association*

Building on the 1996 Antiterrorism Act, the PATRIOT Act expands guilt by association, a McCarthy-era philosophy which the Supreme Court has condemned as "alien to the traditions of a free society and the First Amendment itself,"[2] but which has been making a strong comeback in recent years under the guise of cutting off funding for terrorism. Under the immigration law that existed before September 11, aliens were deportable for engaging in or supporting terrorist *activity*. The PATRIOT Act makes aliens deportable for wholly innocent associational activity with a "terrorist organization," irrespective of any nexus between the alien's associational conduct and any act of violence, much less terrorism.[3] The new law defines "terrorist activity" to include virtually any use or threat to use violence, and defines "terrorist organization" as any group of two or more persons that has used or threatened to use violence. Thus, the Act's proscription on associational activity potentially encompasses every organization that has ever been involved in a civil war or a crime of violence, from a pro-life group that once threatened workers at an abortion clinic, to the African National Congress, the Irish Republican Army, or the Northern Alliance in Afghanistan.

Like the criminal "material support" provisions of the 1996 Antiterrorism Act, the new law contains no requirement that the alien's support have any connection whatsoever to a designated organization's violent activity. Thus, an alien who sent coloring books to a day-care center run by a designated organization would apparently be deportable as a terrorist, even if she could show that the coloring books were used only by 3-year olds. Indeed, the law apparently extends even to those who seek to support a group in the interest of *countering* terrorism. Thus, an immigrant who offered his services in peace negotiating to the IRA in the hope of furthering the peace process in Great Britain and forestalling further violence could be deported as a terrorist if the Secretary of State chose to designate the Irish Republican Army (IRA) as terrorist.

The PATRIOT Act expands the "guilt by association" provisions of the 1996 Antiterrorism Act in several ways. It makes associational support a deportable offense, whereas the 1996 Act imposed criminal penalties. Unlike the 1996 Act, the new law makes no exception even for medicine or religious materials. And it expands the government's authority to blacklist groups, by permitting the designation of domestic groups, requiring no notice to Congress, and providing no opportunity for groups to challenge their designation.

Some argue that the threat from terrorist organizations abroad, and the fungibility of money and support, require us to compromise the constitutional principle that prohibits guilt by association. But the principle prohibiting guilt by association was developed in the crucible of a battle against what appeared to be an even more formidable foe—the Communist Party, an organization that Congress found to be, and the Supreme Court accepted as, a foreign-dominated organization that used sabotage and terrorism for the purpose of overthrowing the United States by force and violence.[4] If association with such an organization deserves protection, surely association with much less powerful groups that have threatened or used some violence at some point deserves similar protection.

The fungibility argument rests on a faulty factual assumption. It maintains that because money is fungible, even a donation of blankets to a hospital will free up resources that will then be devoted to terrorism. But this argument assumes that a group engaged in a political struggle that uses both legal and illegal ends will necessarily devote every marginal dollar to its illegal ends. On this assumption, every dollar donated to the African National Congress (ANC) for its nonviolent opposition to apartheid freed up a dollar that the ANC would then spend on violent, terrorist ends. While some groups may be so committed to violence that all else is only a front for terrorism, that is not likely to be true for most organizations that use violence. For most groups, violence is but one means to a political end. This is not to excuse the violence in any way, but to insist that one must distinguish between a group's lawful and unlawful activities.

Consider Hamas, for example, which has been designated as a terrorist group. The Israeli government itself estimates that Hamas devotes 95 percent of its resources to legal social service activity and only 5 percent to violent or military activity. For that reason the State Department in 1994 opposed making membership in Hamas a ground for denying visas. If Hamas sought to devote every marginal dollar to terror, one would expect to see the distribution between illegal and legal activities reversed. Should a person who sends blankets or medicine to a Hamas-run hospital be condemned as a terrorist? Is it really plausible that every blanket provided will lead to more money being spent on terrorist attacks? If it could be shown that a group's "legitimate" activities were a cover for its illegal activities, action against its legitimate enterprises would be justified, just as federal law allows the government to seize legitimate businesses if it can show that they are fronts for organized crime. But short of such a showing, we can and should distinguish between lawful and unlawful activities.

The fungibility argument also proves too much as a legal matter. The Supreme Court has repeatedly struck down laws that penalized association with the Communist Party absent proof that the individual specifically intended to further the group's illegal ends. If the provision of material support to a group were somehow different, then all of the anti-Communist measures declared invalid by the Supreme Court could have simply been rewritten to hinge punishment on the payment of dues, the volunteering of time, or any of the other material manifestations of political association. The right of association, in other words, would be left a meaningless formality.

◉ Detention vs. Due Process

The PATRIOT Act gives the Attorney General unprecedented power to lock up any immigrant that he certifies as a "suspected terrorist."[5] Such persons are subject to potentially indefinite detention. While "suspected terrorists" may sound like a class that should be locked up, there are several problems with this measure. It applies to "suspected" terrorists, not "proved" terrorists. It allows the Attorney General to lock up individuals where he has "reasonable grounds to believe" that they have committed any of a wide range of immigration violations, without a hearing to determine whether they actually pose any real threat. And the legislation defines "terrorist activity" so expansively that it includes virtually every immigrant who is suspected of being involved in a barroom brawl or domestic dispute, as well as aliens who have never committed an act of violence in their lives, and whose only "crime" is to have provided humanitarian aid to an organization disfavored by the government. The law further provides that such persons may be detained indefinitely, even if they are "granted relief from removal," and therefore have a legal right to remain here permanently. The INS has never before had power to detain persons that it has no authority to expel, yet this law gives it exactly that.

To appreciate the extraordinary breadth of this unprecedented power, one must consider that under pre-existing law, the INS already had authority to detain any alien in deportation or exclusion proceedings who presented either a threat to national security or a risk of flight. Thus, what the new legislation adds is the authority to detain aliens who do *not* pose a current danger or flight risk, and who are *not* removable because they are entitled to asylum or some other form of relief.

This provision raises several constitutional concerns. First, it permits preventive detention of persons who pose no threat to national security or risk of flight. The Supreme Court has upheld preventive detention of accused criminals, but only where there is a specific reason for the detention— namely, that they pose a danger to others or a risk of flight.[6] Under the PATRIOT Act, however, if the Attorney General says that he has reasonable grounds to believe that an alien has threatened to use a weapon, the alien is presumptively detained, whether or not he poses any continuing threat to anyone. Preventive detention without a showing that the alien needs to be detained violates due process.

Second, the legislation allows the government to detain aliens indefinitely, *even where the alien has prevailed in his removal proceedings.* But once an alien has prevailed in his removal proceeding, and has been granted relief from removal, he has a legal right to remain here. At that point, the INS has no legitimate reason to keep him in jail. Detaining such a person would be akin to keeping a prisoner locked up even after he has been pardoned for all of the charges against him. The INS's authority to detain has always been incidental to its authority to deport, yet under this provision, the INS would have freestanding authority to detain indefinitely persons never convicted of a crime and legally residing here.[7]

Third, the evidentiary standard for detention raises serious constitutional concerns. It is important to keep in mind that the law authorizes potentially *indefinite* detention. That is a far more severe deprivation of liberty than holding a person for interrogation or trial. Yet the INS has in litigation argued that the "reasonable grounds to believe" standard now required for detention is essentially equivalent to the "reasonable suspicion" required for a brief stop and frisk under the Fourth Amendment. But if "reasonable suspicion" does not even authorize a full arrest in criminal law enforcement, it surely cannot authorize indefinite detention in immigration law enforcement.

Fourth, and most importantly, it is critical to the constitutionality of any detention provision that the government bear the burden of justifying any preventive detention promptly in a scrupulously fair proceeding. Few intrusions on liberty are more severe than being locked up. Yet the PATRIOT Act imposes no affirmative burden of proof on the government, provides for no hearing, and authorizes detention on the Attorney General's say-so. The only "process" the alien is afforded is the right to go to federal court and sue the government for its actions. But due process requires that the agency seeking to deprive a person of his liberty afford him a fair procedure in which to be heard; the availability of a lawsuit after the fact is not sufficient.

Finally, the PATRIOT Act permits detention of certified aliens for up to seven days without the filing of any charges. Yet the Supreme Court has ruled in the criminal setting that charges must be filed within 48 hours except in the most extraordinary circumstances.[8] The new law extends blanket authority to detain for seven days on mere certification that an alien was at one time involved in a barroom brawl. Such over-broad authority does not meet the Supreme Court's requirement that any preventive detention authority be accompanied by heightened procedural protections and narrowly drawn laws.[9]

◉ Ideological Exclusion

The PATRIOT Act also expands ideological exclusion, authorizing the government to deny entry to aliens for pure speech.[10] It excludes aliens who "endorse or espouse terrorist activity," or who "persuade others to support terrorist activity or a terrorist organization," if the Secretary of State determines that such speech undermines U.S. efforts to combat terrorism. It also excludes aliens who are representatives of groups that "endorse acts of terrorist activity" in ways that similarly undermine U.S. efforts to combat terrorism.

While the Supreme Court has long ruled that aliens outside our borders—in contrast to aliens living among us—have no constitutional rights, such ideological exclusions nonetheless raise constitutional concerns. The First Amendment is designed to protect a wide-open and robust public debate, and if our government can keep out persons who espouse disfavored ideas, our ability as Americans to hear and consider those ideas will be diminished. More broadly, excluding people for their ideas is contrary to the spirit of freedom for which the United States stands. It was for that reason that Congress repealed all such grounds in the Immigration and Nationality Act in 1990, after years of embarrassing politically-motivated visa denials. We are a strong enough country, and our resolve against terrorism is strong enough, to make such censorship wholly unnecessary. Yet we have now returned to the much-criticized ways of the McCarran-Walter Act, targeting people not for their acts but for their words.

❧ Secret Searches without Criminal Probable Cause

The PATRIOT Act also makes many changes in the rules that govern the collection and sharing of information by law enforcement and intelligence agencies. The Administration argued that it needed broader search and seizure authority, and needed to be able to share the information it gained through criminal investigations more broadly with intelligence agencies. While some of the Administration's criticisms about existing law made sense, the changes adopted in most instances go far beyond what was needed to respond to terrorism. In many instances, the changes are not limited to terrorist investigations at all, but apply across the board to all criminal investigations. And while Congress imposed a four-year sunset on some of the changes, permitting reevaluation in light of their implementation, many of the surveillance and information-gathering provisions are permanent. The changes to the rules governing surveillance, information-gathering, and intelligence-sharing potentially affect all citizens, although their principal targets, at least initially, are likely to be Arab and Muslim immigrants.

One of the most significant changes has the effect of authorizing warrants for secret searches (so-called black bag jobs) and wiretaps in criminal investigations without probable cause of criminal conduct.[11] The Fourth Amendment generally permits the government to conduct searches or wiretaps only where it has probable cause to believe that an individual is engaged in criminal activity or that evidence of a crime will be found. But the PATRIOT Act allows the government to evade that requirement wherever it says that its investigation also has a significant foreign intelligence purpose.

The PATRIOT Act does this by amending the Foreign Intelligence Surveillance Act (FISA).[12] FISA creates a limited exception to the probable cause rule for foreign intelligence gathering. It authorizes the FBI to conduct electronic surveillance and secret physical searches without a criminal predicate, on the theory that foreign intelligence gathering is not designed to detect crimes but to gather information about foreign agents. Accordingly, it authorizes warrants not on a showing of probable criminal conduct, but on a showing that the target of the intrusion is an "agent of a foreign power." "Agent" is defined broadly to include any member of a foreign organization, so that a member of Amnesty International could be an "agent." If the suspected agent of a foreign power is a U.S. citizen or permanent resident alien, the government is not allowed to base its warrant on First Amendment-protected activities, but even as to citizens the standard is looser than that applicable to ordinary wiretaps in criminal cases. The First Amendment limit does not apply to noncitizens here on temporary visas.

Searches and wiretaps under FISA may be kept secret from the target, in most cases forever. (Targets of criminal searches and wiretaps, by contrast, must be notified eventually of the search.) Under FISA, a person is notified of surveillance only if he or she is later prosecuted using the evidence seized. Even then, defendants have little opportunity to challenge the validity of the search, for they are not provided the affidavit that served as the basis for the surveillance. Where individuals are not prosecuted—those cases where the likelihood of government overreaching is greatest—notice is never provided, and therefore the search cannot be challenged.

The extraordinary authority provided by FISA was justified on the ground that intelligence gathering is different from criminal law enforcement, and that the FISA authority would not be used for the purpose of investigating crime. Congress recognized, however, that evidence of crimes might be obtained during foreign intelligence gathering—espionage, for example, is a crime—and therefore allowed the use of FISA evidence in criminal cases. But in order to obtain a FISA warrant, the "primary purpose" of the investigation had to be the collection of foreign intelligence, *not* criminal law enforcement. Otherwise, the statute would serve as an end-run around the probable cause requirements of the criminal wiretap statute.

In the PATRIOT Act, Congress eliminated the primary purpose test, amending FISA to allow wiretaps and physical searches without probable cause in criminal investigations so long as "a significant purpose" of the intrusion is to collect foreign intelligence. The express justification for this amendment was to permit the government to initiate wiretaps under FISA's lower standard where the investigation's primary purpose was to collect criminal evidence. The potential scope of this loophole is enormous. For example, in an investigation of foreign contributions to a US political campaign, the Justice Department could conduct a criminal investigation involving FBI wiretapping and secret searches without probable cause of criminal conduct. If it did not initiate a prosecution, the government would never need to notify the politician whose phones were tapped or offices were searched. Yet, as will be detailed later, the FBI could share that information with the CIA, the National Security Council staff, and the Pentagon. And as this example shows, this extraordinary expansion of surveillance authority is in no way limited to the investigation of terrorism, but applies to any federal criminal investigation in which the government can also assert a "significant" foreign intelligence interest.

❧ "Sneak and Peek" Searches

Another provision of the PATRIOT Act expansively alters the rules that govern searches in ordinary criminal invesdgations. Criminal searches have long been subject to the "knock and announce" rule, under which law enforcement officers executing a search warrant must generally knock on the door of the place to be searched and give notice to the owner that the search is to be conducted. The purpose of this longstanding requirement has been to allow owners to ensure that the warrant is being executed at the proper address, to monitor the scope of the search to ensure that it does not extend beyond the terms of the warrant, and in the case of a prolonged search, to seek judicial intervention to narrow the scope of the search.

The PATRIOT Act effectively threw out this concept.[13] It allows the FBI to delay notification of searches whenever notification would "seriously jeopardize" an investigation. Government officials could almost always claim that notice would jeopardize the investigation, and thus this exception to the "knock and announce" rule threatens to swallow the rule. Under a "sneak and peek" warrant, FBI agents can secretly enter an apartment or home while the owner is asleep or away, take, alter or copy things, and not tell the owner that they were there for a "reasonable period thereafter." The Justice Department has stated in its *Field Guidance on New Authorities (Redacted) Enacted in the 1002 Anti-Terrorism Legislation* that 90 days could be a "reasonable period."[14]

Instead of crafting specific standards for such searches, Congress merely incorporated by reference a delayed notice provision governing the reading of stored e-mail, a less intrusive search. And the provision is not limited to terrorism cases, but applies to any federal crime, from drug cases to giving false information on a student loan application. Moreover, it is not subject to the 4-year "sunset" provision, but marks a permanent change. Thus, in this instance, the Administration used the emergency atmosphere generated by the September 11 attacks to make a permanent, fundamental change in law enforcement procedures having nothing to do with terrorism.

❧ Eliminating Barriers between Law Enforcement and Intelligence

One of the purposes of the PATRIOT Act was to promote the sharing of information between law enforcement agencies and intelligence agencies. That goal is not illegitimate. Many experts suggested that one of the reasons for our failure to learn about the September 11 plot before the damage was done was that the many federal agencies that engage in intelligence and law enforcement did not communicate among themselves very effectively. One reason for this, and probably the most difficult to address, is the turf wars that large bureaucracies inevitably engender. But another reason consisted of legal barriers to the sharing of certain information. The PATRIOT Act did nothing to address the first problem, but did seek to address the second. However, in doing so Congress may well have overcompensated, creating the risk that intelligence agencies such as the CIA will now have substantial access to domestic criminal law investigatory tools. And history suggests that when the CIA gets involved in domestic activity, abuses are likely to follow. The agency is simply not trained in adhering to domestic legal limits on its conduct, because its principal field of operation is espionage overseas, where domestic rules do not apply. The PATRIOT Act allows law enforcement officials to share with the CIA the fruits of its grand jury investigations, its wiretaps, and any other information it collects if it constitutes "foreign intelligence." These changes give the CIA and other intelligence agencies a much greater domestic role, while leaving them shrouded in secrecy and largely immune to judicial or public oversight.

When the Central Intelligence Agency was created in 1947, Congress explicitly said that the Agency was to have no subpoena or domestic police powers.[15] Congress did not want this secret intelligence agency engaged in domestic security activities. Instead, the CIA's operations were intended to be directed overseas, focused on foreign nationals, in the world of spy-versus-spy and relations between states, where the criminal law was largely inapplicable. The information the CIA secretly collected was intended to inform the President in carrying out foreign affairs and national defense, not to be used to arrest people or prosecute crimes. The secrecy with which the CIA operated—collection activities could go on for years, even decades, without being publicly revealed—was fundamentally incompatible with the criminal justice system, where investigations must have a clear criminal objective, and the information collected and the means by which it is acquired must in most cases ultimately be shared with the accused and tested in open court.

Since the CIA was not supposed to engage in law enforcement, and since its agents were not supposed to appear in court, the CIA was not granted law enforcement powers. Those law enforcement powers are awesome—in some ways more awesome than the powers of the intelligence agencies—but they are subject to checks and balances unknown to the world of foreign espionage.

One of the most powerful tools of the criminal justice system is the grand jury—an institution originally designed to protect against prosecutorial abuse but since turned into an investigative tool. The grand jury can compel anyone to testify before it under oath. Anyone who refuses to testify can be sent to jail. A witness who lies can be prosecuted for perjury. The grand jury can compel anyone with any record or tangible thing to produce it, irrespective of probable cause, again with the threat of jail time for those who refuse. Neither the Fourth nor the Fifth Amendment protects against the compelled disclosure of records. Witnesses before the grand jury are not entitled to have a lawyer with them in the room while they testify. In practice, the grand jury operates as the arm of the prosecutor who convenes it. While technically subject to the oversight of a judge, the prosecutor issues subpoenas without the prior approval of the judge. In fact, the subpoenas are often issued in blank to FBI agents, who fill them in, serve them, and collect the records. The judge usually never sees what is turned over. Much of it is never shown to the grand jurors.

These powers are subject, however, to two important controls: anything from the grand jury that the government uses in a criminal case must satisfy the full panoply of due process protections, while anything not used in open court can be disclosed only for law enforcement purposes and otherwise must be kept secret.[16] The rules of due process ensure that evidence collected by the grand jury cannot be used against a person without the full vetting guaranteed by the confrontation clause, and must ultimately satisfy the government's burden of proof beyond a reasonable doubt. The rule of grand jury secrecy has two purposes. First, it protects the innocent: much of what the grand jury collects turns out to be about innocent conduct. Some of the testimony is wrong, honestly or intentionally so, some is misleading, some irrelevant. If disclosed, especially if taken out of context, it could lead to wrong conclusions and harm reputations. A second reason for grand jury secrecy is security: witnesses could be endangered if the substance of their testimony were disclosed and investigations could be derailed if news of their direction were prematurely released.

The PATRIOT Act cast aside this set of limitations and controls, giving the CIA the benefit of the grand jury's powers with none of the protections of the criminal justice system.[17] Section 203 amends Rule 6(e) of the Federal Rules of Criminal Procedure to allow information collected by grand juries to be shared with the CIA and other intelligence agencies, as well as any national defense or national security official, without the prior approval of a judge. In effect, CIA agents working with law enforcement officers can now jointly draw up subpoenas, obtain the fruits of the grand jury's power, and never have to appear in open court or explain how they used the information.

At its core, this provision addresses a real problem. The grand jury that investigated the role of Osama bin Laden and al Qaeda in the bombing of the U.S. embassies in Africa, for example, collected some of the most comprehensive information available anywhere in the U.S. government on the operations of al Qaeda. The CIA could have used such information to pursue leads overseas beyond the scope of the criminal case. Thus, information sharing is justified in certain settings.

But Section 203 creates no limits on the sharing of information. A better solution would have required judicial approval for the sharing of grand jury information, but Congress acceded to the Bush Administration's insistence that law enforcement agencies should be free to act without judicial approval. In addition, the sharing of information should have been limited to cases of terrorism. But the PATRIOT Act allows the government to share any grand jury information that "involves" foreign intelligence or counterintelligence. And foreign intelligence is expansively defined to include any "information relating to the capabilities, intentions, or activities of foreign governments or elements thereof, foreign organizations, or foreign persons."[18] Thus, while the sharing of information makes sense, Congress essentially removed any checks on the mixing of intelligence and law enforcement functions, failing to address the very real concerns that the foreign intelligence approach may lead to serious invasions of liberty of people residing here.

❧ Intelligence Access to Records— The Dragnet Approach

Finally, the PATRIOT Act greatly expands the government's ability to collect information under the rubric of investigating terrorism or clandestine intelligence activities. Section 215 of the Act authorizes the government to seize "any tangible things (including books, records, papers, documents, and other items)" where those items are sought for an investigation "to protect against international terrorism or clandestine intelligence activities."[19] The subject of the order need not be suspected of any criminal wrongdoing whatsoever; indeed, the order need not be limited to the records of a particular person but may encompass entire collections of data related to many individuals.

In general, the government can obtain a person's records from a bank, credit bureau, telephone company, hospital, or library only if there is reason to believe that the individual is engaged in some wrongdoing or that the records are evidence of a crime. Over time, Congress has given the FBI power to compel disclosure of various records for intelligence and counterintelligence investigations. Each of these authorities was carefully considered by Congress and was enacted based on a showing by the FBI that the particular category of records was especially relevant to the conduct of counterintelligence investigations. For example, telephone toll records may be useful in identifying members of the circle around a known or suspected hostile foreign agent. Bank and credit records have obvious utility in tracing the money flow, and, in the case of suspected spies, identifying any unexplained income or spending. But in each instance, Congress applied a simple rule: the government had to have reason to believe that the records being sought pertained to an agent of a foreign power—an intelligence officer, for example, or a member of an international terrorist organization.

The PATRIOT Act eliminated the "agent of a foreign power" standard from all of the authorities giving the FBI access to specific categories of records in intelligence investigations, and created a massive catch-all provision, giving the FBI the ability to compel anyone to disclose any record or tangible thing that the FBI claims is relevant to an investigation of international terrorism or "clandestine intelligence activities," even if the record does not pertain to a suspected spy or international terrorist.

The implications of this change are enormous. Previously, the FBI could get the credit card records of anyone suspected of being a foreign agent. Under the PATRIOT Act, the FBI can get the entire database of the credit card company. Under prior law, the FBI could get library borrowing records only by complying with state law, and always had to ask for the records of a specific patron. Under the PATRIOT Act, the FBI can go into a public library and ask for the records on everybody who ever used the library, or who used it on a certain day, or who checked out certain kinds of books. It can do the same at any bank, telephone company, hotel or motel, hospital, or university—merely upon the claim that the information is "sought for" an investigation to protect against international terrorism or clandestine intelligence activities.

These changes permit the FBI in international terrorism cases to cast its net far wider than ever before. As we have shown above, the FBI has historically focused far too much of its counterterrorism effort on the monitoring of overt political activity. The issue is not whether the FBI can investigate people who say that they want to kill Americans—they can clearly be investigated. The issue is whether the FBI can investigate people who merely say that they support a Palestinian state. What was striking about the September 11 attackers is that they had no overt political inclinations—they never engaged in the type of political or associational activity that the FBI has traditionally made the focus of its counterterrorism efforts. Yet the new authorities in the PATRIOT Act will almost certainly result in broader collection of data on persons suspected of no wrongdoing and engaged only in political activity. The FBI and the other intelligence agencies are already awash in information that they cannot digest. Drawing in even more information on more innocent people is unlikely to make the picture any clearer.

In sum, the PATRIOT Act radically transformed the landscape of government power, and did so in ways that virtually guarantee repetition of some of law enforcement's worst abuses of the past. The PATRIOT Act itself, however, was only part of the government's response to September 11. Other actions, detailed below, raise still further questions about the appropriate balance between liberty and security.

❧ Ethnic Profiling

One of the most dramatic responses to the attack of September 11 was a swift reversal in public attitudes about racial and ethnic profiling as a law enforcement tool. Before September 11, about 80 percent of the American public considered racial profiling wrong. State legislatures, local police departments, and the President had all ordered data collection on the racial patterns of stops and searches. The U.S. Customs Service, sued for racial profiling, had instituted measures to counter racial and ethnic profiling at the borders. And a federal law on racial profiling seemed likely.

After September 11, however, polls reported that 60 percent of the American public favored ethnic profiling, at least as long as it was directed at Arabs and Muslims. The fact that the perpetrators of the September 11 attack were all Arab men, and that the attack appears to have been orchestrated by al Qaeda, led many to believe that it is only common sense to pay closer attention to Arab-looking men boarding airplanes and elsewhere. And the high stakes—there is reason to believe that we will be subjected to further terrorist attacks—make the case for engaging in profiling stronger here than in routine drug interdiction stops on highways. Thus, Stuart Taylor, a columnist for Newsweek, the National Journal, and Legal Times, wrote shortly after the attacks in favor of ethnic profiling of Arab men on airplanes.[20]

Press accounts made clear that whether as a matter of official policy or not, law enforcement officials were paying closer attention to those who appear to be Arabs and Muslims. And in November, the Justice Department announced its intention to interview 5,000 young immigrant men, based solely on their age, immigrant status, and the country from which they came. Virtually all of those interviewed were Arabs and Muslims, and the list looked uncomfortably like one generated to identify Arab and Muslims without explicitly relying on ethnicity. Several police departments around the country refused to participate in the interviews on the grounds that they appeared to constitute ethnic profiling.

There is no question that the immediate aftermath of September 11 called for greater urgency than the ongoing war on drugs, and that the immediate threat posed to our national security was greater. But that does not answer whether ethnic profiling is a legal, much less an effective, response. The argument that we cannot afford to rely on something other than racial or ethnic proxies for suspicion, after all, is precisely the rationale used to intern 110,000 persons of Japanese ancestry during World War II. While subjecting an individual to closer inspection and a possible search is less extreme than detention, the rationale—that we should rely on ethnic background as a proxy for suspicion—is the same.

Precisely because of the history of racial discrimination in this country, the Equal Protection Clause of the Constitution presumptively forbids government authorities from relying on explicit racial or ethnic distinctions. Such actions trigger "strict scrutiny," a stringent form of court review that requires the government to justify its racial distinctions by showing that they are "narrowly tailored," or "necessary," to further a "compelling government interest." There is no question that protecting citizens from terrorism is a compelling government interest, but so too is drug interdiction—in fact, all criminal law enforcement would likely be viewed as a compelling state interest.

The real question from a constitutional perspective is whether the means adopted—reliance on ethnic appearance as a proxy for suspicion—is narrowly tailored to further that interest. It is highly unlikely that profiling could satisfy that scrutiny. First, the vast majority of persons who appear Arab and Muslim— probably well over 99.9 percent—have no involvement with terrorism. Arab and Muslim appearance, in other words, is a terribly inaccurate proxy for terrorism. In the sex discrimination context, where the Supreme Court applies less stringent scrutiny than it does to ethnic or racial discrimination, the court held that statistics showing that 2 percent of young men between the ages of 18 and 21 had been arrested for drunk driving did not justify denying men of that age the right to purchase an alcoholic beverage.[21]

Second, the use of ethnic stereotypes is certainly not "necessary" to effective law enforcement. In fact, it is likely to be bad law enforcement. When one treats a whole group of people as presumptively suspicious, it means that agents are more likely to miss dangerous persons who take care not to fit the profile. In addition, the fact that the vast majority of those suspected on the basis of their Arab or Muslim appearance are innocent will inevitably cause agents to let their guard down.[22] Overbroad generalizations, in other words, are problematic not only because they constitute an unjustified imposition on innocents, but because they undermine effective law enforcement.

Profiling undermines effective law enforcement in still another way. It is virtually certain to alienate members of the targeted communities. Studies of policing have shown that it is far more effective to work with communities than against them. Where a community trusts law enforcement, people are more likely to obey the law, and more likely to cooperate with the police in identifying and bringing to justice wrongdoers in their midst. If we have reason to believe that there are potential terrorist threats within the Arab and Muslim community in the United States, we should be seeking ways to work with the millions of law-abiding members of those communities to help identify the true threats, not treating the entire community as suspect.

The ethnic profiling issue is complicated in the wake of the September 11 attacks by the fact that some use of ethnicity is probably permissible. When a bank reports a robbery, and describes the robbers as three white men in their thirties wearing blue shirts, the police can rely on race in seeking to identify and catch the suspects. In that setting, the use of race does not carry negative stereotyped connotations, but is simply an identifying marker, like the fact that they were wearing blue shirts. Moreover, as one of the few identifying characteristics, reliance on race in that setting is narrowly tailored to the compelling interest of catching the robbers. Ethnic or racial profiling, by contrast, consists of the reliance on race as a generalization about future behavior—the assumption that because an individual is black, he is more likely to rob a bank. Such reliance on generalizations is probably always impermissible, whereas reliance on race as an identifying criterion is usually permissible.

In the aftermath of September 11, it was often difficult to separate out these two uses of ethnicity. If law enforcement agents had reason to believe that there were others involved in the planning and carrying out of the attacks or that their associates might have been planning further attacks, and that these others were Arab or Muslim men, then relying on ethnic criteria to identify the guilty parties may have been permissible.

However, to the extent that law enforcement agents rely on ethnicity as a predictor of future behavior, they are using impermissible generalizations. Where the perpetrators are thought to be planning future attacks, the distinction between an identifying criterion and a prospective generalization is particularly difficult to draw. Therefore, where ethnicity is being accorded a dominant role in investigative activities, two other factors become very important. First, the use of an ethnic identifying factor becomes more objectionable when it is applied on a nationwide basis over an extended period of time. It is one thing to say that the police, having only the information that three white men robbed a bank, can stop and question all white men in the vicinity of the bank immediately after the robbery. It would be another matter for the police nationwide to keep interviewing white males until they find the bank robbers.

Second, when the government relies on ethnic identifying characteristics, it is critical that it act quickly to resolve its suspicions and to determine whether other, non-ethnic factors justify or disprove its selection of certain people for scrutiny. What is particularly troubling about the government's response to September 11 is that government officials seemed determined to apply ethnic profiling on a nationwide, seemingly arbitrary basis and failed to resolve promptly their selection of certain individuals for the worst form of ethnic-based action: detention without serious criminal charges.

Endnotes

[1]Pub. L. No. 107-56.

[2]NAACP v. Claiborne Hardware Co., 458 U.S. 886 (1982).

[3]PATRIOT Act, Section 411. The Act defines as a deportable offense the solicitation of members or funds for, or the provision of material support to, any group designated as terrorist. There is no defense available for those who can show that their support had no connection to furthering terrorism. The government is free to designate any organization that uses or threatens to use violence as terrorist. In addition, the law makes aliens who support even nondesignated groups deportable if the group has engaged in violence, unless the alien can show that he neither knew nor reasonably should have known that his support would further the group's violent activity.

[4]*See, e.g.,* Scales v. United States, 367 U.S. 203 (1961); United States v. Robel, 389 U.S. 258, 262 (1967); Keyishian v. Board of Regents, 385 U.S. 589, 606 (1967).

[5]PATRIOT Act, Section 412.

[6]United States v. Salerno, 481 U.S. 739, 746-47 (1987).

[7]The Supreme Court recently held that even aliens who have been finally ordered deported have a constitutionally protected liberty interest in remaining free, and that the INS's authority to detain them is therefore limited. Zadvydas v. Davis, 121 S. Ct. 2491 (2001).

[8]County of Riverside v. McLaughlin, 500 U.S. 44 (1991).

[9]United States v. Salerno, 481 U.S. 739.

[10]PATRIOT Act, Section 411.

[11]PATRIOT Act, Section 218, amending 50 U.S.C. §§ 1804(a)(7)(B) and 1823(a)(7)(B).

[12]50 U.S.C. §1801 et seq.

[13]PATRIOT Act, Section 213, amending 18 U.S.C. §3103a.

[14]A copy of this manual is available at http://www.cdt.org/security/011030doj.

[15]The prohibition is now codified in 50 U.S.C. §403-3(d)(1).

[16]Fed. R. Crim. P.6(e).

[17]PATRIOT Act, Section 203.

[18]PATRIOT Act, Section 203(a), incorporates by reference the definition of "foreign intelligence" contained in 50 U.S.C. §401a.

[19]PATRIOT Act, Section 215, amending 50 U.S.C. §§1862 and 1863.

[20]Stuart Taylor, *Never Say Never,* LEGAL TIMES, Sept. 24, 2001 at 70.

[21]Craig v. Boren, 429 U.S. 190 (1976).

[22]Malcolm Gladwell, writing in The New Yorker shortly after September 11, argued that it is cognitively impossible to remain alert in reviewing metal detectors at airports, because the fact that the vast majority of luggage will pose no threat inevitably causes the security personnel to let their guard down.

[23]Whitney v. California, 274 U.S. 357, 375 (1927).

Questions

1. What is the USAPA? How was this law created?

2. How do the authors critique the USAPA?

3. How has the government's response to the September 11 terrorist attacks involved ethic profiling?

4. What three principles do the authors propose to guide the U.S. response to terrorism?

5. If you were a lawmaker, would you change the USAPA? If so, how? If not, why not?

The Fall and Rise of Restorative Justice

JOHN BRAITHWAITE

One of the most powerful reforms in the criminal justice system involves the idea of restorative justice, which seeks to bring justice and well-being to the community as a whole, not just to punish the offender. In this chapter, John Braithwaite, a leading proponent of restorative justice, defines the concept and its core values, discusses its use in historical and cross-cultural contexts, and gives interesting examples of its use in modern criminal justice systems as well as in traditional rites.

☺ Historical Decline of Restorative Justice

This book conceives of restorative justice as a major development in human thought grounded in traditions of justice from the ancient Arab, Greek, and Roman civilizations that accepted a restorative approach even to homicide (Van Ness 1986, pp. 64–68); the restorative approach of the public assemblies (moots) of the Germanic peoples who swept across Europe after the fall of Rome (Berman 1983, pp. 53–56); Indian Hindus as ancient as the Vedic civilization (6000–2000 B.C.; Beck 1997, p. 77) for whom "he who atones is forgiven" (Weitekamp 1989); and ancient Buddhist, Taoist, and Confucian traditions that one sees blended with Western influences today in North Asia (Haley 1996).

Contemporary Nobel Peace Prize–winning Buddhists Aug San Suu Kyi of Burma and the Dalai Lama are reteaching the West that the more evil the crime, the greater the opportunity for grace to inspire a transformative will to resist tyranny with compassion. They follow in the footsteps of Hindus like Ghandi and Christians like Tutu. In the words of the Dalai Lama: "Learning to forgive is much more useful than merely picking up a stone and throwing it at the object of one's anger, the more so when the provocation is extreme. For it is under the greatest adversity that there exists the greatest potential for doing good, both for oneself and for others" (Eckel 1997, p. 135). Or as Saint Paul put it, "Where sin abounded, grace did much more abound." The implication of this teaching for criminologists is that preventing crime is an impoverished way of conceiving of our mission. Crime is an opportunity to prevent greater evils, to confront crime with a grace that transforms human lives to paths of love and giving. The ancient Palestinian restorative justice institution of the Sulha, still practiced in Galilee today, is one of the richest survivals of the ideal of using the lesser evil of crime to build the greater good of a loving community (see Box 1).

If we take restorative justice seriously, it involves a very different way of thinking about traditional notions such as deterrence, rehabilitation, incapacitation, and crime prevention. It also means transformed foundations of criminal jurisprudence and of our notions of freedom, democracy, and community.

Box 1: The Sulha Today

If a serious crime such as a murder occurs, the first step in a Sulha is that the offender's family approaches a number of different individuals respected as peacemakers and begs for their help. If they offer it, the peacemakers visit the victim's family: "We are asked by the offender and his family to come and pay you a visit in order to have the honor of offering their repentance and to express their sorrow for what has happened and to ask you to be kind—to have a great deal of honor on your own part and to let us take the case into our hands and see how we can help to restore peace between you" (Jabbour 1997, p. 31).

A wise old man is asked in an ancient Arab story, "How do you make peace between people?" The old man answers, "If a bad man and a good man quarrel, I take from the good man and give to the bad man." Then he is asked, "What if it is two bad men who quarrel?" "If it is two bad men," he replies, "then I take from myself and give to both of them" (Jabbour 1997, p. 45). Elias Jabbour then goes on to tell the story from his hometown of women from the family of a murdered man who poured his ashes over the heads of a delegation of peacemakers. "You have the right to do that. Go on, go on," one peacemaker responded. "You are angry? Don't throw it on your enemy—throw it on us. We will take the anger on ourselves."

Accepting the anger of victims with love no matter what they do, of peacemakers sacrificing themselves to absorb that anger, may bring victims to a state of grace. Kay Pranis draws a conceptual parallel for us to consider with Western restorative conferences: "The coordinator not being paid helps make the victim/offender/family feel more worthy."

When the settlement between the families is brokered, it will normally include *diya* (blood money) to "redeem the blood." The peacemaker says, "It's not the price of your man, for there is no price for a human life" (Jabbour 1997, p. 41). The money is symbolic of priceless blood.

When all details of the peace between the two families are negotiated, a process that may take more than a year, the beautiful ceremony of the Sulha occurs. A leader of the victim's family ties a knot in a white flag of peace and gives this flag to the offender, who carries it, surrounded by the peacemakers, as he moves along a line of the victim's family, shaking the hand of each. Community leaders then each make knots in the white flag to symbolize a peace that cannot be untied. Speeches of reconciliation are made by both the victim's and the offender's family. Often the victim family will return the *diya*. Then the mayor or other notable will pronounce something like: "Thank you. You two families were kind and very generous to accept this, and now we are going to open a new chapter . . ." (Jabbour 1997, p. 54). The victim family then takes the offender's family for a cup of bitter coffee. The final step is that the offender's family invites the victim's family to share a meal with them. When all goes well, the violence has become an opportunity to bring a community closer together through each understanding the suffering of the other.

Restorative justice has been the dominant model of criminal justice throughout most of human history for perhaps all the world's peoples. A decisive move away from it came with the Norman Conquest of much of Europe at the end of the Dark Ages (Van Ness 1986, p. 66; Weitekamp 1998).[1] Transforming crime into a matter of fealty to and felony against the king, instead of a wrong done to another person, was a central part of the monarch's program of domination of his people. Zehr (1995, p. 99) points to the irony that the origins of many of the words of contemporary retributive discourse may have had rather more restorative origins concerning civil wrongs: "The Greek *pune* refers to an exchange of money for harm done. Similarly, *guilt* may derive from the Anglo-Saxon *geldan,* which, like the German word *Geld,* refers to payment." In some parts of Europe where kings were weaker, restorative justice survived the medieval period (see Box 2). An important moment in the institutionalizing of restorative ideas was the development in the late sixth century by Celtic monks of a new manner of reconciliation with God—private penance with auricular (told privately in the ear) confession. The penitentials heightened notions of personal responsibility for crime and tackled the ancient idea that failure to exact vengeance was a matter of shame if a member of one's family had been wronged. Continuation of blood feuds became a matter for confession and penance. Specific restorative penances were also instituted. For ex- ample, a master who raped his slave was required in certain cases to make amends by freeing the woman from slavery (Rouche 1987, p. 530).

Beyond the parts of the globe ruled by European kings (among the Indigenous peoples of the Americas, Africa, Asia, and the Pacific), restorative traditions persisted into modern times (as did the retributive practices of blood feuds), remaining today as a resource of cultural diversity that can be drawn upon by European peoples whose justice traditions have been more homogenized and impoverished by central state power (see Box 3). So in 2001 we saw white South Africans embrace a new youth justice bill that in its preamble set the Indigenous restorative notion of *ubuntu*—the idea that our humanity is relationally tied to the humanity of those we live with—as the fundamental objective of the legislation. *Ubuntu* is the notion that enabled Nelson Mandela to construe even the supporters of apartheid as inextricably its victims. Those who think such African ideas of limited relevance in the West might pause to consider the irony that Abraham Lincoln reinvented his people's identity at Gettysburg with the nation-building idea that all Americans, North and South, black and white, must now transcend their suffering together as victims of slavery.

Box 2: Celtic Persistence with the Restorative

Traditional Scottish disputing retained a reparative character until well into the nineteenth century. It is ironic that a place so near the heart of the British Empire should have been one of the last places to have its restorative traditions crushed by formally retributive state law. Historians seem to think restorative traditions were sustained later in Scotland than in England or on the Continent because Scotland was a place where kings were weak and local kin networks strong. Ian Whyte (1995) in *Scotland before the Industrial Revolution* tells us that for serious crimes, "Settlements often involved formal public reconciliations as part of a religious service and sometimes a marriage between opposing families to try and cement the peace" (p. 217). The reason for reconciliation being highly public was to lock kin in to ending a blood feud.

Jenny Wormwald (1980) documents the widespread sixteenth-century Scottish practice of contractual obligations to submit differences between and within kin groups to "wyss [wise] freindis" or "by siche [sight] of frendis or lawe as they think expedient" (p. 72). Even murder was standardly dealt with by the payment of compensation, apology, masses for the soul of the dead, and pilgrimages. In one case in 1554, William Chalmer of Leidcreif could not pay compensation for a murder he had committed because he had been bankrupted by lawsuits. Instead he offered the kin of the victim his bond of manrent, promising allegiance and service to the family for life. Second, his son and cousin were promised to marry the daughter and sister of his victim, without dowry. The second compensation was the key one, as Wormwald explains: "It was fundamental to the system of compensation that when crime was committed, what mattered was not punishment as retribution or deterrent, but reparation in a form which would as far as possible restore the *status quo* which the crime had upset. In this case Chalmer had deprived his victim's daughter and sister of their natural protector, the head of their family. It was now his responsibility to redress that loss by making provision for them" (p. 74). If the actual outcome seems bizarre to us today—marrying the son of the murderer to the daughter of his victim—the principle of restoration and publicly ending bitterness that can foment further violence should still make sense.

According to Wormwald, all the Stewart kings except James III believed that "the most effective justice was still primarily local justice, and that compromise and compensation might be a better answer to crime than a penal code" (p. 79). Better to secure a "lettre of slanis" than to take a serious crime to the courts in Edinburgh for a state-imposed solution, especially when securing the king's peace without the knowledge of the kin of a slain man meant that the kin still had a right of vengeance. The lettre of slanis was issued by the kin of the victim, stating that full and acceptable assythment had been made. *Slanis* is often thought to derive from the Anglo-Saxon *slean,* meaning "to slay." But Wormwald points out that Irish Celtic origins are more likely, *slan* and its variants "signifying health, safety, wholeness; spiritual salvation" (p. 62). In short, the Celtic institution has a profoundly restorative meaning.

Box 3: The Nanante

An Afghan criminologist at the University of Edinburgh, A. Ali Serisht, pointed out after the publication of *Crime, Shame and Reintegration* (Braithwaite 1989) that the Pushtoon, the largest ethnic group in Afghanistan, had an institution called Nanante similar to the conferencing notion I discussed in that book. The Nanante is a ceremony in which the criminal offender brings flour and other food and kills a sheep for a community feast. Often this will be held at the victim's house, where the victim will participate in cooking the food the offender brings. At the ceremonial part of the event, the offender will not be told that he is bad and in need of reform, but rather that "you have done an injustice to this person." At the same time the offender will be assured that "you are one of us and we accept you back among us." The police and courts have virtually no presence in communities that rely on the Nanante.

While restorative justice may have been the dominant model of justice, it simplifies too much to say that restorative justice remained the dominant practice in societies beyond the direct rule of European kings. Most premodern societies sustained side-by-side restorative traditions and retributive traditions that were in many ways more brutal than modern retributivism. In early medieval Europe, for example, castration was a common modality of private justice against wrongdoers, one that the Christian church resisted. Even in the eighth century Charlemagne was finding it difficult to stamp out castration by imposing heavier fines for engaging in the practice (Rouche 1987, p. 456). Long before the Inquisition, church leaders were among those who sought to secure their power through retributive affliction on the bodies of their flock, as in the ninth-century case of the bishop of Le Mans, who was so unhappy with his priests that he had them castrated (Rouche 1987, p. 498). Indeed the canon law constructed in Bologna on the rediscovery of Roman law from the twelfth century laid the foundations for state laws that formally shifted criminal law away from its restorative framework. It was the Church that established prosecution as a central authority to assert its will and crush heresy. The barbarism of the Inquisition was justified because crime was committed not against a victim but against the moral order of the Church. Early Christian practice that had emphasized forgiveness of wrongdoing, reconciliation, and redemption began to lose ground (Zehr 1995, p. 113). The tug-of-war between restorative Christian teachings and insecure rulers who sought to signify their power through vivid displays of inscribing their power on the bodies of felons increasingly favored horrific corporal punishment in early modern times (Foucault 1977). Elsewhere I have hypothesized from the historical literature five stages in the history of Western regulation:

1. A pre-state stage where restorative justice and banishment are dominant

2. A weak state stage where corporal and capital punishment dominate

3. A strong state stage where professional police and penitentiaries dominate

4. A Keynesian welfare state stage where new therapeutic professions such as social work colonize what becomes probation-prison-parole

5. A contemporarily evolving new regulatory state phase of community and corporate policing (with a revived restorative justice) (Braithwaite 2001)

However, in that essay I go on to find that this rather complex sequence, while identifying some important substantive shifts, is in fact too simple. For our purposes here the important point to note is a late modern revival of restorative justice that has its deepest roots in a shift from most regulatory activities having individuals and their bodies as their objects to a world where more of the wrongdoing is done by organizations that are regulated in a mostly restorative fashion.

◉ The Rise of a New Social Movement for Restorative Justice

Interest in restorative justice for individual wrongdoers rekindled in the West from the establishment of an experimental victim-offender reconciliation program in 1974 in Kitchener, Ontario (Peachey 1989). Umbreit (1998) reported that by the mid-1990s there were at least 300 of these programs in North America and over 500 in Europe. By 2000 at the United Nations Congress on the Prevention of Crime and Treatment of Offenders, the Canadian delegation was claiming that there were 400 restorative justice programs in Canada alone.

The 1990s saw the New Zealand idea of family group conferences spread to many countries, including Australia, Singapore, the United Kingdom, Ireland, South Africa, the United States, and Canada, adding a new theoretical vitality to restorative justice thinking. Canadian First Nations' notions of healing circles (James 1993) also acquired wide influence, as did the Navajo justice and healing ceremony (Yazzie and Zion 1996). Less visible was the rich diversity of African restorative justice institutions such as the Nanante. By the 1990s these various programs came to be conceptualized as restorative justice. Bazemore and Washington (1995) and Van Ness (1993) credit Albert Eglash (1975) with first articulating restorative justice as a restitutive alternative to retributive and rehabilitative justice. As a result of the popularizing work of North American and British activists like Howard Zehr (1985, 1995), Mark Umbreit (1985, 1994), Kay Pranis (1996), Daniel Van Ness (1986), Tony Marshall (1985), and Martin Wright (1982) during the 1980s, and the new impetus after 1989 from New Zealand judges such as Mick Brown and Fred McElrea and Australian police, notably Terry O'Connell and northern police leaders converted by O'Connell, such as Thames Valley's Sir Charles Pollard, restorative justice became the emerging social movement for criminal justice reform of the 1990s (Daly and Immarigeon 1998). Since 1995, two organizations, Ted Wachtel's (1997) Real Justice in the United States and John McDonald and David Moore's Transformative Justice Australia have offered training in conferencing to thousands of people worldwide. An evaluation research community also emerged in association with the social movement. This community is much more dominated by Belgians, Germans, Austrians, and Canadians, though Burt Galaway and Joe Hudson (1975) in Minnesota and Canada were the early and persistent role models of this research community. During the 1990s Lode Walgrave, Alison Morris, Gabrielle Maxwell, Kathy Daly, Heather Strang, and Lawrence Sherman were particularly important early leaders of traditions of critical yet constructive research. Even more important are the many local program developers and evaluators steering new tributaries that give restorative justice its vitality. It is this localism that makes the restorative movement to justice as jazz is to music.

Box 4: Postimprisonment Restorative Justice

"Danny was 15 years old. Late one evening he left home with a can of spirits and a box of matches and set fire to the school library. He had taken great care to see that no people would come to harm, but the damage amounted to £26,000, and the library was out of action for several weeks.

Six days later Danny walked into the police station, saying he wanted to "get something off my chest." His parents were invited to a formal interview where he confessed; he said that he had been worried about forthcoming exams and thought that disrupting the library might buy him more time. He said that he had confessed voluntarily because he realized the damage he had caused and the impact on other people, and was full of guilt and remorse.

Before the case came to the Crown Court, a psychiatrist reported that Danny's behavior could be attributed to acute adolescent depression. Danny was sentenced to two years in a young offenders institution—a shorter sentence than he would have received otherwise, because he had no previous convictions and had given himself up. Just afterward, he commented, "Well, if I've learnt anything from all this, then it's not to tell anyone if I do something wrong!"

He wanted to give an explanation of what he had done, and he was being ridiculed and bullied in the prison for having confessed. Meanwhile, the headmaster had unanswered questions but also wanted to say directly to Danny that it was not the wish of the school that he be sent to prison. Danny's parents, too, were struggling to come to terms and wanted to express a sense of shared responsibility. After several visits to each of the parties, it was agreed that they should meet. The conference took place at the school and brought together Danny (who had been granted special leave from the prison), his parents, one of his friends, the headmaster, and the mediator. The librarian and a prison officer were invited but did not attend. The conference lasted for over two hours: they talked about how people had been affected by the crime, Danny answered questions and described his regret and remorse, and forgiveness was expressed. The head was very moved by Danny's account; after the meeting he walked with his hand on Danny's shoulder to the library building, which had been rebuilt, so that Danny could see the scars that had been healed, and said, "Now we all have to make sure that you can heal from this experience." Danny's father, walking behind them, said, "To be honest with you I couldn't see that this would do any good, and have wondered if it might make things worse . . . but isn't it wonderful to see those two chatting away . . . like the best of friends."

Source: Case notes from Guy Masters in Wright 1999, pp. 187–88

During the 1980s, there was also considerable restorative justice innovation in the regulation of corporate crime (Rees 1988; Braithwaite 1995b). Clifford Shearing's (1997, p. 12) historical analysis is more about governmentalities of post-Fordist capitalism than village moots: "Restorative justice seeks to extend the logic that has informed mediation beyond the settlement of business disputes to the resolution of individual conflicts that have traditionally been addressed within a retributive paradigm. . . . In both a risk-oriented mentality of security [actuarialism] and a restorative conception of justice, violence loses its privileged status as a strategy to be deployed in the ordering of security."

The next section of this chapter seeks to conceptualize what restorative justice is against the background of these histories. The final section outlines my engagement with restorative processes in business regulation (nursing homes, corporate crime) and in Asia and the Pacific in an effort to give the reader a grounded feel for restorative justice and the distinctive biography I bring to it.

⊛ What Is Restorative Justice, and Why Is It Beginning to Take Off?

Restorative justice is most commonly defined by what it is an alternative to. Juvenile justice, for example, is seen as seesawing back and forth during the past century between a justice and a welfare model, between retribution and rehabilitation. Restorative justice is touted as a long-overdue third model or a new "lens" (Zehr 1995), a way of hopping off the seesaw, of heading more consistently in a new direction while enrolling both liberal politicians who support the welfare model and conservatives who support the justice model.

The appeal of restorative justice to liberals is a less punitive justice system. The appeal to conservatives is its strong emphasis on victim empowerment, on empowering families (as in "family group conferences"), on sheeting home responsibilities, and on fiscal savings as a result of the parsimonious use of punishment. When restorative justice is applied to white-collar crime, pro-business politicians also tend to find the approach more appealing than a retributive approach to business wrongdoing. Every one of these bases of political appeal is subject to horrible perversions.

In New Zealand, the country with the most developed programmatic commitment to restorative justice, the mainstream conservative and social democratic parties have been joined by Christian pro-family parties of the Right in their support for restorative justice. In New Zealand (Maxwell and Morris 1993) and Australia (Moore with Forsythe 1995), the evidence is surprising on how supportive of restorative justice can be the police, that traditional ally of law-and-order politicians. The strongest opposition has come from lawyers, including some judges, under the influence of well-known critiques of the justice of informal processing of crime. At the same time, in both New Zealand and Canada, judicial leadership has been at the vanguard of restorative justice reform. In 2001, the Lord Chief Justice of England became a public supporter of restorative justice.

In the 1990s, restorative justice became a unifying banner, sweeping up various traditions of justice as "making amends" (Wright 1982); reconciliation (Dignan 1992; Marshall 1985; Umbreit 1985); peacemaking (Pepinsky and Quinney 1991); redress (De Haan 1990); relational justice (Burnside and Baker 1994); transformative justice (Morris 1995; Moore with Forsythe 1995, p. 253); and republican justice (Braithwaite and Pettit 1990). During the same period, similar ideas were also being developed by feminist abolitionists (Meima 1990) and in other feminist analyses that emphasized denunciation of the harm and help for victims as more central than punishment (Lacey 1988, pp. 193–94; Harris 1991; Braithwaite and Daly 1994; Roach 1999; Coker 1999). Feminist thinking about crime has been a dialectic of Portia (an ethic of justice) and Persephone (an ethic of care; Heidensohn 1986), out of which some feminists want Portia and Persephone each to check the excesses of the other (Masters and Smith 1998).

The most influential text of the restorative tradition has been Nils Christie's (1977), which defined the problem of criminal justice institutions "stealing conflicts" from those affected. Centuries earlier the philosophies of New Zealand Maori (Pratt 1996), Native American (Krawll 1994; Aboriginal Corrections Policy Unit 1997a), Christian (Van Ness 1986), and Japanese/Confucian/Buddhist (Haley 1996; Masters and Smith 1998) restorative justice became the sources of the deepest influences on the contemporary social movement.

Paul McCold (1997) convened a Delphi process on behalf of the Working Party on Restorative Justice of the Alliance of NGOs on Crime Prevention and Criminal Justice to see if these disparate strands of the emerging alternative might settle on a consensual conception of restorative justice. A Delphi process iteratively solicits expert opinion, in this case on the best way to define restorative justice. The consensus was not overwhelming. The most acceptable working definition was offered by Tony Marshall: "Restorative justice is a process whereby all the parties with a stake in a particular offence come together to resolve collectively how to deal with the aftermath of the offence and its implications for the future." This definition does stake out a shared core meaning of restorative justice. Its main limitation is that it does not tell us who or what is to be restored. It does not define core values of restorative justice, which are about healing rather than hurting, moral learning, community participation and community caring, respectful dialogue, forgiveness, responsibility, apology, and making amends (see Nicholl 1998). I take those who have a "stake in a particular offence" to mean primarily the victim(s), the offender(s), and affected communities (which includes the families of victims and offenders). So restorative justice is about restoring victims, restoring offenders, and restoring communities (Bazemore and Umbreit 1994; Brown and Polk 1996). One answer to the "What is to be restored?" question is whatever dimensions of restoration matter to the victims, offenders, and communities affected by the crime. Stakeholder deliberation determines what restoration means in a specific context.

Some have suggested dimensions of restoration that are found to be recurrently important in restorative justice processes. For example, I have defined the following dimensions of restoration as important from a republican perspective: restoring property loss, restoring injury, restoring a sense of security, restoring dignity, restoring a sense of empowerment, restoring deliberative democracy, restoring harmony based on a feeling that justice has been done, and restoring social support (Braithwaite 1996).

◉ Restorative Values

The process idea of restorative justice as a method of bringing together all stakeholders in an undominated dialogue about the consequences of an injustice and what is to be done to put them right is important. But so is the idea of restorative justice as an alternative that has a very different values framing than punitive justice. A perfect restorative process in which all stakeholders have their say can result in an undominated democratic decision of the conference to impose an extremely punitive outcome. An approach that is impoverished from the perspective of a process definition of restorative justice—for example, mediation between a single offender and victim by shuttle diplomacy (without meeting face-to-face)—might result in a richer result in terms of restorative values such as apology, repairing of harm, forgiveness, and reconciliation. In evaluating how restorative a program is, we need to analyze both the restorativeness of its processes and its values.

My argument in this book will be that in certain respects restorative values must trump restorative process, but in other respects restorative process should trump restorative values. I use republican normative theory (Braithwaite and Pettit 1990) to specify what these different contexts are. From this republican perspective, the first thing we must say is that just as it is dangerous to allow a court to impose a punishment beyond the maximum allowed by law, so it should be forbidden for a restorative justice process to impose a punishment beyond that which would be imposed by the courts for that kind of wrongdoing. If there is not an upper constraint on the punishment that can be imposed in a democracy, then citizens cannot be free in a republican sense. They live in fear of the tyranny of the majority. This constraint imposes no limits on mercy, however, which is in fact a republican virtue, as it is according to most of the world's great religions. So there is no problem with properly constituted restorative justice processes imposing lesser punishments than those courts would impose. It will be argued that in fact restorative justice processes should be constrained by all the rights that are foundational to liberal legalism.

The sphere in which restorative process should trump restorative values is where the outcome of the restorative process involves no breach of fundamental rights. We might disapprove of a conference or circle that decides on an unreasonably punitive outcome that is unforgiving and does nothing to repair the harm suffered by victims. But so long as that punishment is not cruel or degrading and does not exceed in quantum what the courts allow, a republican must accept the decision of the conference. The analogy is to democratic elections. When the people elect a tyrant who will undermine democratic values, the republican obligation is not to take up arms but to work for overthrow of the tyrant at the next election and to constrain the tyrant while in power to comply with the Constitution. When we say that a civic republican must accept the decision of a restorative process to flout restorative values, that does not mean that she should be silent about the decision. On the contrary, her obligation is to speak out on why she thinks the decision of this conference or circle was wrong, while defending its right to make it.

I have said that fundamental human rights should set legal limits on what restorative processes are allowed to do. But I also suspect that UN human rights instruments can give quite good guidance on the values restorative justice processes ought to observe. Integrating the rights-constraining and values-guiding requirements for restorative justice under the banner of UN human rights instruments might make for simplicity. It also might make for decent and practical global social movement politics for the movement for restorative justice. This is because while no one thinks these UN rights are perfect, they are the distillation of decades of deliberation in which all nations have participated to build a consensual foundation.

The first clause of the preamble of the Universal Declaration that most states have ratified is "Whereas recognition of the inherent dignity and of the equal and inalienable rights of all members of the human family is the foundation of freedom, justice and peace in the world." Obviously freedom, justice and peace have a lot of appeal to someone who values republican freedom to frame the pursuit of justice and peacemaking in restorative justice. Equally, there is appeal to those like Amartya Sen (1999) and Martha Nussbaum (1995), who value freedom in the Aristotelian sense of freedom to achieve capabilities for human flourishing. On their view consensus around a determinate conception of the good at a high level of generality should be developed from "reasonable procedures" (Nussbaum 1995, p. 74). Nussbaum's "thick, vague conception of the good" requires "rich sensitivity to the concrete context, to the characters of the agents and their social situation" 1995, (p. 94). Citizens are left a lot of latitude to specify concretely how to make sense of the thick, vague and "ever-revisable" (p. 107) conception of the good. In all these senses, freedom as nondomination and freedom as capability for human functioning can be seen as complementary though not mutually exhaustive. They both mean that citizens can make a lot of contextual sense of the highly general yet determinate vision of the good in international human rights.

In its thirty articles the Universal Declaration defines a considerable number of slightly more specific values and rights that seem to cover many of the things we look to restore and protect in restorative justice processes. These include a right to protection from having one's property arbitrarily taken (Article 17), a right to life, liberty, and security of the person (Article 3), a right to health and medical care (Article 25), and a right to democratic participation (Article 21).

From the restorative justice advocate's point of view, the most interesting article is the fifth: "No one shall be subjected to torture or to cruel, inhuman or degrading treatment or punishment." Of course, all states have interpreted Article 5 in a most permissive and unsatisfactory way from a restorative justice point of view. The challenge for restorative justice advocates is to take the tiny antipunitive space this article creates in global human rights discourse and expand its meaning over time so that it increasingly acquires a more restorative interpretation (see Power 2000). This is precisely how successful NGO activists have globalized social justice agendas in many other arenas—starting with a platitudinous initial rights and values framework and injecting progressively less conservative and more specific meanings into that framework agreement over time.

We can already move to slightly more specific and transformative aspirations within human rights discourse by moving from the Universal Declaration of 1948 to the less widely ratified International Covenant on Economic, Social and Cultural Rights of 1976 and the International Covenant on Civil and Political Rights of 1966. The former, for example, involves a deeper commitment to "self-determination" and allows in a commitment to emotional well-being under the limited rubric of a right to mental health. The Second Optional Protocol of the Covenant on Civil and Political Rights of 1989 includes a commitment of parties to abolish the death penalty, something restorative justice advocates would regard an essential specific commitment. Equally most restorative justice advocates would agree with all the values and rights in the United Nations Declaration on the Elimination of Violence against Women of 1993 and the Declaration of Basic Principles of Justice for Victims of Crime and Abuse of Power adopted by the General Assembly in 1985. The latter includes some relevant values not so well traversed in other human rights instruments such as "restoration of the environment" (Article 10), "compassion" (Article 4), "restitution" (various articles), and "redress" (Article 5) and includes specific reference to "restoration of rights" (Article 8) and "informal mechanisms for the resolution of disputes, including mediation, arbitration and customary justice or indigenous practices," which "should be utilized where appropriate to facilitate conciliation and redress for victims" (Article 7).

So my proposal for a starring framework for a debate on the content of restorative justice values (and standards for evaluation and peer review) is as follows.

1. *Restorative justice programs should be evaluated according to how effectively they deliver restorative values, which include:*
   Respect for the fundamental human rights specified in the Universal Declaration of Human Rights, the International Covenant on Economic, Social and Cultural Rights, the International Covenant on

Civil and Political Rights and its Second Optional Protocol, the United Nations Declaration on the Elimination of Violence Against Women and the Declaration of Basic Principles of Justice for Victims of Crime and Abuse of Power.

2. *Restorative values include the following values to be found in the international human rights agreements listed in number 1:*

  Restoration of human dignity
  Restoration of property loss
  Restoration of injury to the person or health
  Restoration of damaged human relationships
  Restoration of communities
  Restoration of the environment
  Emotional restoration
  Restoration of freedom
  Restoration of compassion or caring
  Restoration of peace
  Restoration of empowerment or self-determination
  Restoration of a sense of duty as a citizen

As a list of specific restorative values this is unsatisfactorily incomplete, for example, in the noninclusion of the crucial healing values of apology, mercy, and forgiveness, which are nowhere to be found as values in these UN documents. I have argued that these are emergent values of restorative processes, not values we should actively seek to persuade citizens to honor in restorative processes (Braithwaite, forthcoming).

Many will find these values vague, lacking specificity of guidance on how decent restorative practices should be run. Yet standards must be broad if we are to avert legalistic regulation of restorative justice, which is at odds with the philosophy of restorative justice. What we need is deliberative regulation where we are clear about the values we expect restorative justice to realize. Whether a restorative justice program is up to standard is best settled in a series of regulatory conversations (Black, 1998) with peers and stakeholders rather than by rote application of a rule book.

The social movement for restorative justice is so young that it is premature for anyone to have settled views on what should be conceived as restorative values. There has simply not been enough time for sifting through competing views, for the kind of "listening project" that Harry Mika and Howard Zehr with funding from the Open Society Institute, currently are conducting with victims groups across the United States.

I simply want to emphasize one distinction that seems important in this values debate. There are values that we ought to urge participants in restorative justice processes to honor. Respectful listening is an example. But there are other important values where we do not ask anyone to pursue them directly, yet we hope that restorative processes can be designed so that indirectly these values will be realized. Forgiveness is the prime example. Many of us believe that if we can create spaces that give victims an opportunity to discover how they might bring themselves to forgive, this is the most important thing we can do to promote the healing of both the victims themselves and of those who hurt them. Yet it is wrong to ask victims to forgive and very wrong to expect it of them. Forgiveness is a gift victims can give. We destroy its power as a gift by making it a duty. Mercy is another value of this type. In a different way remorse on the offender side has the same quality. Remorse that is demanded is remorse that is destroyed. Creating spaces where wrong-doers might be persuaded of the need for remorse is a good institutional objective. Demanding, coercing, or even expecting remorse or apology may be a bad objective.

The most fraught issue in the values debate is whether values such as retribution, just desserts, and fair punishment should be accommodated in a restorative justice framework. Many of the most distinguished restorative justice thinkers think they should. My own inclination is to think they should not. While all societies seem to have both restorative and retributive values and practices, and while a good case can be made that both have been necessary to the survival of peoples historically, in this book I argue that in the conditions of late modernity our retributive values are more a hindrance to our survival and flourishing than a help. Hence restorative justice should be explicitly about a values shift from the retributive/punitive to the restorative. Retributive emotions are natural, things we all experience and things that are easy to understand from a biological point of view. But, on this view, retribution is in the same category as greed or gluttony; biologically they once helped us to flourish, but today they are corrosive of human health and relationships. The contrary view is that a more rationalist conception of retribution can be reconciled with restoration, however, and indeed must be if restorative justice is to be a pragmatic program (Daly and Immarigeon 1998; Van Ness and Strong 1997, pp. 27–28).

❂ Broadening Our Vision of Restorative Justice

While most of the writing on restorative justice focuses on the comparatively small crimes of juvenile delinquents, in this book I emphasize its relevance to adult crime as well, including war crimes and crimes at the commanding heights of business power (as in corporate restorative justice) and political power (as in Archbishop Desmond Tutu's Truth and Reconciliation Commission in South Africa, which he explicitly saw as a restorative justice process). On this view, organizations like Transcend that specialize in peacemaking training for international violence are part of the social movement for restorative justice (see www.transcend.org).

Most restorative justice advocates came to the approach through juvenile crime as a result of evidence of the failures of the welfare and justice models. The path that led me and a number of my colleagues who are experts in corporate crime to restorative justice is quite different and instructive. Many young criminologists began to study white-collar crime after Watergate to resurrect Edwin Sutherland's (1983) project. We wanted to document systematically how the crimes of the powerful were unpunished. What we found, in effect, was that the regulation of corporate crime in most countries was rather restorative. The reasons for this were far from ennobling, being about corporate capture combined with high costs of complex corporate crime investigations that states were unwilling to pay. Nevertheless, some of us began to wonder whether we were wrong to see our mission as making corporate crime enforcement more like street crime enforcement through tougher sanctions.[2] Instead we began to wonder whether street crime enforcement might be more effective if it were more like corporate criminal enforcement.

In my case, engagement with restorative approaches to corporate crime was entangled with my active engagement with social movement politics—particularly the consumer movement, but other social movements as well. In turn, my engagements with regulatory agencies—concerned with nursing homes, occupational health and safety, antitrust, environment, consumer protection, tax, and affirmative action—were as much connected to my history as an NGO activist as with a research background in these domains. I will now describe two examples of restorative justice praxis to open up an understanding of the interface among activism, theoretical innovation, and evaluation: Asian community policing, and restorative justice conferences.

⊛ Asian Community Policing

After Brent Fisse and I did some limited fieldwork on how Japanese companies and regulators secured compliance with regulatory laws (Braithwaite and Fisse 1985), I became interested in Japanese social control more broadly. The work of many other scholars suggested that it was based rather heavily on dialogue about collective obligation and relationships as opposed to punishment. This seemed true from social control of the largest corporations (which we were studying) down to the regulation of the petty delinquencies of children in schools. As with nursing homes, Guy Masters's (1995, 1997) work shows that Japanese schools use methods of social control very similar to the family group conferences discussed later (see Box 5). There was plenty of degradation and punitiveness in Japanese policing as well, especially when cases move from local *koban* policing (Bayley 1976) to policing by detectives and prosecutors (Miyazawa 1992).[3] Yet it seemed to me then, and still does, that the restorative elements of Japanese social control are more influential and sophisticated than in the West. We have much to learn from them (Masters 1997).

Box 5: Delinquency in the Japanese Classroom

"The students would then be asked by their home room teacher to explain their actions. This would often be done at the child's home in front of the parents. Finally, a meeting with all the students and parents would be arranged, and with any other people that might be involved. For instance if a fight had occurred with students from another school, or an item had been stolen, then these individuals would also be present. The Police might also attend, and make comments. In these meetings, the teachers would start by talking about the student and then the incident. Those involved would be expected to talk about the effect that it had had. The students would be expected to explain why they did it, and to apologise to everybody there. The parents would often then apologise to the injured party, as would the teachers. The students would then have a separate meeting with their home room teacher again, to discuss that meeting, and, as teachers said to me, to stress what the individual student had learnt from the situation. The more serious the incident the more meetings would be arranged . . . For these incidents there was never any specific punishment per se, just the process of the meetings . . . There was a strong feeling that students should not be given up on . . . Even with the persistent trouble makers a common comment was always that, 'This time—I think that they might learn.' . . . When talking about persistent trouble makers one teacher commented that: 'Young children make mistakes. They do bad things, but that doesn't make them bad people. Our job is to look after them when they make these mistakes, until they learn to look after themselves.' It would appear that they look after them by showing them how serious what they have done is, and how it has hurt others" (Masters 1995, pp. 27–29). Lewis (1989, p. 35) identified the following four principles from her observations of discipline in Japanese classrooms: "(1) minimising the impression of teacher control; (2) delegating control to the children; (3) providing plentiful opportunities for children to acquire a "good girl" or "good boy" identity; and (4) avoiding the attribution that children intentionally misbehave."[4]

In an earlier draft of *Crime, Shame and Reintegration*, I also had a section on Chinese community policing (Braithwaite 1989). I threw it in the bin because Chinese informal justice seemed to involve so much more stigmatization and punitiveness than Japanese justice. Vagg's (1998) Hong Kong data capture well the concerns that beat a path to my wastebasket. Chinese Peoples' Courts, especially as they were projected to us in the Cultural Revolution, seemed a model of how not to do restorative justice. Yet Hong Lu's (1998) research in Shanghai shows that the most important contemporary restorative justice institution in China, *bang jiao* meetings (*bang* means "help"; *jiao* means "education" and "admonition") tend to start as rather stigmatizing encounters but to end as reintegrative ones (see also Wong 1999). Indeed *bang jiao* often follows upon stigmatization by state punishment, as in two case studies from Hong Lu's dissertation (Box 6).

Box 6: *Bang Jiao:* Shanghai, 1996

Case one:
A sixteen-year-old boy was sent to a work-study school for rehabilitation because of repeated thefts. Two years later, after recommendations from his *bang jiao* team and work-study school principals, he was transferred to a normal school. Too ashamed to be seen by his neighbors, he went back home after dark every day. After his mother finally talked to the *bang jiao* team members, the members visited his neighbors and found that they did not ridicule or abhor the boy but wanted to communicate with him, but did not know how. They then discussed ways to help the boy overcome psychological barriers. A young girl suggested holding a painting exhibition at the activity center because she knew that the boy was good at painting and had won an award. They approached the boy to ask him to decorate the room and to collect and select a painting of his own and other paintings to be exhibited at the room. Three weeks later, a neighborhood painting exhibition was held at the center. All the neighborhood boys and girls, along with their parents, were invited. The boy's work was highly praised by the neighbors. This experience has totally changed the boy. Since then, he has been heavily involved in neighborhood activities, writing stories for the newsletter and contributing drawings for the bulletin boards. His mother was so thankful for the *bang jiao* team and said that "without their help, my son would not be what he is today."

Case two:
A twenty-seven-year-old young man killed his own father five years earlier out of rage at seeing his father beating his mother very badly. He was sentenced to prison for eight years. Due to his good performance in the labor camp, he was released after serving a five-year sentence. But his brother and sister-in-law, along with his grandmother, did not forgive him. He slept in the joint area of the kitchen and the bedroom. *Bang jiao* team members realized

that it was a difficult situation because of mixed feelings about the young man, in addition to the added burden of an already crowded household. They made frequent visits to the home and tried to persuade the family to forgive and accept the young man. Yet, after only two weeks of his release, he was caught stealing at the local store. When his *bang jiao* team members arrived at the local police station, he begged them not to interfere, saying that he would rather go back to the labor camp. After they realized that he stole because his family members did not give him money and living necessities, *bang jiao* members donated their own money to buy clothes and food for him and persuaded local police to drop the charges. A month later, they arranged a job for him at the community-run factory. He saved every dime of his salary to buy fruits and nutritious products for his grandmother. And during his sister-in-law's pregnancy, he spent hours upon hours taking care of her. After the birth of a baby daughter, he took care of all three generations because his brother works long hours as a truck driver. *Bang jiao* team members also volunteered their time to help out with the family. After two agonizing years, the family members were finally moved by the young man's sincerity and accepted him as a family member. They were honored with a "model family" award. The young man was grateful for the help of *bang jiao* members, saying that, without them, he probably would have committed suicide.

Source: From Hong Lu 1998

Chinese restorative justice, in both its positive and its negative aspects, deserves more attention because China has by far the largest and most diverse programs: 155,000 local mediation committees, which accounted for over 6 million cases, compared with under 4 million cases that went to court in 1994 (Wong 1999). Many of the mediations were of family or neighbourhood disputes that were not necessarily criminal. China also is the home of Confucius (551–479 B.C.), arguably the most influential thinker about restorative justice the world has known (see Box 7).

From the perspective of a European republican philosophy (Braithwaite and Pettit 1990; Pettit 1997), there is much of value to draw on in Confucian

Box 7: Confucius

One of Confucius's best-known views is that "if the people be led by laws, and uniformity sought to be given them by punishments, they will try to avoid the punishment but have no sense of shame" (Confucius 1974, p. 16). In opposition to his contemporaries, he was against capital punishment (pp. 92–93, 98). Reciprocity, mutuality, and harmony were central to his ways of seeing.

[XXIII] Tsze-kung asked, saying, "Is there one word which may serve as a rule of practice for all one's life?" The Master said, "Is not RECIPROCITY such a word? What you do not want done to yourself, do not do to others," (p. 123).

Confucius's quest can be read in part as a search for practices of good government that enable people to understand the effects their actions have on one another and that naturally expose the virtue of the virtuous so that others will follow them. Virtue is inculcated by quiet good example rather than by denunciation.

[XXIV] Tsze-kung said, "Has the superior man his hatreds also?" The Master said, "He has his hatreds. He hates those who proclaim the evil of others" (p. 143).

Obversely, it is wise "to find enjoyment in speaking of the goodness of others" (130). For Confucius, then, shame rather than punishment is the key to social control; but shame is not something we do to wrongdoers so much as something wrongdoers discover through the respectful treatment they receive from virtuous people who manifest in the fiber of their being the example of a transparently superior way of living.

thought but also much that might be dangerous. Confucian communitarianism was patriarchal and hierarchic. Perhaps a settled sense of deference was not so dangerous in a stable world where family, village, and a unitary state were the only institutions that mattered. But in a more complex world where there are many levels of government, up to the International Monetary Fund (IMF) and World Trade Organization (WTO), many cross-cutting institutions of civil society to which we belong, a world in which we and our parents are geographically mobile, we need strong, independent individuals as well as strong families and communities. Individuation is vital as a practice of socialization if individuals are to be strong enough to resist tyranny as they move from one site of domination to another in a complex world. Moreover, if we do not move away from the notion of society as a holistic unity to the notion of the separation of powers and an important place for the rule of law, a liberal-republican constitutional order, the lesson of this century's history is that we will get tyranny—"political power out of the barrel of a gun."

Yet we can read the great sweep of Chinese history as a dialectic of learning and unlearning this lesson. I refer in particular to the great historical struggle between the legalists and the Confucians, and to the dialectic between both legalism and Confucianism and the dialectic of freedom in Taoism, to the disastrous abandonment of the rule of law in the Cultural Revolution and the partial return to it since (Gernet 1982; Huang 1988).

One reason it was an intellectual mistake to scrap the China section of *Crime, Shame and Reintegration* is that the study of Chinese history may hold one key to a macrosociology of restorative justice. In the dialectic of Chinese history between the domination of Confucian and legalist ideas, a high-water mark of legalist influence was the Ch'in dynasty. What brought about the fall of the Ch'in empire in 211 B.C.

> was not the alienation and hatred of the scholar class, nor the bitter enmity of the surviving remnants of the aristocracy, but the growing popular discontent and mounting outrage over the cruelty of the system of punishments and the intolerable burden of taxes and levies imposed for the massive public works that the emperor commanded. Crime increased as did the number of those condemned, tortured, mutilated, and exiled to labor gangs. As long as the emperor was alive, fear of his powerful and demoniacal personality held the empire together; after his death all the restraints broke, and the empire exploded in rebellion. (Michael 1986, p.66)

Today the movement of the Confucian-legalist dialectic is in the reverse direction, with the "rule of law" rebounding as a dominant value. Given the continued trampling of human rights and freedoms in China, this may be a hopeful development, yet part of it is a sharp decline of the proportion of criminal cases dealt with by mediation as opposed to criminal trials. What a pity that so few Western intellectuals are engaged with the possibilities for recovering, understanding, and preserving the virtues of Chinese restorative justice while studying how to check its abuses with a liberalizing rule of law.

Whatever its rights and wrongs, the legalist-restorative contest is more central to the dynamic of Chinese history than to the histories of other nations and therefore more central to the development of a macrosociology of the fluctuating fortunes of restorative justice.

Restorative Justice Conferences

In *Crime, Shame and Reintegration,* I made reference to the desirability of insti-tutionalizing something like the restorative justice conference for criminal offenders (Braithwaite 1989, pp. 173–74). After reading this, John McDonald of the New South Wales police came to me and said this had already been done in New Zealand. Terry O'Connell showed me videotaped interviews with people like Maori chief judge of the New Zealand Youth Court, Michael Brown. These revealed that one of the rationales for restorative justice in the Maori tradition was the simultaneous communication of "shame" and "heal-ing" or "embrace." It was a depressing revelation that what I thought was the only limited originality in *Crime, Shame and Reintegration* had been preceded by several hundred years of Polynesian oral tradition, not just in New Zealand. Indeed, I concluded that Maori ways of thinking about *whakama,* or shame, were in some important ways an advance on my own thinking. After *Crime, Shame and Reintegration* became a widely read book, many people from Africa, Melanesia, Asia, and the Americas contacted me about restora-tive justice conferences that were part of their tradition. I learned that the Native American healing circle seeks to institutionalize equality rather than hierarchy and "puts the problem in the center—not the person" (Pranis 1996, p. 46, quoting Melton 1995). These stories challenged assumptions I strongly held until the mid-1990s, for example, that traditional Western criminal process was superior at fact-finding with justice than restorative processes (see Box 8).[5]

New Zealand remained of preeminent importance, however, because it mainstreamed the conferencing innovation into a Western juvenile justice system (and into the care and protection of abused and neglected children as well). The importance of New Zealand was not its adoption of Maori restora-tive philosophies; indeed, Pakeha (non-Maori) New Zealanders tended to reject much of both the restorative and retributive aspects of Maori philoso-phy, initially justifying the practice of "family group conferences" in terms of a move from the welfare model to the Western justice model! When its in-novation became internationally celebrated, New Zealand wisely and more

Box 8: Hollow Water

Healing circles in the Manitoba Ojibway community of Hollow Water began to deal with what many thought of at first as an epidemic of alcohol abuse. As citizens sat in these circles discussing the problems of individual cases, they realized in 1986 that there was a deeper underlying problem, which was that they lived in a community that was sweeping the sexual abuse of children under the carpet. Through setting up a complex set of healing circles to help one individual victim and offender after another, in the end it had been discovered that a majority of the citizens were at some time in their lives victims of sexual abuse.[6] Most of the leading roles in this process were taken by women of Hollow Water (Bushie 1999). Fifty-two adults out of a community of 600 (Jaccoud 1998) formally admitted to criminal responsibility for sexually abusing children, 50 as a result of participating in healing circles, 2 as a result of being referred to a court of law for failing to do so (Ross 1996, pp. 29–48; Lajeunesse 1993). Ross (1996, p. 36) claims that the healing circles have been a success because there have been only two known cases of reoffending. Tragically, however, there has been no genuinely systematic outcome evaluation of Hollow Water.

What is more important than the crime prevention outcome of Hollow Water is its crime detection outcome. When and where has the traditional criminal process succeeded in uncovering anything approaching 52 admissions of criminal responsibility for sexual abuse of children in a community of just 600? Before reading about Hollow Water, I had always said that the traditional criminal investigation and trial process is superior to restorative justice processes for justly getting to the truth of what happened. Restorative justice processes were only likely to be superior to traditional Western criminal process when there was a clear admission of guilt. The significance of Hollow Water is that it throws that position into doubt.

accurately reinterpreted family group conferences as restorative justice. Indeed, for all of us practice was ahead of theory, and it was well into the 1990s before the North American label *restorative justice* subsumed what had been developing elsewhere for a long time.

The way conferences work is very simple. Once wrongdoing is admitted, the offender and his or her family are asked who they would like to have attend a conference as supporters. Similarly, the victim is asked to nominate loved ones to attend. The conference is a meeting of these two communities of care. First there is a discussion of what was done and what the consequences have been for everyone in the room (the victim's suffering, the stress experienced by the offender's family). Then there is a discussion of what needs to be done to repair those different kinds of harm. A plan of action is agreed upon and signed by the offender and usually by the victim and the police officer responsible for the case. Conferencing advocates believe that asking the offender to confront the consequences of his wrongdoing (and talking them through in the presence of those who have suffered them) has a variety of positive effects in terms of taking responsibility, experiencing remorse, and offering practical help and apology to the victim and the community to right the wrong.

Beyond this common core, conferences vary from place to place in how they are run. In Australia, Wagga Wagga was the first conferencing program from 1991 and an important site of early research and development on a culturally pluralized conferencing process suitable for both Western and Australian Aboriginal cases. This R and D is being carried forward by the RISE Experiment in Canberra in which 1,300 adult and juvenile cases have been randomly assigned to conference versus court by Lawrence Sherman and Heather Strang (Sherman et al. 1998). Drunk driving, property crimes, and violent crimes are covered by the experiment.

◉ *L*earning from *P*lurality

Western nations need to open themselves to learning not only from the restorative practices of their own Indigenous peoples but also from Asian, Polynesian, African, and other cultural traditions of restorative justice. Of course one reason they should do this is that they have large numbers of citizens from these other parts of the world who crave a more meaningful experience of justice. But another is that out of seeking to understand diversity in the practice of justice, we acquire a richer understanding of how justice becomes real in the lived experience of citizens. The same point applies to learning lessons from nursing home regulation on how better to regulate burglary (and vice versa). We get richer theory from a more plural inductive base. Yet that theory must be adapted and tested in a way that makes sense in a local cultural context.

This book argues that in most cases justice works best by empowering affected communities to deal with the consequences of injustice and transform private troubles into public issues, as by advocacy of preventive measures. We will enrich crime prevention and enable healing by empowering plural deliberation about the injustice.

Endnotes

[1] Barnett (1977, p. 352) cites Diamond's (1935) research as sustaining his conclusion that of the 50 to 100 tribal communities from which data are available, 73 percent call for a pecuniary penalty for homicide, while only 14 percent demand death. In Europe all the Early and Middle Codes to A.D. 1100 called for pecuniary penalties for homicide, while all of the Late Middle Codes made death the exclusive sanction for intentional homicide.

[2] Critics indeed might enjoy the irony that Watergate offender Charles Colson, now of Prison Fellowship Ministries, is a prominent restorative justice advocate.

[3] I am indebted to Christopher Murphy for pointing out that on the basis of his considerable observation of Japanese policing, Bayley and Miyazawa may both be right in this way, like the blind Hindus in the legend, feeling different parts of the elephant. That is, Japanese policing may be more reintegrative at the *koban* level, more stigmatizing in the hands of detectives and prosecutors.

[4] On the greater commitment to restoration in Japanese versus American conceptions of justice and responsibility, the work of Hamilton and Sanders (1992) is instructive.

[5] A conversation with Gale Burford about his work on conferencing family violence with Joan Pennell also has me wondering. In a third of their cases, sexual abuse of children came out during conferences. Gale said: "So violence programs that exclude sexual abuse don't really. They just say if they have sexual abuse don't talk about it or you'll be out of the program."

[6] LaPrairie (1994, p. iii), in a sophisticated study of this problem from a restorative justice perspective in another context, found that 46 percent of inner-city native people in Canada had experienced child abuse. For an outline of the Hollow Water procedures for dealing with sexual abuse, see Aboriginal Corrections Policy Unit 1997b, especially pp. 221–30. At Canim Lake, the site of another

innovative Canadian First Nations healing circle approach to sexual abuse, "The research showed us that up to eighty percent of our people had been sexually abused at one point in their lives" (Warhaft, Palys, and Boyce 1999, p. 171).

References

Aboriginal Corrections policy Unit. 1997a. *The Four Circles of Hollow Water.* Aboriginal Peoples Collection. Ottawa, Canada: Solicitor General.

————. 1997b. *Responding to Sexual Abuse: Developing a Community-Based Sexual Abuse Response Team in Aboriginal Communities.* Ottawa, Canada: Solicitor General.

Barnett, R. 1977. "Restitution: A New Paradigm of Criminal Justice." In *Assessing the Criminal: Restitution, Retribution and the Legal Process,* edited by R. Barnett and J. Hagell, Cambridge, Mass.: Ballinger.

Bayely, David H. 1976. *Forces of Order: Police Behavior in Japan and the United States.* Berkeley: University of California Press.

Bazemore, G., and M. Umbreit. 1994. *Balanced and Restorative Justice: Program Summary: Balanced and Restorative Justice Project.* Washington, D.C.: U.S. Department of Justice, Office of Juvenile Justice and Delinquency Prevention.

Bazemore, G., and C. Washington. 1995. "Charting the Future of the Juvenile Justice System: Reinventing Mission and Management." *Spectrum,* Spring: 51–66.

Beck, Guy L. 1997. "Fire in the Atman: Repentance in Hinduism." In *Repentance: A Comparative Perspective,* edited by Amitai Etzioni and David E. Carney. New York: Rowman and Littlefield.

Berman, Harold J. 1983. *Law and Revolution: The Formation of the Western Legal Tradition.* Cambridge, Mass.: Harvard University Press.

Black, Julia. 1998. "Talking about Regulation." *Public Law,* spring: 77–105.

Braithwaite, John. 1989. *Crime, Shame and Reintegration.* Cambridge: Cambridge University Press.

————. 1995b. "Corporate Crime and Republican Criminological Praxis." In *Corporate Crime: Ethics, Law and State,* edited by F. Pearce and L. Snider. Toronto: University of Toronto Press.

————. 1996. "Restorative Justice and a Better Future." Dorothy J. Killam Memorial Lectures, Dalhousie University, 17 October.

————. 2001a. "Crime in a Convict Republic." *Modern Law Review,* 64:11–50.

————. 2001b. "Reconciling Models: Balancing Regulation, Standards and Principles of Restorative Justice Practice." In *International Perspectives on Restorative Justice Conference Report,* edited by H. Mika and K. McEvoy. Belfast: School of Law, Queens University.

————. Forthcoming. "Domination, Quiescence and War Crimes" In *Handbook on Multi-National Policy toward Peace, Prosperity and Democracy,* edited by S. Nagel. Lexington, Ky.: Lexington Books.

————. Forthcoming. "Principles of Restorative Justice." In *Restorative Justice,* edited by A. Von Hirsch. Oxford: Hart Publishing.

Braithwaite, John and K. Daly. 1994. "Masculinities, Violence and Communitarian Control." In *Just Boys Doing Business,* edited by T. Newburn and E. Stanko. London: Routledge.

Braithwaite, John, and Brent Fisse. 1985. "Varieties of Responsibility and Organizational Crime." *Law and Policy* 7:315–43.

Braithwaite, John, and Philip Pettit. 1990. *Not Just Deserts: A Republican Theory of Criminal Justice.* Oxford: Oxford University Press.

Brown, M., and K. Polk. 1996. "Taking Fear of Crime Seriously: The Tasmanian Approach to Community Crime Prevention." *Crime and Delinquency* 42:398–420.

Burnside, Jonathan, and Nicola Baker, eds. 1994. *Relational Justice: Repairing the Breach.* Winchester: Waterside Press.

Bushie, Berma. 1999. "Community Holistic Circle Healing: A Community Approach." Proceedings of Building Strong Partnerships for Restorative Practices conference, Vermont Department of Corrections and Real Justice, Burlington, Vermont.

Christie, Nils. 1977. "Conflicts as Property." *British Journal of Criminology* 17:1–26.

Coker, Donna. 1999. "Enhancing Autonomy for Battered Women: Lessons from Navajo Peacemaking." *UCLA Law Review* 47:1–111.

Confucius. 1974. *The Philosophy of Confucius.* Trans. James Legge. New York: Crescent Books.

Daly, K., and R. Immarigeon. 1998. "The Past, Present, and Future of Restorative Justice: Some Critical Reflections." *Contemporary Justice Review* 1:21–45.

De Haan, W. 1990. *The Politics of Redress: Crime, Punishment and Penal Abolition.* London: Unwin Hyman.

Diamond, A. 1935. *Primitive Law.* London: Longmans, Green.

Dignan, J. 1992. "Repairing the Damage: Can Reparation Work in the Service of Diversion?" *British Journal of Criminology* 32:453–72.

Eckel, Malcolm David. 1997. "A Buddhist Approach to Repentance." In *Repentance: A Comparative Perspective,* edited by Amitai Etzioni and David F. Carney. New York: Rowman and Littlefield.

Eglash, Albert. 1975. "Beyond Restitution: Creative Restitution." In *Restitution in Criminal Justice,* edited by J. Hudson, and B. Galaway. Lexington, Mass.: Lexington Books.

Foucault, Michel. 1977. *Discipline and Punish: The Birth of the Prison.* London: Pantheon.

Galaway Burt and Joe Hudson, eds. 1975. *Considering the Victim.* Springfield: Ill.: Charles C. Thomas.

Gernet, Jacques. 1982. *A History of Chinese Civilization.* Cambridge: Cambridge University Press.

Haley, John. 1996. "Crime Prevention through Restorative Justice: Lessons from Japan." In *Restorative Justice: International Perspectives,* edited by Burt Galaway and Joe Hudson. Monsey, N.Y.: Criminal Justice Press.

Hamilton, V. Lee, and Joseph Sanders. 1992. *Everyday Justice: Responsibility and the Individual in Japan and the United States.* New Haven, Conn.: Yale University Press.

Harris, M. K. 1991. "Moving into the New Millennium: Toward a Feminist Vision of Justice." In *Criminology as Peacemaking,* edited by H. E. Pepinsky and R. Quinney. Bloomington: Indiana University Press.

Heidensohn, Frances. 1986. "Models of Justice: Portia or Persephone? Some Thoughts on Equality, Fairness and Gender in the Field of Criminal Justice." *International Journal of the Sociology of Law* 14:287–98.

Huang, Ray. 1988. *China: A Macro History.* Armonk, N.Y.: M. E. Sharpe.

Jabbour, Elias J. 1997. *Sulha: Palestinian Traditional Peacemaking Process,* edited by Thomas C. Cook Jr. Montreal: House of Hope Publications.

Jaccoud, M. 1998. "Restoring Justice in Native Communities in Canada." In *Restorative Justice for Juveniles: Potentialities, Risks and Problems for Research,* edited by Lode Walgrave. Leuven: Leuven University Press.

James, T. M. 1993. *Circle Sentencing.* Supreme Court of the Northwest Territories: Canada.

Krawll, M. B. 1994. *Understanding the Role of Healing in Aboriginal Communities.* Ottawa: Solicitor General, Canada Ministry Secretariat.

Lacey N. 1988. *State Punishment: Political Principles and Community Values.* London: Routledge.

Lajeunesse, T. 1993. *Community Holistic Circle Healing: Hollow Water First Nation, Aboriginal Peoples Collection.* Canada: Supply and Services.

LaPrairie, C. 1994. *Seen but Not Heard: Native People in the Inner City*. Victimisation and Domestic Violence, Report 3. Ottawa: Department of Justice.

Lewis, C. 1989. "Co-operation and Control in Japanese Nursery Schools." In *Japanese Schooling: Patterns of Socialisation, Equality and Political Control*, edited by James Shields. University Park: Pennsylvania State University Press.

Lu, Hong. 1998. "Community Policing—Rhetoric or Reality? The Contemporary Chinese Community-Based Policing System in Shanghai." Ph.D. diss., Arizona State University.

Marshall, T. F. 1985. *Alternatives to Criminal Courts*. Aldershot: Gower.

Masters, Guy. 1995. "The Family Model of Social Control in Japanese Secondary Schools." Unpublished manuscript, Lancaster University.

———. 1997. "Reintegrative Shaming in Theory and Practice." Ph.D. diss., Lancaster University.

Masters, Guy, and David Smith. 1998. "Portia and Persephone Revisited: Thinking about Feeling in Criminal Justice." *Theoretical Criminology* 2: 5–28.

Maxwel, Gabrielle M., and Allison Morris. 1993. *Family, Victims and Culture: Youth Justice in New Zealand*. Social Policy Agency and Institute of Criminology, Victoria University of Wellington, New Zealand.

McCold, Paul. 1997. "Restorative Justice: Variations on a Theme." In *Restorative Justice for Juveniles: Potentialities, Risks and Problems for Research*, edited by Lode Walgrave. Leuven: Leuven University Press.

Meima, M. 1990. "Sexual Violence, Criminal Law and Abolitionism." In *Gender, Sexuality and Social Control*, edited by B. Rolston and M. Tomlinson. Bristol, England: European Group for the Study of Deviance and Social Control.

Melton, Ada Pecos. 1995. "Indigenous Justice Systems and Tribal Society." *Judicature* 79: 126.

Michael, Franz. 1986. *China through the Ages: History of a Civilization*. Taipei: SMC Publishing.

Miyazawa, Setsuo. 1992. *Policing in Japan: A Study on Making Crime*. Albany: State University of New York Press.

Moore, David B., with L. Forsythe. 1995. *A New Approach to Juvenile Justice: An Evaluation of Family Conferencing in Wagga Wagga*. Wagga Wagga: Charles Sturt University.

Morris, Ruth. 1995. "Not Enough!" *Mediation Quarterly* 12: 285–91.

Morrison, Brenda E. 2000. "The Role of Affect and Identity in Resolving Social Dilemmas: Insights from Restorative Justice." Paper presented at the annual conference of Australasian Social Psychologists, Perth, Western Australia, 27–30 April.

Nicholl, Caroline G. 1998. *Implementing Restorative Justice.* Washington, D.C.: Office of Community Oriented Policing Services, U.S. Department of Justice.

Nussbaum, Martha. 1995. "Human Capabilities: Female Human Beings." In *Women, Culture, and Development,* edited by M. C. Nussbaum and J. Glover. Oxford: Clarendon Press.

Peachey, D. E. 1989. "The Kitchener Experiment." In *Mediation and Criminal Justice: Victims, Offenders and Community,* edited by M. Wright and B. Galaway. London: Sage.

Pepinsky, H. E., and R. Quinney, eds. 1991. *Criminology as Peacemaking.* Bloomington: Indiana University Press.

Pettit, P. 1997. *Republicanism.* Oxford: Clarendon Press.

Power, Patrick. 2000. "Restorative Conferences in Australia and New Zealand." Ph.D. diss., Law School, University of Sydney.

Pranis, K. 1996. "A State Initiative toward Restorative Justice: The Minnesota Experience." In *Restorative Justice: International Perspectives,* edited by B. Galaway and J. Hudson. Monsey, N.Y.: Criminal Justice Press.

Pratt, John. 1996. "Colonization, Power and Silence: A History of Indigenous Justice in New Zealand Society." In *Restorative Justice: International Perspectives,* edited by Burt Galaway and Joe Hudson. Monsey, N.Y.: Criminal Justice Press.

Rees, Joseph V. 1988. *Reforming the Workplace.* Philadelphia: University of Pennsylvania Press.

———. 1994. *Hostages of Each Other: The Transformation of Nuclear Safety since Three Mile Island.* Chicago: University of Chicago Press.

Roach, Kent. 1999. *Due Process and Victims' Rights: The New Law and Politics of Criminal Justice.* Toronto: University of Toronto Press.

Ross, Rupert. 1996. *Returning to the Teachings: Exploring Aboriginal Justice.* London: Penguin.

Rouche, Michel. 1987. "The Early Middle Ages in the West." In *A History of Private Life,* edited by Phillipe Ariès and Georges Duby. Cambridge, Mass.: Harvard University Press.

Sen, Amartya K. 1999. *Development as Freedom.* New York: Alfred A. Knopf.

Shearing, Clifford. 1997. *Violence and the Changing Face of Governance: Privatization and Its Implications.* Cape Town: Community Peace Foundation.

Sherman, L. W., H. Strang, G. C. Barnes, J. Braithwaite, N. Inkpen, and M. M. Teh. 1998. *Experiments in Restorative Policing: A Progress Report.* Canberra: Law Program, RSSS, Australian National University.

Sutherland, E. H. 1983. *White Collar Crime: The Uncut Version.* New Haven, Conn.: Yale University Press.

Umbreit, Mark. 1985. *Crime and Reconciliation: Creative Options for Victims and Offenders.* Nashville, Tenn.: Abington Press.

———. 1998. "Restorative Justice through Juvenile Victim-Offender Mediation." In *Restoring Juvenile Justice,* edited by Lode Walgrave and Gordon Bazemore. Monsey, N.Y.: Criminal Justice Press.

Umbreit, M., with R. Coates and B. Kalanj. 1994. *Victim Meets Offender: The Impact of Restorative Justice and Mediation.* Monsey, N.Y.: Criminal Justice Press.

Vagg, Jon. 1998. "Delinquency and Shame: Data from Hong Kong." *British Journal of Criminology* 38:247–64.

Van Ness, Daniel. 1986. *Crime and Its Victims: What We Can Do?* Downers Grove, Ill.: Intervarsity Press.

———. 1993. "New Wine and Old Wineskins: Four Challenges of Restorative Justice." *Criminal Law Forum* 4:251–76.

Van Ness, Daniel, and Karen Heetderks Strong. 1997. *Restoring Justice.* Cincinnati, Ohio: Anderson Publishing.

Wachtel, Ted. 1997. *Real Justice. How We Can Revolutionize Our Response to Wrongdoing.* Pipersville, Pennsylvania: Piper's Press.

Warhaft, E. Barry, Ted Palys, and Wilma Boyce. 1999. "'This Is How We Did It': One Canadian First Nation Community's Efforts to Achieve Aboriginal Justice." *Australian and New Zealand Journal of Criminology* 32: 168–81.

Weitekamp, E. 1989. "Restitution: A New Paradigm of Criminal Justice or a New Way to Widen the System of Social Control?" Ph.D. diss., University of Pennsylvania.

———. 1998. "The History of Restorative Justice." In *Restoring Juvenile Justice,* edited by Lode Walgrave and Gordon Bazemore. Monsey, N.Y.: Criminal Justice Press.

Whyte, Ian D. 1995. *Scotland before the Industrial Revolution.* London: Longman.

Wong, Dennis. 1999. "Delinquency Control and Juvenile Justice in China." *Australian and New Zealand Journal of Criminology* 32:27–41.

Wormwald, Jenny. 1980. "Bloodfeud, Kindred and Government in Early Modern Scotland." *Past and Present* 87:54–97.

Wright, M. 1982. *Making Good: Prisons, Punishment and Beyond.* London: Hutchinson.

———. 1999. *Restoring Respect for Justice: A Symposium.* Winchester: Waterside Press.

Yazzie, Robert, and James W. Zion. 1996. "Navajo Restorative Justice: The Law of Equality and Justice." In *Restorative Justice: International Perspectives,* edited by Burt Galaway and Joe Hudson. Monsey, N.Y.: Criminal Justice Press.

Zehr, Howard. 1985. *Retributive Justice, Restorative Justice.* New Perspectives on Crime and Justice: Occasional papers of the MCC Canada Victim Offender Ministries Program and the MCC, U.S. Office of Criminal Justice. Vol. 4. Elkhart, Ind.: Mennonite Central Committee; Kitchener, Ontario: Canada Victim Offender Ministries Program.

————. 1995. "Rethinking Criminal Justice: Restorative Justice." Unpublished paper.

☺ ☺ ☺

Questions

1. How would you define restorative justice?

2. Why was restorative justice no longer the dominant model of justice at the end of the dark ages?

3. Who most often opposes restorative justice programs?

4. What are the values of restorative justice?

5. Would a criminal justice system based exclusively on restorative justice principles be possible? Why, or why not?